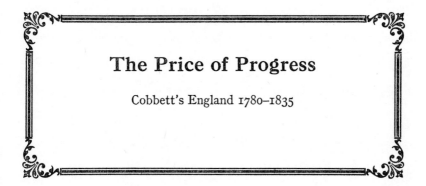

# The Price of Progress

Cobbett's England 1780–1835

# The Price of Progress
## Cobbett's England 1780–1835

**John Clarke**

HART-DAVIS, MACGIBBON
**GRANADA PUBLISHING**
London Toronto Sydney New York

Published by Granada Publishing
in Hart-Davis, MacGibbon Ltd 1977

Granada Publishing Limited
Frogmore, St Albans, Herts AL2 2NF
and
3 Upper James Street, London W1R 4BP
1221 Avenue of the Americas, New York NY 10020 USA
117 York Street, Sydney, NSW 2000 Australia
100 Skyway Avenue, Toronto, Ontario, Canada M9W 3A6
Trio City, Coventry Street, Johannesburg 2001, South Africa

ISBN 0 246 10604 2

Printed in Great Britain by
Butler & Tanner Ltd
Frome and London

To Celia

# Contents

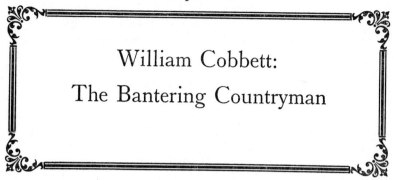

# Chapter One

# William Cobbett:
# The Bantering Countryman

## The Ideal

In the 1770s there was an ale house at Farnham in Surrey called The Jolly Farmer. The landlord, Mr Cobbett, had a son named William who was destined to become one of the most loved and hated men of his generation. The words 'Jolly Farmer' sum up the England Cobbett believed in, a country of hard work, honesty, healthy outdoor occupations, rural sports, independence of outlook and an abundance of wholesome food and strong beer. Looking back from the grim world of his old age, William Cobbett saw the years of his childhood as a sort of Indian summer of the life style implied by the name of his father's public house. Old men are liable to remember the good things of the past and forget the bad; Cobbett was no exception. But good or bad, there is no doubt that the life of William Cobbett coincided with some of the most dramatic changes ever experienced by the people of England. By the 1830s, the world of the 1780s must have seemed as remote as the Middle Ages.

In appearance, many of the customers at The Jolly Farmer did indeed belong to the Middle Ages; vagaries of fashion had passed them by and most of them still wore the off-white yoked smocks favoured by peasants for centuries. There must have been similar scenes in ale houses throughout England. Local matters probably dominated conversations but occasionally the arrival of a tattered and out-of-date news sheet, carefully read aloud for the benefit of those who could not read for themselves, provoked some discussion of wider issues. Cobbett recalled that his father, a supporter of General Washington, had fierce arguments about the American Revolution with a loyalist gardener named Martin.[1]

The outside world obtruded, but it seems unlikely that the men in
The Jolly Farmer were talking about the abstract principles of the
American Revolution. Like peasants everywhere and like Cobbett
himself, they viewed new and abstract ideas with hostility and suspicion.
They knew that there was a catch in schemes for universal happiness
based on a few self-evident principles. In later life Cobbett mellowed
somewhat in his attitude to the United States but even in the 1830s he
could still speak of that country as held 'in everlasting subjection to the
prejudice and caprices of the democratical mob'. Cobbett was even less
enthusiastic for the French Revolution and when he met Talleyrand,
the ci-devant Bishop of Autun, had no hesitation in calling him 'this
modern Judas, an apostate, a hypocrite and every other name of
which he was deserving'.[2] Neither Cobbett nor the men of Farnham
had any interest in democracy, republics or congresses, but this did not
mean that they were hostile to the American rebels–they simply
interpreted outside events in the light of their own experience. The
customers at The Jolly Farmer were certainly on the side of the under-
dog. Folk memory, nurtured by ballads, chap-books and woodcuts, was
still extraordinarily long; local men had been involved in the Peasants'
Revolt of 1381, in Jack Cade's rebellion of 1450, in the disturbances of
1549 and in the Digger movement of the 1640s. The spirit was not dead
and in 1830 the men of Surrey were again to take to rick-burning and
rebellion.[3]

But the hallmark of these movements had been a readiness to resort
to violence in order to restore a glorious past, not to speed progress into
a more logical and 'higher' stage of society. A passionate belief in the
'good old days' is one of the most enduring features of the Englishman's
outlook and one which is well represented by William Cobbett. The
ideal society can be anything from Edwardian England to King Arthur
and Avalon; the only essential is that it is in the past. Cobbett thought
that the best times had been in the fourteenth and fifteenth centuries.
The choice was a popular one and in the nineteenth century William
Morris's *News from Nowhere* completed the apotheosis of 'Medieval
Socialism'. The book would have appealed to William Cobbett who had
a great capacity for believing what he wanted to believe.

Cobbett's choice may seem crazy–was not his ideal time one of
devastating epidemics of the Black Death, of debilitating wars at home
and abroad, a time of over-mighty subjects with private armies degrading the Crown and plundering town and country alike, a time of
corruption and worldliness in the church, a time of heresy hunting and
burning? Compared to such a nightmare world, was not the early nineteenth century a very paradise on earth? William Cobbett thought not;

although some things had gone wrong even before his birth, he believed that Farnham in the 1780s was close enough to the ideal to give at least some notion of what things had really been like in the good old days.

During Cobbett's youth, social tensions were never absent from the countryside but they were probably less acute in Farnham than elsewhere. Relative harmony was the result of prosperity and the buttresses of Farnham's wealth were its hops and its palace. Cobbett never missed the chance to praise Farnham hops as the finest in England. The fertile greensand valley, sheltered by a chalk ridge, stretched for twelve miles from Farnham to Wrecclesham and Bentley. The hops were sold at Weyhill Fair and always commanded high prices, while the River Wey, improved by Sir Richard Weston in the seventeenth century, provided excellent access to the London market.

The vale of Farnham delighted many observers, including the agricultural expert Arthur Young, who described it as the finest ten miles in England. The area gave an impression of precision and neatness; the valley seemed like a garden and hop growing had the status of a craft. There was intense pride in work–hedges cut with shears and every square foot of ground tilled to the best advantage. The hop season gave an added jollity to life. When the crop was gathered in, the pickers decked themselves out in ribbons and finery. The average size of the hop gardens was small and no great social divide separated tenant and labourer. Together they would dance through the streets of Farnham led by fiddlers. William Marshall, like Young an agricultural specialist, found the 'finishing frolicks' of the Farnham hop pickers an unusual example of glee and merriment 'in those decorous times'.[4] Cobbett was to have a good deal to say about 'those decorous times'.

The fiercely independent Farnham hop grower was the ideal member of society for Cobbett but the great palace of the Bishop of Winchester exercised a very powerful influence on his thinking. Winchester was the second richest see in the country and its bishops had once enjoyed almost as much power as the ecclesiastical princes of Germany. Farnham Castle, dominating the town from the chalk ridge, retained its twelfth-century keep and fifteenth-century curtain walls. Although some of the fortifications were gone, destroyed by Parliamentary troops in 1643, the castle was still an impressive symbol of the church's former power. At the national level, the Anglican church might be no more than a milch cow for politicians, the complacent parasite of the Hanoverian usurpation, but in the town of Farnham the illusion of ecclesiastical independence could still be maintained. The Bishop of Winchester kept what amounted to a private court in Farnham Castle. The Bishop, Dr Thomas, may have been a lesser man than his twelfth-century predecessor, Henry of Blois, but he still kept up the practice of alms at the Castlegate, he maintained a private theatre and employed local craftsmen to make alterations to his palace. The bounty of Bishop Morley, who in the years after the Restoration had spent £8000 in repairing the ravages of the Parliamentary ruffians, was still fresh in local memory.

Cobbett was once employed as a gardener at the castle. To the little boy clipping the yew hedges in the formal gardens, Dr Thomas was surely a figure of terrifying importance. When work was over there were more reminders of the glories of the past. The ruins of Waverley Abbey produced feelings of melancholy for what had once been. It was not surprising that a clever child should have been intrigued by the pre-Reformation church and later expressed contempt for those who dared to call the great days of castle and cathedral building 'The Dark Ages'.

Looking back over his long life, Cobbett singled out some important features of his childhood. He imagined himself a little boy again–going along by the side of a field near Waverley Abbey in the barley-sowing season. There were primroses and bluebells springing up in the banks on either side while it seemed that there were a thousand linnets singing in the spreading oak over Cobbett's head. Over the hedge came the sounds of jingling brasses and plough boys whistling and then the ultimate delight of a pack of hounds in full cry to be followed mile after mile across open country.[5]

These had been good years when country people had had enough to eat while small towns and craft industries flourished. Grandees like Dr Thomas spent their money locally and knew that they had obligations as well as rights and that the poor had rights as well as obligations. It was a world of ideal types, ideal bishops and ideal farmers unpolluted by upstart bankers, stock-jobbers, Jews and Quakers. Such parasites confined themselves to the City of London and did not presume to set themselves up as country gentlemen. Counties enjoyed virtual independence from central government, taxation scarcely affected ordinary people and wages were paid in coin which kept its value.

Life was tolerable even for the very poor. Cobbett's grandmother, the widow of a farm labourer, had to make do with a turf fire and a rush dipped in grease for light, but she was able to give her grandchildren milk and bread for breakfast, an apple pudding for dinner and a piece of bread and cheese for supper. Men in work were better off. In those so-called 'Dark Ages', it was unheard of for a labouring man to leave home in the morning without taking a bottle of beer and a satchel containing cheese or bacon to hang upon his crook.[6]

Many of the houses were tiny but the little thatched cottage where Cobbett's grandmother lived had a good garden. The house had only two windows, a damson tree shaded one and a clump of filberts the other.[7] Even those without gardens could find fruit, firewood and an occasional rabbit in the large tracts of open land around Frensham Ponds. Clothes were home-made but hard wearing. Country labourers' wives would spin and knit whenever they had a spare moment from the work of the farm. They made the stockings and gloves needed by their family and Cobbett's grandmother continued to knit stockings even after she had gone blind.[8] Like the landscape, the appearance of the people was neat and modest. The fairs Cobbett went to as a boy were always made especially attractive by the white smock frocks and red handkerchiefs of countrymen and the clean clothes of the girls.[9]

In Cobbett's youth it seemed there were virtually no machines and certainly no prospect of 'technological unemployment'. Everyone had a job, however humble, and could feel they were making a worthwhile contribution to the village community. Cobbett himself could not remember the time when he did not earn his living. At an age when he was scarcely tall enough to climb gates and stiles, he went out into the fields to drive birds off the peas and turnips. Later, he was sent to pull tares from wheat fields and then to lead a single horse harrowing barley. Cobbett had three brothers, and by the time the eldest was fifteen, their father was boasting that his four boys did as much work as the most industrious men in Farnham.

Such an upbringing gave little time for formal education. Cobbett had a dim memory of going to a cottage 'dame school' where an old woman tried to teach him the alphabet. But it was Cobbett's father who instructed his sons in reading, writing and arithmetic on winter evenings. Cobbett senior had taught himself some branches of mathematics and acquired a knowledge of land surveying which meant that he was often asked to draw plans of disputed field boundaries. It was knowledge like this which gave a man standing and respect in the community. The value of classroom education was questionable and Cobbett had only contempt for 'those frivolous idiots that are turned out from Winchester or Westminster School or from any of those dens of dunces called colleges and universities'.[10] Real education meant the school of life–precious memories of rolling down a sandhill with the boys of Farnham, or walking alone in the fields and gradually gaining knowledge of animals, plants and weather lore.

It was not just the amount of education or the material standard of living which concerned Cobbett, but whether people had been *happier*. Although work was hard, there was none of the grinding monotony of a factory existence. There were rural sports to join in; fox hunting was less socially exclusive than it was to become in the nineteenth century. The old-fashioned 'Farmers' Hunts' which Mr Jorrocks tried to reform were flourishing in the 1780s. There was no nonsense about correct dress and many members came without horses. Anyone at all could take part in a hare hunt. Impudent Scots economists might talk about 'Dark Ages' but there was no denying that there had been more holidays in Cobbett's young days. A fair held anywhere in the district meant a day off from work. There was time off at Christmas, Easter and Whitsun as well as a day or two at Candlemas and at Hollantide in November. Even cricket matches, single stick matches and other sports were regarded as legitimate reasons for not going to work.[11]

## The State of People's Minds

Life in Cobbett's childhood seemed to have had a static, almost medieval quality about it, even if it fell short of the glories of the Middle Ages proper. With such a view of his past it was natural that Cobbett should be suspicious of any changes, however much vaunted by others. In fact Cobbett had no doubt that every change had been made for the worse. Where were the labourers now who carried beer to work? Cobbett had seen scarcely half a dozen examples in the twenty years after 1814. When he revisited the country fairs which had given him so much pleasure in his youth, he found them poorly attended; the country people looked ragged and dirty while some of the girls were decked out in tawdry machine-made cottons which made them seem more like town prostitutes than honest country girls. According to Cobbett the change was a pretty fair sample of what had happened throughout England.[12] It was Cobbett's life work to expose the humbug of those who talked of 'vast improvements' and had the effrontery to claim that things had got better.

Cobbett returned to his attack time and time again. Everywhere honesty and good craftsmanship were being replaced by deceit, ugliness and pretence. In *Rural Rides* Cobbett noted the large number of estates bought up by bankers and stock-jobbers. The later enthusiasm for 'Regency Taste' would have horrified Cobbett; to him the years after 1810 were times of 'villainous gingerbread houses'. Everything was designed to make the maximum impression for the minimum outlay. Plaster Gothic was very different from the thick walls of Farnham Castle, and bankers' architecture was scarcely more substantial than bankers' securities. In October 1821 Cobbett visited a banker's park near Newbury: 'Of all the ridiculous things I ever saw in my life, this place is the most ridiculous. In one of the gravel walks we had to pass under a Gothic arch, with a cross on top of it, and in the point of the arch a niche for a saint or a virgin, the figure being gone through the lapse of centuries. But the good of it was, this Gothic arch, disfigured by the hand of Old Father Time was composed of Scotch Fir wood, as rotten as a pear, from a distance, like the remnants of a ruin! I wonder how long this sickly, this childish taste is to remain?'[13]

The very apogee of Regency Taste was to be found at Brighton, the creation of the prince himself. Cobbett had poor opinion of the Pavilion, a building he always called 'The Kremlin'. 'The Kremlin lies in a gorge. Take a square box the sides of which are three feet and a half and the height a foot and a half. Take a large Norfolk turnip, put the turnip in the middle of the box. Then take four turnips of half the size and put them on the corners of the box. Then take a considerable number of bulbs of the crown imperial, the narcissus, the hyacinth, the crocus and others...put all these, pretty promiscuously, but pretty thickly on the top of the box. Then stand off. There! That's a *Kremlin*!'[14]

The occupants of such places were easy to spot. Cobbett said that he could always tell them by their lank jaws, the stiffeners round their necks, their stays, their false shoulders, hips and haunches, their half whiskers and 'by their skins, colour of veal kidney suet, warmed a little and then powdered with dirty dust'.[15] There was a world of difference between such disgusting creatures, who were so sadly typical of the new era, and the type of man Cobbett regarded as the true Englishman. Never unduly modest, he would have been delighted to see himself in that role.

In 1817 the Lancashire Radical Samuel Bamford met Cobbett at his office in Newcastle Street, London. Cobbett looked very much the gentleman farmer in town–six foot tall, plump with round weathered cheeks and bright grey eyes. He was wearing a blue coat with a swansdown waistcoat and topped boots and Bamford was particularly impressed by his immaculate linen. Cobbett seemed the perfect example of what he had always professed to be, 'the well liked, stout hearted, bantering countryman'.[16]

Cobbett may have been the bantering countryman but that does not mean that he lacked sensitivity; few men have described the countryside as vividly as he. In *Rural Rides*, the reader can almost see the dew on the grass and smell the flowers in the hedges. It takes little imagination to join Cobbett as he jogs down a green lane, noticing with him the gypsy camp under the hedge, the beauty of the rising sun and the state of the crops in the surrounding fields. In his way Cobbett was every bit as close to nature as Wordsworth, but his feel for landscape and skies

The Price of Progress

was never allowed to become sentimental. In fact, as Cobbett journeyed around England in the years after 1815, he became increasingly angry and bitter.

Cobbett was to be many things in his life—soldier, government propagandist, anti-government propagandist, journalist, agitator, banker, prisoner, exile, Member of Parliament, farmer, butcher and even scholar—he was to change his opinions on many issues, but he was not an inconsistent man. His determination to expose what was happening in the country he loved so much led him to try to explain why these terrible changes had taken place. Why were the poor less well fed, less well clothed, less happy, less independent and less respected? Why were there more upstarts, more bankers and stock-jobbers? Why were these people more vulgar, more arrogant and more able to manipulate the traditional landowning classes? Why was the face of England being changed by Enclosure of common land and by the building of hideous factory towns? Why were hypocrisy and prudery gaining ground? Why was machinery being invented which was throwing craftsmen out of work? Why was the government making things worse rather than better?

All these vital questions and many more obsessed Cobbett for over thirty years. Of course Cobbett's answers were not always correct. His anger at the iniquities of paper money and the funding system often led him away from an analysis of the more profound forces at work in society. Many of his mistakes were due to his preoccupation with the countryside of southern England; in particular this led him to the erroneous belief that the population of England was falling rather than rising. Although Cobbett was ultimately to become Member of Parliament for Oldham in Lancashire, he knew little of the industrial north, of the cotton towns, of the advances in medicine and of the emergence of a large and self-confident middle class. The implications of new machinery passed him by; he was content to describe steam engines as 'infernal' and leave the matter there. He did not see that efficient production meant that there was a chance of improving living standards for all. The enormous contribution made by exports to economic growth was seen by Cobbett simply as an indication of the loss of national wealth.

Even Cobbett's views on developments in the south were rather wild. To him, the growth of London was 'abominable' and 'The Great Wen' simply a parasite on the rest of the country. The spas and seaside resorts were extensions of 'The Wen' and largely inhabited by 'vermin, tax eaters, prostitutes, government sinecurists and pensioners'. Most of the 'vast improvements' of the time left him cold. Turnpike Trusts were simply a means of making the poor pay for the use of the roads they did not want, in order to line the pockets of speculators. The Turnpikes, 'stock-jobbers' roads', were no more than fingers on the Great Wen obtruding into the countryside. Even in agriculture, Cobbett's ideas were questionable; it is not certain that rural living standards fell between 1780 and 1830 and most historians reject the view that Enclosure actually reduced agricultural output.

Perhaps Cobbett's gravest weakness was in his suggestions for improving living standards. His constant theme was 'we want nothing new' and all his remedies, however radical, were designed to bring about a return to the lost Arcadia whose after-glow had persisted into his childhood. To Cobbett the Industrial Revolution was a terrible but still reversible aberration; he believed that the social and technological developments of the time were caused by political changes, not the other way round. If one could get the politics right, the other ills would cure themselves. By the 1820s, the 'Merrie England' world Cobbett described in such loving detail was gone beyond recall–if indeed it had ever existed. Any serious attempt to recreate Cobbett's ideal would have resulted in disaster.

Yet all these strictures do nothing to undermine the importance of William Cobbett. Although he may have got the answers wrong, he certainly asked the right questions. He raised his vital issues with a force and power which must place him head and shoulders above all other social commentators of his generation. He spoke in language which is still fresh and trenchant; his down-to-earth similes can still give the reader greater insight into a particular problem than whole volumes of explanation by modern historians.

The greatest thing of all was the response Cobbett evoked in others. He is surely the representative of millions of Englishmen who were puzzled, alarmed and slightly bemused by the events we now call the Industrial Revolution. Faced with such bewildering changes, it is not surprising that they too reacted in that most typically English way–by seeking to get back to the good old days. Like William Cobbett and the men in The Jolly Farmer, the ordinary Englishman had little time for things new or theoretical. Cobbett reflected this general mood when he dismissed the Utopian socialism of Robert Owen, the creator of New Lanark, as 'a species of monkery'; even the cry for universal suffrage never really appealed to him. Cobbett's political philosophy can be summed up in one sentence–'A full belly to the labourer is the foundation of public morals and the only real source of public peace.' Even new ideas on diet roused Cobbett's suspicions and he believed persistently in the virtues of white bread, red meat and strong beer. Cobbett's

9

views may have been old-fashioned but his methods were surprisingly modern. The way to understand England was to go about 'Hearing what gentlemen, farmers, tradesmen, journeymen, labourers, women, girls, boys and all have to say; reasoning with some, laughing with others and observing all that passes. At the end of a tramp like this you get impressed upon your mind a true picture, not only of the state of the country, but of the state of people's minds throughout the country.'[17]

Cobbett's influence on ordinary people was exercised through his newsletter, the *Political Register*, affectionately known as 'The Twopenny Trash'. In the years around 1820, copies of 'The Twopenny Trash' were flung down from the London coaches as they rattled through villages and small towns of England. Circulation reached the unprecedented figure of 40,000 copies a week, far larger than that of any other newspaper. 'The Twopenny Trash' was passed from hand to hand in public houses and so the number who learned about Cobbett's ideas was even larger than the circulation figures suggest. If the character of an age is to some extent determined by the man who influences most people, however humble, then the England of the early nineteenth century was certainly the Age of Cobbett.

In general, historians have tended to patronise William Cobbett– finding him an interesting man but one whose impractical plans to return England to an earlier stage of social development really disqualify him from any claim to greatness. What such people fail to appreciate is that those who try to restore the past–and there have been thousands of them in English history–often play an important part in the making of the future. This is certainly true of William Cobbett; in some of his statements Cobbett was far ahead of his time. Others were still claiming that the most useful class in society were the owners of capital, while the working man was less valuable because of his tendency to become a burden on the poor rates. Cobbett would have none of that:

Elegant dresses, superb furniture, stately buildings, fine roads and canals, fleet horses and carriages, numerous stout ships, warehouses teeming with goods; all these and many other objects that fall under our view are so many marks of natural wealth and resources. But all these spring from labour. Without the journeyman and the labourer none of these could exist; without the assistance of their hands, the country would be a wilderness.[18]

For all his mistakes William Cobbett usually knew what he was talking about.

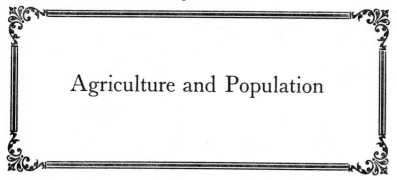

# Chapter Two

# Agriculture and Population

## Goths and Vandals of the Common Fields

William Cobbett's especial concern was for the rural population of England and, in general, he was hostile to changes in agricultural methods. The old ways were certainly tenacious. In the England of George IV there were still villages whose farming practices had not altered significantly since the thirteenth century. The traditional pattern of English landscape would have astonished the modern countryman. There was more waste land, more forest and there were large unfenced fields around villages. The village usually had three large fields–divided into strips worked by various farmers–and an area of commonland. The strips were separated only by a furrow; after the harvest, the land was thrown open and anything that remained was eaten by scavenging animals. Each field was left fallow for one year in three in the hope that it would regain its richness before being used again for wheat.

For those who were concerned about the nation's food supply, the continuation of such an antiquated system was scandalous. Agricultural improvement had long been in the wind. Some new techniques were introduced from the Low Countries in the seventeenth century and expounded in books like John Worlidge's *Systema Agriculturae*. Worlidge advocated the use of leguminous crops like sainfoin (originally Sainte Foine) which helped to fix more nitrogen in the soil and thus enriched it far more than the period of fallow. The new 'artificial grasses' were also valuable as fodder crops. The influence of such teaching may have been wider than is usually imagined. By the beginning of the eighteenth century, farmers in the townships of the large Oxfordshire parish of Spelsbury near Woodstock were making agreements with their landlord, St John's College, to grow sainfoin on part of the open fields.[1]

Although examples of modern techniques can be found, they affected only a tiny fraction of the villages of England. When an enlightened writer such as Jethro Tull could still declare that clover was 'foul food for horses and injurious to cattle' it is surely unlikely that less adventurous spirits would be tempted to experiment. The most persistent and influential critic of the old system was Arthur Young. Young argued that animal disease and the poor quality of beasts in the open fields made drastic changes imperative. A Mr J. Chamberlin told him that in Oxfordshire more sheep died from 'scab and rot' than at the hands of the butcher.[2] Consecutive seasons of disease could easily ruin a farmer. In Oxfordshire, hardier Southdown sheep were gradually replacing the Berkshires, but the absence of proper fences made selective breeding difficult.

Under strip cultivation, maximum advantage could not be derived from drainage. Small, inconvenient land units precluded experiments with drills—which saved valuable seed—and with improved ploughs. Hand hoeing in particular was wasteful in terms of manpower compared to the horse-drawn hoe. A great deal of time was lost to-ing and fro-ing when a farmer had dispersed patches of land all over the village. He would also be unable to maintain a close supervision of his labourers to ensure that they were not slacking. The main objection to the old system was that all the strips in one large field were planted with the same crop which was chosen by agreement. It was obviously difficult for the enterprising man to get the agreement of conservative villagers to try a new crop.[3] The situation has been compared with that of the slowest ship in a convoy determining the speed of the rest. The Open Fields were generally associated with fallow; the old rotation meant that a third of the land was wasted. If this loss alone could be abolished, the gain to agricultural output would be enormous.

Young had a clear-cut answer—*Enclosure*. Enclosure consisted of the amalgamation of the strips into larger fields with permanent boundaries. At the same time, the common land would be taken into intensive cultivation for the first time. With fenced fields of a reasonable size, economies of scale could be implemented and labour properly supervised. Hedges and walls would allow selective breeding and now that farmers had absolute control over their land—without reference to some parish meeting—the age of improved agriculture could begin in earnest.

Young constantly referred to one area of England which was in the forefront of progress—the County of Norfolk. Even in Young's own lifetime, the improvement had been dramatic. In 1804 he could point to land which, forty years earlier, had been used only for sheep walks let at sixpence per acre; the same land now supported the best arable farms in England. Young concentrated on seven points which had transformed Norfolk farming:

FIRST: By enclosing without assistance of parliament
SECOND: By spirited use of marle and clay
THIRD: By the introduction of an excellent course of crops
FOURTH: By the culture of tulips well hand-hoed
FIFTH: By the culture of clover and by grass
SIXTH: By landlord granting long leases
SEVENTH: By the country being divided chiefly into large farms.[4]

Young was so convinced of the virtue of Enclosure that he did not care how it was achieved. After 1775, however, Enclosures required an Act of Parliament; the process was time-consuming and opposition in the Commons could produce serious delays. Young believed that the enormous advantages of Enclosure were in danger of being strangled by red-tape which only served to gratify 'the Knavery of Commissioners and Attornies'. It was surely better to keep costs down by achieving Enclosure by private agreement. Economy was vital because the most crucial spending came *after* Enclosure. The erection of fences did not, in itself, make agriculture more productive; the changes which came with Enclosure were the ones that brought the real gains. There was a danger that Parliamentary Enclosure would absorb too much of the available money in legal costs and leave nothing over for things like the purchase of better stock.

In his advocacy of marling, Young was stressing the importance of preparation and improvement of the soil to the right consistency. In most parts of Norfolk, clay was found below the sandy soil. Once every twenty years or so, marl was ploughed into the soil to give it extra body. The process could be done to excess, but Norfolk farmers quickly worked out the precise amounts required. Perhaps the greatest contribution of Norfolk farming was the introduction of four-course rotation which removed the problem of fallow. The rotation usually adopted was (1) turnips, (2) barley, (3) clover or rye grass and (4) wheat. The beauty of this system was that it led to a more balanced system of mixed farming. Although barley and wheat were probably the only cash crops, turnips and clover were crucial. Clover prepared the land for an exhausting grain crop and turnips provided winter fodder for animals. The presence of more animals meant that more dung was produced–which in turn enriched the soil and allowed more crops to be grown.

Young was also concerned with the organisation of Norfolk farming. If a tenant faced the possibility of being turned out of his farm simply at the caprice of his landlord, there was no incentive to make improvements which would only benefit his successor. The farmer had to be given some security in the shape of a long lease. It was absurd to expect an incoming tenant to spend up to £5 per acre on improvements when he was liable to be turned out at one year's notice. Similarly, it was obvious that landlords should divide their estates into large farms and let them to men with plenty of capital. Improvements were too expensive for the small man. Recent work has emphasised just how much English agriculture owed to large tenant farmers. Those who actually contributed to agricultural knowledge–Bakewell, Tull and Collings–tended to be tenant farmers rather than landowners. The landlord would pay for Enclosure but new stock and marling were clearly the responsibility of the tenant.

Of course, improved agriculture was increasing in places other than Norfolk. Between 1793 and 1801, 182 Acts of Parliament were passed providing for the Enclosure of 273,891 acres of common pasture and waste. Young was responsible for publishing a *General View* of the farming of most counties of England. As Secretary to the Board of Agriculture he was a man of influence who was often consulted by cabinet ministers. It was partly Young's criticism of the costs of Enclosure which persuaded the government to introduce a General Enclosure Act in 1801. Unfortunately, the legal profession was well represented in Parliament; lawyers' concern for their fees meant that the Act was so hedged about with provisos that there was no significant reduction in costs. Still, the progress of Enclosure went on; between 1802 and 1815 there were 564 enclosures covering 739,743 acres.

Young may have been a successful propagandist, but he was a disastrous farmer. He took a 'very fine Essex Farm' of 300 acres, called Stamford Hall, tried various experiments, lost money and was finally reduced to paying a local farmer £100 to take it off his hands. The farmer then proceeded to make his venture extremely profitable. This unfortunate result exemplified a significant truth; although there was much of value to be found in Young's writings, his solutions were too dogmatic to fit the infinite complexities and varieties of English farming.

In essence, Young's picture was distorted because the Norfolk system which he so much admired was not always successful when attempted elsewhere. The *sine qua non* of the Norfolk system was the four-course rotation, but the Norfolk rotation worked well only in areas of light, dry soil. Nathaniel Kent, author of *Hints to Gentlemen* and himself a land agent, recognised the importance of turnip husbandry but was careful to add 'but wet ground will not admit it'. Wet ground and waterlogged clay soil was probably a greater enemy to agricultural progress than the common fields. Kent's dictum–'till the land be laid dry 'tis in vain to bestow any kind of manure upon it'–has more sense than whole volumes of Young's *General Views*. There is a case for believing that the increased output of English agriculture was due to greater cultivation of light soil–which drained easily and needed fewer horses for ploughing–than to Enclosure itself. Enclosure of heavy land for arable purposes was of questionable economic value until the appearance of cheap earthenware drainage pipes in the 1830s and 1840s. A rotation based on swedes and mangels sometimes worked, but turnips were far too delicate for clay soils. In wet years they were liable to rot in the ground.

Perhaps Young's greatest weakness was his failure to pay significant attention to market forces; there was no point in going in for expensive improvements unless they produced a profit. The farmers of Norfolk had a variety of incentives for investing in agricultural improvement. East Anglia was well placed to receive new ideas from the Low Countries and, at a time when sea transport was far cheaper than by land, Norfolk farmers had a clear edge over their Midlands rivals in competition for the vital London market. In fact, ease of access to London was probably the main stimulus to agricultural progress. In good years, Norfolk also sent grain exports to the Continent and in 1794 the county exported more grain than the rest of England put together. The great ports of Norfolk were King's Lynn and Yarmouth. In 1793 Lynn exported agricultural foods valued at £262,650. It was at the outlet of more inland navigation than any port except London and was third after London in its import of sea coals.

Even in land communications with London, Norfolk was better placed than the clay lands where shortage of stone impeded good quality road building. In 1775 Parson Woodforde described the road from London to Norwich as the best in England. The great advantage of the Norfolk roads was that they allowed flocks of sheep, cows and even turkeys and geese to be driven to the Great Fair at St Ives or to Smithfield market and to arrive in better condition than flocks from other parts of the country. By 1800 Norfolk was sending 20,000 cattle and 30,000 sheep to London every year.

To add to Norfolk's many advantages, it was blessed with excellent land agents like Kent and his partners Claridge and Pearce. The personal qualities of an agent could determine the economic and social tone of a large neighbourhood. Above all, the agent was the intermediary between the landlord and the tenant. In periods of agricultural prosperity, as in the Napoleonic wars, rents tended to lag behind prices but, after 1815, grain prices fell more sharply than rents. Inevitably, some tenants were unable to pay. The land agent's role in advising the employer on when to evict or when to reduce rents was crucial.

But good land agents needed good landlords. The most famous landlord in the Age of Cobbett was Thomas Coke of Holkham. In 1776 at the age of twenty-two, Coke inherited a Norfolk estate of 43,000 acres. Few envied him; the land was then so poor that it was not even self-sufficient in grain and in 1776 10,000 quarters of wheat had to be brought into the district. The land was so light that attempts to grow wheat on it resulted in the top soil just blowing away. One cynic remarked that the best way to plough the land would be to use rabbits drawing a pocket knife. Yet the population of Holkham grew from 200 in 1776 to 1100 in 1818; in that year, the estate had a surplus of 11,000 quarters of wheat. Coke's estate yielded an income of only £2200 in 1776 but in 1818 it produced £20,000. The Holkham annual sheep shearing fair began in 1778 and continued until 1821. What began as a small agricultural show eventually attracted visitors from all over the world. Coke put on display the best breeds of sheep, the best cattle, the best kinds of seeds and new types of machinery. Cobbett was not a man to praise 'improvements' and he had a positive distaste for Coke's political views. In 1822, however, even Cobbett was forced to admit: 'Here at Holt as everywhere else, I hear every creature speak loudly in praise of Mr Coke. It is well known to my readers that I think nothing of him as a public man, but it would be base in me not to say that I hear from men of all parties, and sensible men too, expressions made use of towards him that affectionate children use towards the best of parents. I have not met with a single exception.'[5]

All over the country, where conditions were favourable, landlords, tenants and land agents planned improvements. In the west, the foundation of the Bath and West of England Agricultural Society in 1777 was a sign of interest in new techniques. The great work of draining the Sedgemoor marshes, begun in the seventeenth century, was taken up again. Floods in 1794, 1798 and 1800 swept away some of the drainage works but set-backs only emphasised the spirit of improvement. Careful studies were made into the correct sighting of sluices and a new South Drain was eventually constructed to solve the problem. Farmers in Sedgemoor came to see the value of steam engines for agricultural improvements. In the draining of the southern levels, the whole idea of gravitational drainage was given up in favour of steam pumping. The first steam engine was installed in Westonzoyland in 1830; a twenty-seven-horse-power scoop wheel pump showed that it was capable of draining no less than two thousand acres.[6]

It is certainly arguable that the emphasis of writers like Young on the achievements of Norfolk has led historians into concentrating too much on discussions of arable farming. Animal husbandry was always very important and Norfolk did not excel in all its departments. William Marshall denounced the Norfolk method of cheese making as 'execrable': '*Rennet*. The curd which happens to be contained in the stomach of the calf when butchered, together with the hairs and dirt which are inseparable from it are used by the dairy women in this county to coagulate their milk; hence, probably the rancid flavour of the Norfolk cheese.'[7]

In addition to the large herds of cattle in rural areas, a surprising number of cows were kept in sheds in large towns to provide fresh milk. In urban conditions, hygiene was even more important than in the country. Marshall was forced to make a very obvious suggestion which was clearly not yet the normal practice. 'A dairymaid should not be allowed to sit down under a cow with a pail a fine lady would scruple to cool her tea in; nor until she has washed the teats of the cow and her own hands; and for the purpose clean water and a cloth should always be at hand.'[8]

Such comments suggest that it would be unwise to exaggerate the changes in English agriculture during the first decades of the nineteenth century. There were villages unenclosed in 1830 and some enclosed parishes actually retained the wasteful system of leaving one-third of the land as fallow. It has been estimated that during the eighteenth century agricultural production rose by 43 per cent but that only 10 per cent can be attributed to increased productivity per acre. Between 1760 and 1800, nearly three million acres of waste, common or woodland was taken into cultivation; it was this development which was responsible for most of the increased output. Old-fashioned practice persisted. In 1796 William Marshall was horrified at Devon farmers winnowing corn in the open air, instead of using a fan. Devonshire farm labourers were dismissed as a sad collection of 'drunken idle fellows'.

The Age of Cobbett saw few innovations; at a time of rapid technological progress elsewhere the lack of new agricultural machinery is surprising. The only really new features, the threshing machine and the application of steam power to agriculture, did not become significant until the end of the 1820s. In some counties there was a temporary scarcity of labour during the wartime boom. In Essex, farmers sometimes gave £50 to find substitutes so that their own labourers would not be drafted into the army.[9] One would expect scarce, and consequently dear, labour to stimulate the invention of labour-saving machinery. Numerous patents were taken out between 1788 and 1816–for drills, reaping, sowing, hay-making and winnowing machines, but few were developed far enough to overcome teething troubles. In general farmers were conservative men and, in any case, there was no shortage of labour in many counties. Yet despite its many imperfections, the period between 1780 and 1830 remains the best candidate for the 'Age of Agricultural Revolution'. Changes previously confined to one farm or one village now affected whole counties.

## The Power of Population

The advocates of agricultural change believed that improvements were necessary to save England from starvation. The social implications of Enclosure might be good or bad but even if they were bad, this was surely a lesser evil than the alternative of permanent famine. Some writers, who agreed with Cobbett that the living standards of ordinary people were deplorably low, could not follow him when he claimed that this state of affairs was caused by the greed of the political and social establishment. Many thought that the situation resulted from the folly of the poor themselves or was due to factors beyond human control. In 1798 the Revd Thomas Malthus, a young Fellow of Jesus College, Cambridge, delivered a serious blow to the idealised picture of rural England. He pointed out that the children of peasants had little in common with the rosy cherubs described in romantic novels. Sons of labourers were apt to be stunted and were a long while in arriving at maturity. Boys who looked fourteen or fifteen were found to be eighteen or nineteen years old. Even lads who drove the plough, surely a healthy exercise, rarely had any appearance of calves to their legs. The only possible explanation was lack of adequate nourishment.[10]

Malthus believed that low living standards were caused by rapid population growth. If there were more mouths to feed, there would be less for each person to eat. If unchecked, populations doubled every twenty-five years; for one generation at most, resources might keep pace with population, but agriculture would soon reach a level where the whole of England was cultivated like a garden and no further improvements would be possible.[11] It was naïve to believe that agricultural improvements could provide the answer. The best land, the clay areas of the Midlands and the south of England, was already under intensive cultivation. Further improvements could not be expected there and any gains could come only from taking previously barren areas into cultivation. It was inevitable that such areas would never be so productive as the clay lands so that, for the country as a whole, the yield per acre would fall. The inevitable increase in food prices would

18

leave most people without any means to purchase the products of industry and commerce. Collapse of home demand would lead to the abandonment of factories. Malthus, like Cobbett, saw the Industrial Revolution as merely a temporary phase in English history.

Malthus believed that populations naturally expand to the very limit of resources, with the poorer classes hovering on the subsistence level. The equilibrium was always precarious. If population expanded beyond the limits of resources, retribution would soon come. After a period of rapid population growth, one could expect a time of famine and epidemics. It seemed that nature would audit her account with a red pencil and Malthus had no doubt that the main cause of death would be shortage of food. The only way to check the 'power of population' without 'positive checks' involving all the frightfulness of famine, was to strengthen 'preventive checks'. It should be the aim of governments to discourage marriage among the lower classes, particularly among those receiving poor relief. In 1798, however, Malthus believed that 'preventive checks' were not strong enough and that the British population would shortly be reduced to famine of the most appalling kind.

Many found these ideas distasteful, and Cobbett saw Malthus's book, *The First Essay on Population*, as another tentacle of evil 'Scotch Feelosophy' designed to deprive the poor man of his bread and of the legitimate pleasures of family life. Of course, Malthus was nonsensical if the population was not increasing. Cobbett, for one, with his evidence derived from the south of England, rejected talk of 'the surplus population'. Those who believed such absurdities need only make the journey from High Clere to Hambledon in Hampshire as Cobbett did in November 1822. Everywhere they would find huge churches like the one at East Meon, surrounded by large numbers of small paddocks, each of which had once contained a cottage. The cottages were no more, and the present inhabitants could occupy scarcely one-quarter of the church. Surely, once upon a time, the church had been filled with villagers; how then could Malthus and his like speak of the increase in population? All observations and reason were against this notion. There were some who actually claimed that between 1801 and 1821 the population of Great Britain had increased from 10 to 14 million. A man who could suck this in would 'believe, literally believe, that the moon is made of green cheese'. The whole thing was too monstrous for anyone to accept who had not been utterly brainwashed by the 'Pitt system'.[12]

Cobbett was expressing a widely held opinion. The scholarly Dr Richard Price FRS thought that the population of Great Britain had fallen by a quarter during the century after 1688. Price pointed to an apparent decline in the number of houses in the country and put particular blame on the expansion of London. A study of the London Bills of Mortality showed a considerable excess of burials over baptisms. The expansion of London could only be explained by a large migration of people from other parts of the country to the capital. London was literally consuming the people of England.[13] Estimates of the total population varied from Price's low figure of 5 million to Sir Frederick Eden's guess at 11 million in 1800.[14] It was obviously important to find out what had been happening and Parliament authorised a census, taken in 1801, which showed the population of England, Scotland and Wales to be 10·7 million–considerably larger than most people expected. Modern researches suggest a figure of about 7,500,000 for 1781, an increase of 23 per cent in twenty years. Later censuses showed that the population was not only increasing, but that the rate of growth was actually accelerating; the 1831 figure was no less than 16·4 million.[15] Malthus was vindicated and Cobbett's attempts to discredit him flew in the face of scientific evidence.

Strangely enough, Malthus's own views became more optimistic as time went on. 'Malthusian crises' have indeed occurred in the Ireland of the 1840s and in modern Africa and Asia. In England, however, the catastrophe did not come, and the population was able to increase without serious check. Malthus was too gloomy about agriculture. His arguments assumed a static technology and virtually ignored the developments of the Agricultural Revolution. Further, there was no reason why marginal land should always remain less productive than areas already in cultivation as the new techniques on the farms in the light soil country of Norfolk showed.

But it was not just a question of resources; there were things about the patterns of population growth itself which saved England from the Malthusian trap. Despite population growth of 1·7 per cent per annum in the early nineteenth century, this figure is a far cry from Malthus's notion of the population doubling in twenty-five years and it is substantially less than rates of growth experienced today in Africa and Asia. Malthus underestimated the influence of 'preventive checks' in eighteenth-century England. In European societies, the responsibility for the care of children is traditionally carried by the parents–rather than by the whole community as in much of Africa. There are, thus, strong pressures to prevent marriage until the couple concerned are capable of supporting children. There is usually a considerable gap between the age of puberty and the average age at marriage and this explains much of the difference between the maximum biological birth rate and the actual birth rate. Concern to preserve one's living standards and social status was recognised by Malthus as a powerful reason for the postponement of marriage. A bachelor of good education and an income just sufficient to enable him to associate with gentlemen would know that the expenses of family life would mean that he could no longer afford to mix with his former companions. After marriage, his circle would be a less cultivated world of small farmers and tradesmen. Domestic servants 'living in' in a great house often had little incentive to marry.[16] Many enjoyed easy work, and their food was almost as luxurious as the dishes served at their master's table. Yet they were without knowledge or capital for business or farming and the best prospect they could hope for if they left gentleman's service was to become the landlord of a miserable ale house. It is not surprising that large sections of the population never married at all.[17]

At the level of labourers, however, Malthus feared that 'stronger passions or weaker judgements would prevail' but the age at marriage among the labouring classes was surprisingly high. In the Devonshire village of Colyton, containing a high proportion of farm labourers, the average age of brides was nearly twenty-seven between 1720 and 1770, and twenty-six between 1770 and 1800.[18] There were some years when the average was close on thirty. With a generally early menopause–soon after forty–families were likely to be fairly small by Victorian standards. To some extent, of course, the effects of late marriage were offset by illegitimate births. A large proportion of children were conceived out of wedlock, but local authorities were quite likely to pressurise a putative father to marry his girl and thus prevent her child being a burden on the rates. Reluctant bridegrooms were sometimes brought to church in handcuffs. On 25 January 1787, the East Anglian clergyman, James Woodforde, wrote in his diary: 'Rode to Ringland this morning and married one Robert Astick and Elizabeth Howlett by licence, the man being in custody and the woman being with child by him. The man was a long time before he could be prevailed on to marry her when in the churchyard; and at the altar behaved very unbecoming. It is a cruel thing that any person should be compelled by law to marry. I received of the officers for marrying them 10/6d. It is very disagreeable to me to marry such persons.'[19]

By means of such strong-arm tactics, illegitimate births counted for no more than 6 or 7 per cent of the total. Within marriage, intervals between births tended to be longer than was usual in the nineteenth century. There was a fairly small chance of a woman conceiving while she was still breast-feeding a previous child and in the eighteenth century babies were not weaned until they were nearly two years old. Some contraceptive devices certainly did exist. Pessaries were used by some upper-class women and leather condoms are often mentioned, although they seem to have been associated with casual relationships and their main purpose was to protect the wearer from venereal disease. For the rural poor, the most usual means of family limitation was coitus interruptus. In years of exceptional economic difficulty there was probably some recourse to abortion and licensed midwives were required to promise not to give 'any counsel or administer any herb, medicine, or potion or any other thing to any woman being with child whereby she should destroy or cast out that she goeth withal before her time'.[20]

It seems certain that there was a sharp increase in birth rates towards the end of the eighteenth century. Various factors may have caused this change–a higher proportion of the population marrying, a lower average age at marriage or a shorter interval between pregnancies. In the case of Colyton, there was no significant variation from usual patterns before the 1790s but by the early nineteenth century a higher proportion of the brides were teenagers. There were important regional differences. New industrial areas experienced particularly high birth rates because they were populated by people who had recently moved and these immigrants were likely to be concentrated in the child-producing age group. Age at marriage in towns and in areas of rural industry had always been lower than in purely agricultural districts. As towns grew, a higher proportion of the total population was likely to marry early. In the towns wages were higher and men could set up a household earlier in life. In places where child labour was in demand, the possession of a large family could be an economic advantage. Arthur Young asked bluntly: 'Is it not evident that the demand for hands must regulate the number of the people?'

In the country areas, many farm houses were rebuilt at the end of the eighteenth century and there was usually less accommodation provided for farm workers to live in. That part of the population least liable to matrimony was thus reduced. But perhaps the most important change was the decline of many small farmers to the level of labourer. A man expecting to inherit a farm or a business would wait for his parents to die before he considered marriage; his period of maximum earning would come relatively late in life. The same consideration would apply to highly skilled tradesmen or to those in the professions. A labourer on the other hand reached his maximum earnings fairly early, and was thus likely to marry accordingly.

To many contemporaries, the reason for the increased birth rate was obvious; the cause of misery and over-population was traced to the Pelican Inn at Speenhamland in Berkshire. On 6 May 1795 a meeting of JPs resolved on a policy which was gradually adopted throughout southern England. Under this system the poor rates were used to supplement wages; married men received more than bachelors and the allowance increased with the size of the family. The scale recommended by the Berkshire magistrates was:

A single man according to his labour.
A man and his wife not less than 6s a week.
A man and his wife with one or two small children, not less than 7s a week.
And for every additional child not less than 1s a week.[21]

It was now economically more attractive to be married than single, whereas previously it had been the other way round. Malthus hated a system which gave 'Direct constant and systematical encouragement to marriage by removing from each individual that heavy responsibility which he would incur by the laws of nature for bringing human beings into the world which he could not support.'[22]

Local opinion saw a clear connection between early marriage, high birth rates and the Speenhamland system. D. O. P. Okeden, reporting on the parish of Duns Tew in Oxfordshire, declared that 'early marriage of mere boys is frequent for the avowed purpose of increasing their income by allowance for increase of children'.

It was widely believed that the Speenhamland system also increased the number of illegitimate births. Parish authorities collected what money they could from the father and handed it over to the mother. An unscrupulous woman could collect a number of such payments from different men until she became a local heiress and in a position to make an advantageous marriage. Under affiliation orders, unmarried mothers frequently enjoyed a higher allowance than widows with legitimate families. When the father could not be found the parish was compelled to support the girl and her child. With such good security, mothers were instrumental in having their daughters seduced in order to rid themselves of the expense of supporting them. Girls had little motive for saying 'no'; magistrates noted that women applying for affiliation orders seemed quite pleased with themselves. Explanations were predictably feeble. One girl when asked why she had consented replied blandly: 'Why Sur, he wudn't tak enny denial.'

Yet it seems difficult to attribute more than marginal importance to the system of poor relief as a reason for rising birth rates. The full Speenhamland system with allowances for every child was an exception even in the south of England and the economic difficulties of the 1820s forced many more parishes to abandon the system. By 1834, only

0·2 per cent of the parishes in England and Wales made payments for the first two children. There is little evidence to suggest that birth rates varied markedly in parishes with similar economies but different systems of poor relief. The Kent villages of Lenham and Barham support this view. In Lenham, a man with eight children had his wages made up to no less than £1 per week whereas in Barham there was no wage supplement. The only significant difference in population trends seems to be that mortality figures were rather lower in Lenham. In any case, birth rates were highest of all in the industrialising northern counties which did not operate the Speenhamland system. Increased birth rates then did affect population growth in the period 1780–1830, although the explanation most favoured by contemporaries seems to have little to support it. The change is probably best ascribed to the shift from rural to urban life and a definite trend towards early marrying.

But despite the difficult years and the over-population of some parts of the country, the possibilities of improved farming were so great that after 1815 agricultural production was increasing substantially faster than population growth. In the following twenty-five years, food prices drifted downwards, contrary to Malthus's predictions, and England was able to remain virtually self-sufficient in food until the middle of the nineteenth century.

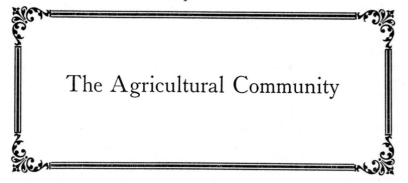

# Chapter Three

# The Agricultural Community

## Giles Jolterhead Esq

On the face of it then, farmers and landowners had made an enormous contribution to providing a solution to one of England's most serious problems. But even the defenders of the landed classes had to admit that cheap food and good harvests, obviously in the interests of the rest of the nation, were not welcomed either in manors or in farmhouse parlours. The farmers thought times were 'good' when the price of corn was over a hundred shillings per quarter–an average maintained between 1809 and 1812. Good or bad, the state of the harvest was still the most important factor in the general economic condition of the country. The weather was the thing that really mattered; employment fluctuated with the seasons rather than with a trade cycle. The last four months of the year were the busiest while January to April were the slackest; the rhythm of life was essentially agricultural. T. S. Ashton had the best insight into the real priorities: 'What was happening at Westminster was of little importance compared to what was happening in the Heavens.'

Agriculture could not be entirely separated from other forces at work in society, forces which were fast destroying William Cobbett's ideal world. Cobbett recognised that some of the pressures for change had been building up for centuries. The first major blow to Cobbett's ideal world had come in the sixteenth century; much of England's troubles could be traced to the Dissolution of the Monasteries by 'that matchless tyrant' Henry VIII and 'the devastating ruffians of the miscreant Thomas Cromwell'. Cobbett believed that the monasteries had maintained their philanthropic role until the end–'the relief of travellers, strangers and persons in distress'. Above all, the celibate monks had been generous landlords, aware of their responsibilities to their neighbourhood and willing to return the proceeds of their rents to the community by buying locally. Their lay successors, on the other hand, obsessed with the idea of amassing wealth to leave to their descendants, merely extracted the absolute maximum from their tenants. Such money as the landlords did spend was more likely to be frittered away on the dubious pleasures of London than spent on wages for local craftsmen.

Families who had grown rich on the plunder of the monasteries now thought themselves the grandest in England. Some, like the Russells, had the effrontery to claim that they had always been in the vanguard of liberty; in fact they had been in the vanguard of avarice. At a village near Petworth, Cobbett told a group of labourers that before the Reformation, wages had been fivepence a day–at a time when bacon cost a halfpenny a pound. The wages of 1825 would scarcely buy even a pound of bread. In short the vaunted advantages of Protestantism seemed questionable.

The place where Cobbett definitely parted company with conventional historians was in his evaluation of developments from 1688. 'Whig' enthusiasm for the 'Glorious Revolution' was derided and the accession of William and Mary portrayed as the imposition of a 'Venetian Constitution' by a parasite aristocracy ready to exploit and degrade throne and people for its own benefit. Taxes raised on the necessities of life were used to give pensions and sinecure offices to those who were already rich. According to Cobbett, it was the creation of the National Debt under William III which first made speculation respectable, and resulted in the proliferation of unstable paper fortunes which owed more to trickery than to honest industry. First shares, and then everything else, were bought in the hope of capital appreciation rather than for their intrinsic worth. The Age of the Banker and Stock-Jobber was about to begin.

But it was the long war against Revolutionary France which really transformed the situation. By 1815, the National Debt had reached £600 million, held in various types of 'Consols'. Even interest payments on a sum like this consumed a substantial part of the national income. Despite its borrowing, government spending on the war far exceeded its income from all sources and it became impossible to maintain a gold coinage. After 1797 more and more paper money appeared, and the increased money supply was one reason for the rising food prices of the Napoleonic wars. Not only Cobbett was worried by the effects of paper money. When the war was over, Lord Liverpool's government decided to return to a system of gold coinage. But if anything, 'Peel's Bill' of

1819 made things worse. A return to the gold standard, accompanied by drastic reductions in government spending, brought about a fall in both prices and incomes. The only thing which was not significantly reduced was the National Debt; rather, the cost of interest payments in real terms was increased because taxes took up a higher proportion of a man's reduced income. The lucky fundholder who had loaned only depreciated paper money received his dividends payable in gold worth as much as 40 per cent more.

The implications for the traditional aristocracy were serious. In their desire for gain, the landed classes had thrown in their lot with stock-jobbers and bankers during the war. They had used the alleged threat of Revolution and danger to property to pass Acts of Parliament which tried to stifle protests against the massive war profiteering that was then rampant. But now the unholy alliance was under strain; if the tenant farmer, affected by lower food prices, could not pay his rent, how could his landlord pay his taxes and maintain his existing standard of living?

Suppose Giles Jolterhead Esq. to have twenty farms. In consequence of alteration in the value of the currency wheat falls from 14s. to 7s. a bushel. It is clear that his rents must fall from £4000 to £2000 a year; and if he continued to pay £1000 towards the debt, it is clear that his spending income is, in fact, reduced to £1000 instead of £3000 a year. Well the situation of Squire Jolterhead is truly distressing. He lays down his *hounds* and three out of his four hunters and packs off a couple or three servants to begin with. People ask him why. He *'likes coursing* better'. But, the *greyhounds* are still expensive. The Tax gatherer comes thundering at the door; talks so loud (with his hat on all the while) that the servants hear his voice quite into the Hall. Away go the beautiful greyhounds dancing and capering to the pippin-tree. Four or five more visits from the man with the ink bottle at his button hole send off a brace out of three gardeners, turn the close-shaven lawn into a rough bit of pasture.[1]

Under the present system Squire Jolterhead would lose all his little luxuries and then his estate itself–probably to some war profiteer like Squire Turpentine, the spirit contractor, or Squire Garbage, the meat contractor. It seemed as if the landed classes had merely used their political influence to bring about a situation which would result in their destruction. They would be replaced by a race of vulgar upstarts spending their ill gotten gains on garish country houses, gambling and 'pretty improprieties'.

For all Cobbett's rhetoric, however, changes in the social origins and in the life style of the landowning sections of society were not dramatic.

Cobbett's distinction between the landowning and commercial classes was far too bald. For centuries, the system of primogeniture made it imperative for many younger sons to make a career in trade. A fluid land market was no new thing and successful merchants had aspired to become landowners and aristocrats even during Cobbett's 'ideal' fifteenth century. Some 'old' families found themselves in financial difficulties but few lost everything. In an age before death duties, it required massive extravagance on the scale of the Duke of Buckingham and the Marquis of Hastings to bring about complete disaster. In any case, it really mattered less who owned the land than the use to which it was put. It was certainly vital to increase agricultural output but even those who owned land and were short of ready cash could still improve their estates. Insurance companies were usually ready to advance money on the security of land.

It is certainly true that the 'new men' were likely to have more money to invest in improvement than would have been the case with the previous owners. In that sense, the change that Cobbett so much deplored was highly desirable. But few of the new owners bought estates for economic reasons. The main division in society was gentlemen versus the rest. The precise qualification of a gentleman was left conveniently vague but it definitely helped to be a landowner. The Arkwright family, cotton factory owners, 'Seigneurs of the Twist' *par excellence*, quickly became landed gentlemen. Richard Arkwright, barber, was certainly not a gentleman, but the money he made as a cotton spinner enabled him to buy up land around Cremford in Derbyshire. By a loan of £6000 to pay off the gambling debts of Georgiana Duchess of Devonshire, Arkwright was able to bring pressure to have himself accepted into polite society. Arkwright's son, another Richard, set himself up as a landowner on a large scale; in 1809 he bought the Hampton Court estate near Leominster in Herefordshire for £230,000. In the 1820s many landowners were forced to spoil their property by wholesale timber felling and by installing tenants who simply 'mined' the soil. The Arkwright cotton fortune protected the Hampton Court estate from such depredations.

Agriculture made handsome profits before 1815 but the greatest criticism of farmers and landowners came in the 1820s. Peace coincided with a return of good harvests; in a free market, the reappearance of East European corn and a fall in government purchases would have produced a quite catastrophic fall in prices. It was alleged that the landowners used undue political influence to safeguard their economic interests at the expense of the rest of the nation. Under the terms of the 1815 Corn Bill, foreign corn was excluded from Britain when the price of home-grown corn was less than 80 shillings per quarter. The specific intention was to keep up grain prices. On 6 March 1815 Mr Horace Paul got up in the House of Commons and said that the Corn Laws proved that the government was prepared to starve the people in order to gratify its political supporters. Manufacturers would have to pay higher wages than their foreign competitors in order to keep their work force alive. The effect on Britain's position in the world would be disastrous.

In fact, a good case can be made for the Corn Laws. There were already serious problems of urban unemployment. An even more drastic fall in grain prices than actually occurred would have forced many farmers to convert from arable to pasture. Pasture employed less labour than arable and thus the economic and social problems of unemployment would have been much worse. In general, therefore, one can say that the record of agriculture in its relations with the rest of the community was remarkably good. The big question is whether it was equally good to its own work force.

## The Nourishment of Vice and the Corruption of Youth

It would be naïve to see the agricultural Improvers and Enclosers merely as disinterested philanthropists. Some of the advocates of Enclosure were primarily interested in securing greater social control over the rural population. As we have seen, the claims made for Enclosures were often exaggerated and Cobbett, who was living in Hampshire 'when the madness for Enclosure raged most furiously', refused to believe that more food was being produced. In 1807 and 1808 his afternoon walks took him to a patch of common land called Horton Heath. The Heath was only about 150 acres in extent and was surrounded by thirty cottages, each with its own garden. The Heath gave life to the little community and provided the cottagers with grazing for their animals, rabbits for their pets and brushwood for their fire. Cobbett noted the names of all the cottagers, the number of children, cows, calves, pigs, geese, ducks, fruit-trees and beehives. There were fifteen cows, sixteen pigs and five hundred head of poultry. At the very least, the output from 150 acres was as great as that of 200 acres of enclosed land.[2]

Thus, if Enclosure actually reduced output, one could blame the 'Improvers' for the high prices and near starvation. Above all, the new system hurt the rural poor. It denied them food and employment—how else could one explain the great empty churches? If Horton Heath were to be enclosed, where were the cottagers to go? Their only refuge could be in one of the terrible factory towns. Indeed, Cobbett believed that the main purpose of the 'improvements' was to depopulate the countryside in order to create an industrial proletariat. This idea was later taken up by Marx who made the process into an essential pre-requisite of an Industrial Revolution.

The important thing about Cobbett's ideal yeomen and cottagers was not that they were efficient or inefficient but that they were no man's servant. Although hard-working, they worked to please themselves, and for their own benefit. They were independent and, in the last resort, able to thumb their nose at the squire or the parson. Of course, not everyone could have a farm, but even the landless were provided for by their Commons Rights of grazing and fuel gathering. In such a community, some men were richer than others but there was no crude distinction between the few arrogant and socially pretentious large farmers and the mass of grovelling, dependent wage slaves. Oliver Goldsmith believed that the inhabitants of the old type of community had been 'strangers alike to opulence and to poverty'.

Loyalties were vertical rather than horizontal. Whatever his social standing, a man identified with his local community against all sorts of 'foreigners'. The inhabitants of the next village were fortunate if they were regarded as no more than peculiar. Feuds between villages lasted for centuries, and marriages with the 'enemy' much condemned. Village patriotism reached its height on the day of the Patronal Festival. The feast provided an annual opportunity to check the villainy of a neighbouring parish out to grab a few square yards of extra territory. Parish boundaries were not the orderly affairs drawn up by Victorian reformers. Outlying parts, enclaves five miles or more from the mother parish were frequent. Vigilance to meet the threat of encroachment was vital. The universal practice of 'beating the Bounds' on the day of the Village Festival was no idle ceremony. To men bred up in the Psalms, the necessity of removing the adversary's landmark was self-evident. Pitched battles were frequent on such occasions; everyone, high and low, rich and poor, was expected to defend the communal heritage.

But one must guard against being too romantic about rural life in 'the good old days'. Eulogies about social harmony have to be set against the reality of misery, grossness and cruelty. The Lamb Ales, Whitsun Ales, Morris dancing, spinning feasts, hay homes and harvest homes were all accompanied by heavy drinking and frequently resulted in a crop of bastards for the parish to support. The festivities, with definite pre-Christian overtones, were particularly uninhibited where the village was unenclosed and there was no resident parson or squire. At

Padstow in Cornwall a man dressed as a horse danced through the streets on May Day. The horse sometimes fell and was declared 'dead' and then rose up again. The man who took the part of the horse was naked under his wide skirts and the girls caught under them when he 'died' were assured of fertility in the coming year. Elaborate ceremonies accompanied the Whit Ale at Kidlington in Oxfordshire: 'On the Monday after Whitsun week there is a fat live lamb provided and the Maids of the Town, having their thumbs ty'd behind them, run after it and she that with her mouth takes and holds the Lamb is declared *Lady of the Lamb*, which being dressed with the skin hanging on is carried, on a long pole before the Lady and her companions, to the Green, attended with Music and a Morisco Dance of men.'[3] The church had accommodated itself to 'popular' religion. The fertility role of the priest was emphasised by the fact that well into the nineteenth century, Anglican clergymen were expected to donate a bull and a boar to the village for breeding purposes. In some places, the people were essentially pagan and the influence of organised religion minimal. The impiety of Ottmoor, the unenclosed marshy land between Oxford and Bicester, was notorious. Few acknowledged their duty to worship God and their only attendance at church was at funerals where they usually appeared half drunk.[4]

Perhaps one should approve of such free-thinking but it is hard to find much to say for the terrible cruelty to animals which rural society delighted in. Cock fighting was made illegal early in the nineteenth century but continued in country districts for more than fifty years. Examples of bull baiting are found as late as the 1830s. The Revd Edward Elton, Vicar of Wheatley, Oxfordshire, wrote: 'Rude sports lingered here as in their last resort. Before this the custom was at the Feast or at Whitsuntide to parade a bull through the streets covered with ribbons and during the next day to bait him tied to a stake, i.e. everyone who had a savage dog was allowed to let him loose at the bull. This was done in the old quarry and a brutal scene it was.'[5]

Elton thought there was a connection between unenclosed parishes, idleness and moral turpitude. Official opinion was coming to the conclusion that life was too easy for the poor, particularly those who depended upon Commons Rights. Such riff-raff needed discipline; they were not compelled to work and when they had secured enough to live on, they could do what they liked with the remainder of their time. It was undesirable that the lower orders should have spare time; idleness was wicked in itself but it also led to vice and disaffection. It would be better for the nation and even for the people concerned if they were kept in continual labour. The dangers of the situation were exemplified in the life style of the Ottmoor 'moormen': 'In looking after a breed of goslings, a few rotten sheep, a skeleton of a cow or a mangy horse, the moormen have lost more than they might have gained by their day's work and have acquired habits of idleness and dissipation and a dislike to honest labour, which has rendered them the riotous and lawless set of men they have shown themselves to be.'[6]

'Commoners' even had the effrontery to refuse work; they were liable to reply that they must go and look at their sheep, get their cow out of the pound, or even that they had to take their horse to be shod to carry them to a race meeting, or cricket match. Even milder interests were dangerous. Despite his nostalgia for the past, the Oxfordshire antiquary, William Wing, conceded that the race meetings on 'dear delightful, breezy, naughty old Cottisford Heath' had tended to the 'nourishment of vice and the corruption of youth'. Upper-class opinion did not share Cobbett's enthusiasm for the 'harmless pleasures' of the countryman or for the social attitudes which accompanied such activities. In the new social order, there would be no more 'saucy' commoners; the lower orders would be hard-working and deferential to their betters. Most of the Enclosers genuinely believed that agricultural changes would improve the material lot of the poor–and their claims were largely justified–but there can be little doubt that the main social effect of Enclosure was a more polarised class system. Some welcomed the change; men like Cobbett deplored it. The years between 1780 and 1830 were to see bitter conflict between the beneficiaries and victims of agricultural change.

## Designing Rogues

Initiative for Enclosures usually came from the largest landowner in the parish. After 1775 all the proprietors in a village were supposed to be consulted before a petition was sent to Parliament requesting the appointment of commissioners to decide on a reallocation of holdings. Although there might be substantial local opposition, it was not difficult for the promoters of Enclosure to give a misleading impression in Westminster. The Member who introduced an Enclosure Bill could virtually nominate the committee chosen to discuss details of the measure! Parliament was only likely to pay attention if the objectors included a man of substantial property.

Thus denied legal outlet for their objections, the small farmers and commoners were sometimes ready to threaten violence to preserve their traditional way of life. In February 1799 the promoters of an Enclosure Act at Cheshunt, Hertfordshire, were offering fifty guineas to discover the authors of an anonymous letter:

Whe like horse leaches will cry give, give until whe have split the bloud of every one that wishes to rob the inosent unborn. It shall not be in your power to say 'I am safe from the hands of my Enemy' for whe like birds of pray will prively lye in wait to spil the bloud of the aforesaid Charicters whose names and places of abode are as prutrified sores in our Nostrils. Whe leave it for thy consideration whether thou would like to be sorted out from the land of the liveing.

Once the Act was passed, the commissioners arrived in the village, examined title deeds and claims and began the task of drawing up a new and rational system of field boundaries. In most cases, Enclosure was accompanied by the abolition of remaining manorial rights and tithes; compensation was given in the form of land. The principle adopted was that land was presumed to belong to the Lord of the Manor unless the occupier could prove to the contrary. Those who could produce no satisfactory deeds got nothing in the award, nor was there any provision for the landless Commoners whose rights were extinguished. The commissioners faced considerable temptation to give the best quality land to the richest men and, in case of doubt, to decide in favour of those who could be of use to them in the future. On the whole, however, the Enclosure commissioners carried out their tasks with commendable impartiality. It was alleged that during the Enclosure of Charnwood Forest, Leicestershire, the commissioners had been unduly favourable to the large landowners by awarding them fields near to their houses, but more careful investigation seemed to show that any bias had been in the other direction. The claims of the most influential had been disallowed while those of the poor were admitted even on slender evidence.[7]

The commutation of manorial and tithe rights meant that the share of the village land owned by the Lord of the Manor and, in some cases, by the Rector, was increased. The award to the church was of vital significance; discipline could not be instilled into work-shy villagers unless the message had authoritative spiritual backing. It seemed that only a landowning and rich parson could command proper deference. Revd T. W. Allies, Rector of Launton, Oxfordshire, wrote that his parishioners had no respect for him as a clergyman but they were prepared to give him due deference as a gentleman and a landowner.[8]

In the past, the church lacked the resources to support such a man in every village. Rich clergymen were a small minority; the fortunate few controlled several livings and then delegated their responsibilities to miserably underpaid curates. The old system was slow to change. In his *Legacy to Parsons*, William Cobbett singled out some of the notorious pluralists of his day. In addition to enjoying a government pension of £700 a year, Lord Walsingham was Archdean of Surrey, Prebendary of Winchester, Rector of Calbourne, Rector of Fawley, perpetual curate of Exbury, and Rector of Merton. The conversion of tithes into real property, however, provided an economic basis for the marked revival in church influence at the beginning of the nineteenth century. It was hoped that there would be enough money for a rich and socially impressive resident incumbent in every parish. Richard Davis, frequently employed as an Enclosure commissioner in Oxfordshire, cited the example of a clergyman near Banbury whose income had risen from £105 to £220 per year as a result of Enclosure, and declared that there would be further gains when existing leases fell in.[9] In many cases evidence of this wealth was to be seen in the building of large parsonages to replace the 'mere cottages' which had housed generations of 'hedge priests'.

If Enclosure increased the proportion of a parish owned by the squire and the parson, what of the smaller landowner, the yeoman farmer? Even if the commissioners were fair, the small farmer lost his Commons Rights, which had previously played an important part in the viability of his farm. 'Strip the small farms of the benefit of the commons', said one observer, 'and they are all at one stroke levelled to the ground.' All those who received an award had to pay their share towards the cost of Enclosure. There were legal costs, the expenses of the commissioners, as well as the longer-term prospects of paying for the hedging, ditching and fencing required to make the new landscape. All sorts of people benefited from the passage of an Enclosure Bill. In the House of Commons alone, there were payments to 'Mr Speaker, his Secretary, his Clerk, the Clerk Assistant, the Chief Clerk without doors (being one of the four Clerks without doors, who receives the fees and pays them to the officers of the House), the Sergeant and the Officers under him, the Housekeeper, the two Doorkeepers, the four Messengers, the Clerks of the Committee Clerk's Office and those of the Private Bill.'

In 1800 Enclosure commissioners usually charged two guineas a day for their services and the surveyor about thirty shillings. What really mattered to the small landowner was the cost per acre he would be called upon to carry. Obviously the costs of Enclosure were a problem, but the process rarely involved cataclysmic change: more often it was merely an important step along a well-trodden path. Consolidation of holdings had been going on for centuries and was to continue long after

Enclosure. Enterprising small farmers were able to find the money to pay their share of Enclosure costs and to participate in the boom of the war years. It was only the really small man, with a holding best described as a paddock rather than a farm, who would be inclined to sell up immediately. Twenty-five acres was probably the decisive figure; a holding larger than that was viable without Commons Rights.

The groups most likely to be adversely affected by Enclosure were those who lived by their rights as commoners and those who had 'squatted' upon the common without legal title. It was these people who were believed to be in especial need of the discipline of hard work and who would now provide the labour force for the large farms created by Enclosure. Although the new system of agriculture may have provided more work, in some cases even an improvement in living standards, it also deprived a man of his independence. It is not surprising that the Commoners were the basis of resistance to Enclosure. It was not just a matter of sending anonymous threatening letters; in some places men were prepared to resist by force. In the early months of 1799 the commissioners supervising the Enclosure of the common at Wilbarston, Northamptonshire, encountered continual harassment. On 24 July the Northampton and Althorp troops of Yeomanry were ordered to assemble at Harborough under the command of Major Cartwright and attended, significantly, by the Revd Mr Griffin JP. The Yeomanry were to escort wagons carrying the fencing materials but, as they approached Wilbarston, they were met by a crowd of about three hundred people who had lit a huge bonfire in the middle of the road to prevent the passage of the wagons. The Riot Act was read and the wagons advanced after the arrest of 'one or two of the most active of the mob'.[10]

The affair at Wilbarston was tame compared to the concerted resistance to the Enclosure of Ottmoor, following the signing of the Commissioners' Award on 15 April 1829. The movement was given extra strength and coherence by the fact that small farmers–who in most places either acquiesced in or actively promoted Enclosure–were here prepared to support the 'moormen'. In August 1830 small parties of men gathered at night, blowing horns and roaming the moor with bill hooks and axes to cut down the hated fences. An element of mystery was provided by blacked faces and the wearing of 'women's clothes'. Resistance was well organised; printed handbills appeared signed by 'The King of Ottmoor' urging his people to destroy the Enclosure. Nervous magistrates talked of a carefully planned conspiracy. On 6 September 1830 the Yeomanry arrived and were faced with a crowd of nearly one thousand people, cutting down fences and appealing to the soldiers to join them. In the following confrontation, forty-four people were arrested and put into carts to be taken to Oxford Castle. The streets were full of countrymen visiting St Giles's Fair; a horrified 'Gentleman of Rank' described what happened. 'At some distance from this city, the detachment were met by the mob, which continually increased and which attacked them with stones, bricks, sticks etc., calling out to the prisoners to make their escape. The Fair at St Giles in this city, had assembled vast numbers of the worst description of people, and passing through the streets the yeomanry were assailed with the utmost violence and many of them seriously injured.'[11]

The twenty-nine soldiers under Captain Hamilton knew that if they fired even one round into the air, they would be torn to pieces by the crowds. The escort party simply fled, leaving its prisoners to escape. Hamilton was among the first to flee and only one Yeomanry man, Bartlett, had the courage to try to keep the mob at bay by using the flat of his sword. Agitators roused the visiting countrymen to fury and the streets of Oxford echoed to the sounds of 'Ottmoor for Ever' and 'Down with the Bloody Officers'.

There was rioting all over southern England in the autumn of 1830. The men who pulled up fences or smashed threshing machines often claimed to be carrying out the orders of Captain Swing. Although William Cobbett never gave explicit approval to violence, he was closely associated with Captain Swing. At Battle in Sussex the authorities believed that cases of arson had been caused by 'a lecture lately given here publicly by a person named Cobbett'. At Tadmarton near Banbury, a hay-making machine was destroyed by a chimney sweep named Philip Green who was 'a great admirer of Cobbett whose productions he is in the habit of quoting in the public houses he frequents'.[12] The village of Micheldever in Hampshire was virtually ruled by the rioters for several days; conveniently there was a shoemaker at hand who had read aloud from Cobbett's *Political Register* to a 'small party of Hampshire bumpkins' on Saturday nights.[13] 'Swing' confirmed Cobbett's faith in the true born Englishman; he declared on 13 November 1830:

I know that English labourers would not lie down and die in any number, with nothing but sour sorrel in their bellies (as two did at Acton on the beginning of the summer); and know that they would never receive the *extreme unction* and die of hunger, as the poor Irish did, and be praised for their *resignation* by Bingham-Baring or Baring-Bingham, or whatever else he is. I knew that all the palaver in the world, all the wheedling, coaxing, praying; I knew that all the blustering and threatening, I knew that all these would fail to persuade the honest, sensible and industrious English labourer, that they had not an indefeasible right to live.[14]

The government was so convinced of Cobbett's complicity in the 'Swing Riots' that he was brought to trial on a charge of sedition in July 1831. Cobbett was not a man to be awed by the panoply of the law; he would defend himself powerfully, even arrogantly, arguing that he had only called upon the authorities to change unjust laws which were driving the labourers of England to despair. During the trial he constantly denounced the Game Laws. The slaughter of game was the exclusive monopoly of men with landed estates worth more than £100 per annum; farmers who owned a moderate sized estate were forbidden to kill the game that lived on their own property. Blackstone had declared that these pernicious laws had set up 'a little Nimrod' in every parish. Faced with plump pheasants in gorgeous feathers the starving labourer was supposed to recognise that such things were not for him. Penalties for touching the forbidden food were savage. In 1816 it had been enacted that any person found with a poaching net even if he was not armed could be transported for seven years. If there was any violence or clash with the gamekeepers it might provide work for the public hangman. Cobbett's message was that it was better to poach and risk the noose, or death from the spring gun, than to starve. The case against Cobbett was based on the confession of one of the convicted rioters, Thomas Goodman, who, under the influence of Revd H. J. Rush of Crowhurst in Sussex, had declared 'I, Thomas Goodman, never should of thought of doing aney sutch thing if Mr. Cobet had never given aney lactures; i believe that their never would been any fires or mob in Battel nor maney other places if he never had given aney lactures at all.'[15]

Goodman's confession was elaborated under pressure from the Sussex magistrates. He now claimed that Cobbett had urged every labouring man to keep a gun in his cottage and had given direct encouragement to arson. At the trial, Cobbett destroyed the prosecution's case that 'Swing' had been a carefully planned conspiracy; he showed that Goodman had simply been saving his neck by providing the magistrates with a confession. At the end of the trial Cobbett spoke for four and a half hours; according to Charles Greville 'his insolence and violence were past endurance, but he made an able speech'.[16] He concluded 'If I am compelled to meet death in some stinking dungeon into which they have the means of cramming me, my last breath shall be employed in praying to God to bless my country, and to curse the

Whigs to everlasting; and, revenge I bequeath to my children and to the labourers of England.'

The case against Cobbett had been in ruins from the moment the accused called as a witness Henry Brougham, the Lord Chancellor of England himself. Brougham admitted that he had written to Cobbett at the height of the disturbances asking permission to reprint some articles from the *Political Register* in which Cobbett had urged the people not to resort to violence. If the Lord Chancellor saw Cobbett as a force for moderation, surely there would be an acquittal. The Lord Chief Justice, however, summed up against Cobbett and, in the end, the jury could not agree–but no attempt was made to hold a retrial. The labourers' champion had escaped but the labourers themselves did not. The government set up special commissions to try the rioters–rather like those directed by Judge Jeffreys after the Monmouth Rebellion. At Winchester alone 101 people were sentenced to death, although only six were actually executed. Certainly the riots caused a great deal of damage but no lives had been lost. Among those hanged was Kenny Cook, an illiterate plough boy who had struck off the hat of William Bingham Baring Esquire JP.

In the face of such repression, the rural labourers returned to obedience to their betters. Resistance on Ottmoor lasted longer than in most places and was not quenched until 1835. The Yeomanry were not regarded as sufficiently reliable and the only solution was to have a garrison of regular soldiers on hand to support the civil power. Companies of the finest regiments in the British Army–the Coldstream Guards and Scots Guards–had to be quartered in tiny Oxfordshire villages to prevent any recurrence of 'agrarian outrage', and even then they were not very successful. In general the new rural proletariat acquiesced but very sullenly in their new role; as the *Commercial and Agricultural Magazine* declared: 'Those who have to employ the poor, constantly experience in them the machinations of minds, which have always been intent on a single object; to procure large wages for the least possible work. Their laziness out of sight and bad performance of work so constantly occurs that they are usually looked upon as designing rogues.'[17]

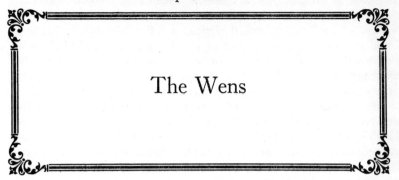

# Chapter Four

# The Wens

## At Once Horrible and Ridiculous

Although changes in the English countryside were important, such developments pale alongside the more fundamental change of increased urbanisation. The Age of Cobbett saw the foundation of new industrial centres in the north of England, but there was also a significant expansion of older settlements like London and Birmingham where traditional crafts still flourished. The problems of rural life were so serious that one would imagine that contemporaries would have welcomed the expansion of towns. Yet Cobbett and other writers regarded urban society as unnatural and corrupting. They believed that the 'real' England was a country of fields, manors and cottages– not of festering slums, factories and upstart bourgeois villas. Distaste for towns was a reflection of the Romantic sentiment of the times; Cowper, Wordsworth and Southey vied in their denunciations. In his *Letters from England* Robert Southey said of Birmingham: 'You will perhaps look with some eagerness for information concerning this famous city, which Burke calls the grand toy-shop of Europe. I am still giddy, dizzied with the hammering of presses, the clatter of engines, the whirling of wheels; my head aches with the multiplicity of infernal noises, and my eyes with the light of infernal fires, I may add, my heart aches at the sight of so many human beings employed in infernal occupations, and looking as if they were never destined for anything better.'[1]

The charge against the cities was not only that they were dirty– towns of the past had certainly been that–but the new industrial dirt seemed 'active and moving, a living principle of mischief' so that visitors felt they needed their throats sweeping like an English chimney.

The Age of Cobbett saw a fantastic advance in human ingenuity; Birmingham provided the spectacle of new processes for the manufacture of small arms, watch chains, necklaces, bracelets, buttons, buckles, snuff-boxes and a host of other things. But it had all been purchased at a frightening cost of health and morality. To those who were appalled and haunted by the course of events in France, the absence of a clear social hierarchy was a certain recipe for disaster.

Southey believed that the urban poor was more easily roused to riot and revolution than its rural counterpart. The town workman had no loyalties or attachments; he merely envied his employer as a man who had grown rich by the labour of others. In times of economic difficulty there was no chance of the townsman raising his own food; he was completely at the mercy of the ups and downs of the trade cycle and liable to respond with desperation and violence. Above all, the townsman was likely to be half educated; he knew just enough of the political world to think himself a politician. The direction of popular fury depended entirely on caprice. In 1794 a Birmingham mob attacked the houses of rich nonconformists who were suspected of disloyalty and then searched everywhere for the scientist Joseph Priestley, carrying a spit on which it was intended to roast him alive. The implication was clear: governments who founded national prosperity upon manufacturing industry were sleeping upon gunpowder. If the new system continued to expand violent revolution was inevitable.[2]

Birmingham was bad enough, but the really monstrous growth was that of London itself. It was estimated that over one thousand new houses were built each year for the middle classes alone. In January 1822, Cobbett found that one of his Rural Rides was far less rural than it ought to have been. 'On quitting the great Wen (London) we go through Surrey. From St George's Fields which are now covered with houses, we go towards Croydon, between rows of houses, nearly half the way, and the whole way is nine miles. What at once horrible and ridiculous this country would become if this thing could go on for a few years! But how is this Wen to be dispersed? I know not whether it be to be done by knife or caustic; but dispersed it must be!'[3]

Neither Birmingham nor London were industrial towns in the modern sense; that is, they were not towns with large factories. Much of their expansion was caused by the growth of traditional industries and, in the case of London, by developments connected with the war against France. In a way, they were part of traditional England and in some respects they provided the brightest spots in an otherwise troubled country. Continental writers could view things in a broader perspective than English pessimists; most of them felt that Londoners had much to

William Cobbett at work on the *Political Register*, the most widely read news sheet in the country   *Radio Times Hulton Picture Library*

Cobbett's childhood home, The Jolly Farmer at Farnham, the model for his vision of old England *Radio Times Hulton Picture Library*

Farnham hop pickers, living in Cobbett's Arcadia, symbolising the beer of 'true' England *Radio Times Hulton Picture Library*

A scene probably similar to Cobbett's grandmother's cottage, showing a family poor but industrious  *Radio Times Hulton Picture Library*

The epitomy of everything Cobbett hated–vanity, pretence and immorality (compare with previous plate)  *The Mansell Collection*

An enclosure map with neat field boundaries–no room here for 'Saucy Commoners'   *Radio Times Hulton Picture Library*

be thankful for and that the last twenty years of the eighteenth century had seen remarkable improvements. Some Germans were surprised that the City authorities in London still permitted 'that absurd and noxious custom of burying their dead among the living, in church yards amidst dwelling houses, and even in churches under the feet of the parishioners.'[4] In all other respects, London had the edge over its rivals. Its western parts, inhabited by the better-off sectors of society, were undoubtedly among the finest residential areas in Europe. It was far better provided for than Paris in pavements, cleanliness and lighting.

English writers, however, tended to portray London as a hot bed of crime and squalor. A London magistrate, Patrick Colquhoun, wrote *Treatise on the Police of the Metropolis* which spoke of 'outrages and acts of violence continually committed', although Francis Place, 'the Radical Tailor of Charing Cross', looking back on his youth in the 1780s, was convinced that crimes had then been more numerous and more atrocious than they were in the 1820s. Place gave much of the credit to street lighting. Even in the 1780s, Archenholtz declared that there were more lamps in Oxford Street alone than in the whole of Paris. The new oil-lamps, covered by crystal globes and hung on posts, were objects of universal admiration. But oil-lamps were dim compared to the gas burners that appeared in Whitecross Street in August 1807 and in Pall Mall a year later. In Paris the lamps were not lit when there was supposed to be a full moon; the fact that the night might be very dark and the moon covered by clouds made no difference.

For the tourist perhaps the most striking feature of London life was the enormous sale of newspapers–by the end of the eighteenth century there were twenty daily papers published in London; people seemed to waste an inordinate amount of time reading them and to accept what they read as absolute truth. Foreigners were astonished at the liberty allowed to the press and the absence of effective censorship. Most extraordinarily, even those who were attacked seemed not to care very much. Yet, despite the avid reading of newspapers it was striking that, even in wartime, there was astonishingly little interest in what was happening in other countries. 'Informed' opinion believed in a 'balance of power' and that England should hold the balance–but that was about the sum of it. Already, the newspapers which concentrated on 'anecdotes of romantic lovers, horrid accounts of robberies, murders, fires and melancholy accidents' were considered to be the most entertaining.

Newspapers could be read in one of the three thousand coffee houses. These establishments were generally well conducted and quiet;

frequenters of coffee houses were not regarded with disapproval as they were in Germany. At a coffee house or a print shop, the tourist could furnish himself with a plan of London, although he had to be careful to specify that he must have the latest edition, because new streets were constantly being created. But no visit to London was complete without seeing the Bethlehem Hospital–Bedlam; moralists justified the visit as a means of humbling human pride and teaching moral man what degradation might be his fate. But foreigners also took some pleasure from the fact that the English seemed more subject to madness than other nations. The Royal Exchange and its stock-jobbers was another source for moralising:

> None of them thinks he has enough; no one is satisfied; and amongst them may, perhaps, be seen a man, who having appeared in the Gazette, yet struts along with so much confidence, that a stranger might be inclined to take him for the richest man there. Not many years elapse before an almost new set of faces appear on the Exchange. The great gulf of London swallows all, and the burying grounds of this great metropolis are stored with the bones of the rich as well as of the poor. The generality of them are soon forgotten, sometimes even by their heirs, when they have rested hardly eight days underground.[5]

After all the public buildings, churches and commercial premises, the visitor was allowed to inspect the pleasure gardens at Vauxhall. Once in the height of fashion, by the end of the century the respectability of pleasure gardens was being questioned. It was still possible to hear good music and singing but there were those who visited the gardens and 'derived from thence cause for a long repentance'. Thus, London was a city to be admired but treated with caution. The idea that London could go on growing was firmly rejected. Sir Richard Phillips declared:

> Great cities contain in their very greatness, the seeds of premature and rapid decay. London will increase, as long as certain causes operate which she cannot control, and after those cease to operate for a season her population will require to be renewed by new supplies of wealth, these failing the houses will become too numerous for its inhabitants and certain districts will be occupied by beggary and vice, or become depopulated. This disease will spread like an atrophy in the human body and ruin will follow ruin, until the entire city is disgusting to the remnant of the inhabitants.[6]

## Prostitution and Plunder

Of course tourists like the German Frederick Wendeborn were concerned with the London of the rich and the middle classes. At all levels of society, including the lowest, people moved to towns in the hope of an easier life. London was a paradise for beggars. It was claimed that any person with an obvious defect or deformity should make his way to London; beggars had free liberty of showing their nauseous sights to terrify people and force them to give money to get rid of them. Begging had reached the proportions of an art. The shallow lay was a well-established custom in which the beggar stood in the street, wearing only a few tattered garments and calling for help and pity from passers-by. If wet weather ruined honest street traders, it was a godsend to the shallow lay. The beggar wanted money; if he was given food or clothing there was a danger that his 'earnings' would be too obvious and his cover destroyed. In the 1830s it was estimated that the shallow lay style of begging produced about three shillings a day, or rather more than the wages of the ordinary labourer. More sophisticated methods required greater investment. Some beggars hired children to accompany them in the hopes of gaining extra sympathy; an ordinary child charged threepence a day, a crippled child sixpence a day, and a badly deformed child as much as four shillings.

But only the unintelligent boys stayed on as beggars as their more stupid sisters remained prostitutes. Wendeborn was right; the big cities were indeed snares for the innocent. Moralists constantly underlined the dangers faced by maids who left their places or by hopeful young women coming up from the country. Many 'Officers of Intelligence', officially employment bureaux for domestic service, were really recruiting agencies for brothels. Wendeborn did not sufficiently appreciate that prostitution was only a secondary source of income; its returns could be substantially improved if it were combined with robbery. Ellen Reece admitted that she lived by 'prostitution and plunder' but she made seven times as much by robbery as by prostitution. For many girls, prostitution was simply a means to an end and a drunken client made the ideal victim.[7] If a prostitute was arrested and accused of robbery, drastic action had to be taken. 'The place for hiding money are pockets in the underside of the stays towards the lower part. Also wrapping it in a piece of rag or paper and putting it in the hair. Also pockets in the stocking below the garter. Also putting it where decency forbids to name–has known thirty sovereigns hidden there at one time. Also swallowing it–has known eleven swallowed. If they don't get it for two or three days, they get opening medicine.'[8]

Ellen Reece was obviously a girl of some resources who claimed to know plenty of lawyers who were prepared to accept payment in kind if she had no money for her defence. But beggars and prostitutes were at the bottom of the criminal world. Pickpockets, 'cracksmen' and high-class confidence tricksters regarded such riff-raff with disdain. Patrick Colquhoun cited the example of a carefully planned seizure of a cartload of raw silk, worth £1200, in the middle of Cheapside; the whole operation and the disappearance of the cart was over in 'the twinkling of an eye'.

Such activities required at least a degree of honour among thieves. Although casual crime existed, there was a distinct criminal class, conscious of its own identity. London slang divided people into two groups—clockmakers (the honest and hard-working) and watchmakers (criminals). Criminal society was rather conservative and old-fashioned; its institutions and rules corresponded closely to those of an old craft guild. Like more legitimate journeymen, criminals had a well-established tramping route which took them away from London during the summer months; from June to October, they would carry on their profession at watering places and at country fairs. Passwords would be issued which would assure a wandering thief a welcome at certain inns which were frequently in more serious business as 'flash houses'. In these establishments, stolen goods were collected, carefully hidden behind false walls and then quietly disposed of. Dickens's character Fagin was probably based on the owner of a 'flash house', the notorious Ikey Solomons, who was finally caught and transported to Van Diemen's Land in 1827. The 'flash house' was often used to instruct promising youngsters. In the training of pickpockets, an overcoat with a hand bell tied to the sleeve was hung from a nail. The first lesson was to take a wallet from the coat pocket without the bell ringing.

Despite Colquhoun's alarmist advice never to stop in a crowd or to look into a shop window, there were solid reasons to support Francis Place's argument that London was becoming more law-abiding. Reforms in the administration of justice had some effect. According to the Irish politician Edmund Burke, the Middlesex Justices were 'generally the scum of the earth, some of whom were notoriously men of such infamous characters that they were unworthy of any employ whatever and others so ignorant that they could scarcely write their names'. The work of a magistrate involved issuing warrants, questioning prisoners and the risk of catching 'gaol fever'. But magistrates were entitled to keep a proportion of the fines they imposed. Samuel Harrison cited the example of an old man called 'Polly' Walker who was a 'Trading Justice' in the 1790s. From his office in Hyde Street, Bloomsbury, Walker had positively incited gang fights between contending bands of Irish in order to increase his income.

The establishment of 'Rotation Offices', where the duties were shared by at least two magistrates, helped to check this abuse and increase public confidence in the administration of justice. The Thames Police Office was established in 1798 owing to pressure from the West India merchants; the office was intended to check the wholesale plundering of ships and warehouses which appeared to threaten the very core of London's prosperity. On land, police work was still in the hands of vestry meetings so that an efficient force for the whole of London could not be created until 1829. But even so, many of the vestries obtained local Acts of Parliament to enable them to lay a 'watch rate' and cure inefficiency and dishonesty rampant under the old system. After 1782, there was a Foot Patrol of at least sixty-eight Bow Street Runners in the streets of London after dark. There was still a long way to go but, under the impetus of the reforming magistrate Sir John Fielding, there had been steady improvement. Francis Place could declare that the 1820s saw a clear connection between the decline of crime and general prosperity: 'We are much better people than we were half a century ago, better instructed more sincere and kind hearted, less gross and brutal, and have fewer of the concomitant vices of a less civilized state.'[9]

The big test of apparent improvement came with the inevitable economic dislocation after the end of the Napoleonic wars. Even Townsend, the most famous of the Bow Street Runners, admitted that things had been much quieter after 1815 than he had anticipated. Of course, one reason why people could be deterred from crime was fear of punishment. In theory, the law was draconian; in 1800 there were about two hundred offences which carried the death penalty. A reduction did not begin until 1808 when the Whig Lawyer Sir Samuel Romilly succeeded in abolishing capital punishment for pickpockets. In fact, the system could be advantageous to the criminal; juries were reluctant to convict a guilty man because they believed that the death sentence was inappropriate in the case of a relatively minor crime. Even those sentenced to death were in little danger of being brought to the scaffold. Between 1805 and 1814 eighty people were sentenced to death at the Old Bailey for the crime of shop-lifting but, in the event, not one was executed.

Hanging days were held at Tyburn eight times a year, occasions when apprentices and journeymen were traditionally excused from work. Public executions at Tyburn were suspended in 1783, much to the annoyance of Dr Johnson who believed that the condemned man was 'supported' by the presence of a large crowd. But this support often took a strange form; an unpopular criminal's last moments were interrupted by 'shouts and execrations, stones, dirt and filth, thrown with violence in every direction'. It was dangerous to attend an execution; limbs were frequently broken and eyes gouged out in the fights which accompanied the macabre scene. Afterwards the crowd would look for more sport, and the harassment of foreigners was a popular follow-up. After such treatment a M. de la Condamine 'shut himself up in the house for a fortnight where he vested his indignation in continual imprecations against England and the English'. Probably Francis Place was right to insist that only thieves, prostitutes and a few twisted characters from high society attended public executions. By 1830 it seemed incredible that, within living memory, people with a claim to respectablity should have been spectators at Tyburn.

## Modesty and Sobriety

Contemporaries who believed that crime was less of a problem than in the past explained the development in terms of the greater respectability of the lower classes. London was certainly not a prudish place in the 1780s. As a boy, Francis Place came to doubt the truth of religion in general and of the Virgin Birth in particular from his reading of *Aristotle's Compleat Master, displaying the Secrets of Nature*. Place also noted that obscene prints were available at most stationers. At Roach's in Russell Court, Mrs Roach tried to interest a boy or girl who came in to buy a school book by asking them if they wanted to see some pretty pictures and then opened a portfolio containing a multitude of obscene prints. By the 1820s such shops were much harder to find and the views expounded by Sir John Fielding in 1773 had gained general acceptance:

And now, gentlemen, give me leave to take notice of one public offence, so mischievous in its effects, that, like a pestilence, it does not only stand in need of your immediate assistance, but that of all good men, to stop its corroding progress; I mean the exposing to sale, and selling such indecent and obscene prints and books as are sufficient to put impudence to the blush. Surely gentlemen, providence has placed too strong propensions in our nature to stand in need of such inflammatory aids as them; on the contrary, in this particular, we rather require restraints than encouragement. By care, you may prevent youth in some degree from frequenting bad company; but alas, what doors, what bolts, what bars, can be any security to their innocence, whilst vice in this deluding form counteracts all caution and bids defiance to the force of precept, prudence and example.[10]

Fielding's warning was taken up by the Society for the Suppression of Vice whose members persuaded the courts to take a sterner view of pornography. In April 1803 one Harris 'a Vender of Ballads and Obscene Books and Prints' was sentenced to two years imprisonment by the Westminster sessions. The same court passed sentence on an Italian named Bertazzi who sold obscene books in 'boarding schools of both sexes'. The same, more puritanical trend was observable in the standards applied to children's games. 'Drop the Handkerchief' and 'Kiss in the Ring' which ended with mock marriages and kisses were smiled on by parents in the 1780s but regarded with horror in the 1830s. Popular songs, too, were changing. Francis Place's father kept The King's Arms in Arundel Street, by the standards of the time a well-conducted public house. The respectable tradesmen who spent their evenings in the parlour would sing songs which later generations found 'very gross'. Place was embarrassed by recollection of these songs in 1835 when he told a Parliamentary committee that he had 'long since forgotten' the words of 'Morgan Rattler' and 'A Hole to Put Poor Robin In'. The songs 'cannot now be more than generally described' and would scarcely be tolerated at any level of society, much less in the presence of children. In short: 'The manners of the heads of families were coarse and vulgar and frequently indecent to an extent scarcely to be credited. Their children were permitted to run about the filthy streets, to hear all sorts of bad language and to mix with whomsoever they pleased. The change in this particular is complete and when I look back and reflect on the conduct of such persons I even am surprised at the change.'[11]

The change in the conduct of apprentices and young women was equally dramatic. In the 1780s 'want of chastity' in the girls was common, and not a matter of reproach if in other respects they were decent in general conduct. At the age of fourteen Francis Place was apprenticed to a leather breeches maker; Mr France had a good business but his daughters were prostitutes and his sons thieves. In his leisure hours, Place found time to join a rowing or 'cutter' club, a sad set of blackguards whose coxswain was later transported for robbery. There were also 'Cock and Hen Clubs' where there was a long table with a chair at one end occupied by a youth and a chair at the other occupied by a girl; 'The amusements were drinking–smoking–swearing and singing flash songs.' The chairs were taken at 8 pm and the boys and girls paired off by degrees, till at 12 o'clock none remained. The girls were not particularly alluring. Francis Place frequently spent his evenings in 'dirty public houses' with some of the local girls. Most of them wore quartered shoes, and large-buckled shoes and stockings were generally clean because it was then the fashion to be 'flashy about the heels'. But the girls did not wear stays (apparently a sign of moral laxity) and their dresses were always open to expose their breasts. Whatever attention the girls may have lavished on themselves to improve on nature, they certainly did not bother about their hair which was usually filled with lice and 'hung in rat's tails' over their eyes.[12]

Even with their very limited means the young people of Place's circle were very fashion-conscious and there were fashions peculiar to particular areas. The boys who aimed at being 'Kiddies' had their hair on the sides of their faces rolled round pieces of lead about four inches long which were probably stolen from a glazier. There were three or four of these ringlets. A lad who aspired to the very height of fashion had a bunch of strings at his knees to fasten his breeches and long striped cotton stockings complete with a dozen buttons. With the hindsight of forty years Place could only consider these fashions quite grotesque.[13]

The influence of fairs on the youth of both sexes was widely deplored. The amateur topographer and engraver James Malcolm wrote in 1808: 'Many of the pernicious customs which disgrace the populace of London may, and indeed must be continued by their attendance at the various Fairs still held near the Metropolis. It is well known that the passions of human nature require the utmost coercion, even in families of undoubted honour and virtue; is it then prudent, much less wise to send apprentices, youths from schools, girls, the offspring of the lower classes, and servants into these regular scenes of riot and systematic violation of order and decency where customs must be acquired which will not bear repetition?'[14] Place recognised that society in his youth had been dissolute by later standards but he was less censorious than Malcolm, who had been 'educated at enormous expense' and came from a rich Quaker family. Both Place and Malcolm were concerned with the connection between crime and drink. Place had first-hand experience of the problem; his eldest sister married James Pain, an excellent cabinet-maker, who could have made four pounds a week all year round. But Pain was an 'ignorant besotted fellow who had never saved a single shilling'. At one time Place hoped that Pain could be reformed and, indeed, it might have been so if Mrs Pain had been a better wife. Place's sister despised her husband; she went to chapel, prayed, sang hymns and attended meetings when she ought to have been at home. Husband and wife had separate consolations–he in drink and she in Methodism. It is far from clear which her brother considered to be the greater moral evil.

Fifty years later, there was an obvious family pride in Francis Place's reference to the days at The King's Arms; he could see no harm in a well-conducted house. The parlour at The King's Arms was furnished with leather-covered benches and mahogany tables and heated by a good fire in winter. The beer was kept in large cool cellars and Simon Place was always on guard against brewers sending new and inferior beer. He made a rule never to draw any beer which had been in his cellars for less than a year and the Brown Stout, for which The King's Arms became famous, was no less than three years old. Of course, people did get drunk, particularly at gatherings in the upstairs club room which was supplied with Simon's punch–but the Cock and Hen Clubs with their associated debaucheries were absolutely forbidden. To James Malcolm, however, public houses and dram shops were centres for 'thieving, plots and murders'. Where there was the greatest misery and the greatest crime, there one would find the largest number of public houses.

The great division among the lower classes was between the skilled and the unskilled; it was the unskilled who seemed more addicted to drink and it was drink which shaped the character of 'Londoners of the lowest class' so much disapproved of by Malcolm:

Observe them absorbed and mark their custom; they wear a round hat, like those of men of fashion, placed far back on the head, covering a collection of long, lank hair which shades the features composed of vacancy and impudence; the neck is cloathed in a coarse muslin cravat folded in ungraceful lines; his coat is generally dark blue or brown lapelled, his waistcoat of white or printed cotton, and his legs are covered either by pantaloons or breeches and white cotton stockings. Their progress through the streets is marked by impetuosity and a constant exertion of strength, making the peaceful citizen and his wife and children retire in order to avoid being hurried forward with them or overturned. Their conversation consists of violent disputes and execrations, often degenerating into whimsical effusions of retort, peculiar to this branch of the great human tree, accompanied by occasional observations on the females who unfortunately pass them.[15]

In addition to these dregs of society, there were many journeymen rendered stupid, fretful and quarrelsome by drink. Such men, perhaps 30,000 of them in London, only worked hard at the end of the week in order to redeem their clothes from the pawnbroker; sedulous votaries of Saint Monday, they celebrated their patron with such quantities of beer and gin as to render them unfit for work on Tuesday. Each night thousands of wretches stumbled back home while their wives devised plans for avoiding a beating. The public house also played a central part in the lives of more respectable men. Journeymen got up before six in the morning and worked until eight when an hour was allowed for breakfast; an hour was taken for dinner between twelve and one and the day's work came to an end at about six in the evening. Public houses were open during all these intervals of labour and even at breakfast time 'large potations of beer' were consumed.

Despite his fulminations, even Malcolm was forced to admit that things had improved, particularly in the running of gin shops. Gin had once been the solace of the hen-pecked husband, the companion of the neglected wife, the bane of chastity, the foe of honesty, the friend of infidelity and the very spirit of sedition. Now it was all rather tame. 'A Gin Shop may generally be scented as the passenger approaches; but he cannot mistake it, as an assembly of drivers of asses with soot, brick dust, cats' meat and vegetables, with a due proportion of low ladies of pleasure always besiege the door. Thanks to the Distillers and Brewers liquor is much less powerful in its operations at present than it was fifty years past; hence the improvement in the conduct of the votaries of Geneva. Those people very seldom exceed low wit, a little noise and abuse of each other; indeed our streets are wonderfully quiet, and riots and quarrels are very rare.'[16]

But did the decline of drinking indicate a greater security of life? It is generally believed that the development of modern capitalism heightened the peaks and depressed the troughs of activity–in other words, it made life more uncertain for the working man. This is not necessarily so. England was involved in major wars for more of the eighteenth century than she was to be in the nineteenth. The transition from war to peace, or vice versa, could have a dramatic effect for good or ill on the prosperity of different trades. Even in towns, a great deal of work remained seasonal and depended on the weather. In London important sections of industry were brought to a standstill if adverse winds in the Thames estuary delayed the arrival of the Newcastle coal convoy. Sudden changes of fashion have a devastating effect. About 1786 the fashion for buckled shoes suddenly collapsed and was replaced by one for lace-up shoes. In 1791 the bucklemakers of Birmingham were petitioning the Prince of Wales on behalf of '20,000 in distress'. The bucklemakers paraded a donkey through the streets, its hooves wearing shoe laces; they insulted people wearing lace-up shoes but all to no avail.

Faced with these incalculable forces, it is not surprising that men took no thought for the morrow. In an economy of small workshops, a master could set up in business with a little capital, he might act as a sub-contractor, half workman and half capitalist. But his reserves were small and in bad years he was liable to go under and throw his employees out of work. Place gave countless examples of men ruined by a mixture of bad luck and their own improvidence:

Mr Woollams was a Hair Dresser and a wig maker in Arundel Street. His business was expensive and lucrative, he might have lived respectably and saved money, but, like many others he spent his time in public houses; his business decayed, he died very poor and left his family in great distress. Duke a Tailor, his course of life was the same, his business decayed and being nearly ruined he sold his niece whom he brought up to a rich old man who came from the East Indies and lodged in his house. His niece was a pretty, modest girl, who pined herself to death and Duke became destitute. Soon after this his wife died and he became a beggar about the streets.[17]

The ups and downs of life produced an obsession with 'chance'. Francis Place's father was ruined by his waste of money on the purchase of tickets for state lotteries. Wendeborn attributed this natural failing to the desire to get rich quick and live an idle life. This was the only possible explanation of the madness which took possession of the London populace during the time when state lotteries were drawn; but the eighteenth-century belief that manliness was best shown in a willingness to take great risks probably had a good deal to do with it. Of course there were terrible crashes in the 1820s, particularly in 1825, but at least among the skilled London tradesmen the trend was towards greater steadiness of conduct and greater regularity of employment.

Chapter Five

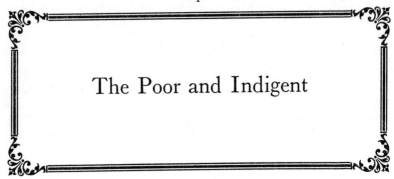

# The Poor and Indigent

## They Die at an Early Period of Life

In the 1790s John Knyveton, then a fashionable society doctor, described an operation of the 1760s when he had been a medical student:

> Assisted Doctor Urquehart with the amputation of a leg taken from an attorney's clerk. The clerk, being bound, the leg was held out firmly by a servant who wedged it against his belly and Doctor Urquehart with a sharp knife cuts half a circle from below the Tubercle and I pull these flaps back and get soaked with blood from the great arteries at which the Doctor laughs. The Doctor a very quick man had the leg off in four minutes and so the clerk was removed at All Peace, he having fainted from the vehemence of his emotions at the cutting of the second flap and I for one very thankful for his screams at first deafened me. So home very sweaty and bloody to change my shirt and cravat.[1]

Gradually surgery became less painful; laudanum was substituted for brandy, and the anaesthetic properties of nitrous oxide, or laughing gas, were discovered in 1800. But these developments did not make surgery any safer; there could be little advance until the discovery of antiseptics. Knives were not always cleaned properly and few doctors even took the simple precaution of passing the blade through a flame before beginning an operation. Some surgeons did know a great deal about anatomy but, well into the nineteenth century, it had to be admitted that 'skill in the performance has far outstripped the success in the result'. In 1801 it was said that hospital gangrene had been like an epidemic of two hundred years in the 'cutting wards' of the *Hotel de Dieu* in Paris. In English hospitals mortality rates in operation patients were considered good if they were less than 50 per cent. It seems certain that the number of lives saved by surgery can have had no effect on the total population.

In non-surgical cases the question is more controversial. Knyveton certainly did not present an attractive picture of the wards in a London hospital. He noted that when Urquehart went into the wards he always put on a short coat–because a full-skirted one would sweep the walls and quickly gather the lice and insects which infested them. Beds usually contained 'not more than three to four patients'–arranged so that the head of one was placed next to the feet of his neighbour. This curious practice was supposed to reduce the dangers of cross infection and to prevent one patient being too much exposed to the 'tainted effluvium' of the next. The stench in the wards was terrible and the windows were never opened. Most doctors carried a sponge soaked in vinegar in front of their nose in an attempt to reduce the smell and to protect themselves from infection.

Some London hospitals had new and better ventilated wards added at the end of the eighteenth century and the introduction of iron beds did much to reduce the problem of lice. A patient would obviously have a better chance of recovery in the wards of the Middlesex hospital, as drawn by Rowlandson in 1808, than in the squalor and chaos shown in the engravings of the 1760s. Given the primitive state of medicine, some hospitals had astonishingly good records; the York County Hospital was able to discharge over 90 per cent of its patients as 'cured' or 'relieved' in the century between 1740 and 1840.[2]

York seems to have been an exception and some historians claim that hospitals actually *increased* death rates. Overcrowding and poor hygiene were the source of 'hospital fever'–usually typhus–which then spread to the surrounding community. Scraps of food left by infected patients were distributed to the poor. There was little attempt to segregate infectious and non-infectious patients inside hospitals; patients entering a hospital with one disease stood a considerable chance of dying from a completely different complaint contracted from other inmates. After the turn of the nineteenth century, isolation was more stringently enforced and may have helped to control epidemics outside. Perhaps the best comment on the role of hospitals is to be found in the practice at St Bartholomew's; until 1828 all patients entering the hospital were required to deposit 19s 6d 'burial fees'.

For patients with sufficient means to bring doctors and nurses to their own houses, prospects were a little brighter. Deaths in childbed were significantly reduced among the upper classes as reasonably well-instructed male obstetricians took over from ignorant, old and frequently drunken women. In 1783 the Royal College of Physicians decided to award a special licence in midwifery but the prejudice against men assisting at childbed died hard. General George Hanger wrote in 1814: 'Custom governs and sanctions everything or how could the most delicate and decent women permit a man midwife six foot high and two feet broad over the loins, to attend them during their pregnancy; taking liberties, but *only professionally*, to whether the child lies right and after that to deliver them.'[3]

The development of forceps in place of the fearful instruments used earlier in cases of difficulty may have helped, but the most important factor was the gradual improvement of hygiene in the labour room. These were not years of important advances in medicines. Mercury was more widely used in the treatment of syphilis, digitalis for heart complaints, cinchona for some fevers and iron as a tonic. In an age when many medicines were lethal enough for adults, the effect of such potions on a child can be well imagined. James Woodforde wrote in September 1790:

The young woman Spincks (who lately had a Bastard Child by one Garthon of Norwich) called on me this morning to acquaint me that her child was dead, died last night, owing to her having given him a Sleeping Pill which she had of her Neighbour Nobbs whose husband is very ill and had some composing Pills from Mr Thornes, one of which Nobbs' wife advised her to give her Child to put him to sleep whilst she was out. The Child slept for about 5 hours then he waked and fell into convulsion fits, which continued for 4 hours and a half and then died in great Agonies.[4]

However unfairly, such tragedies were held against medical men. The public regarded doctors with hostility and distrust. It was likely that even a manifestly successful new treatment would encounter great resistance. The main cause of hostility towards doctors was over the question of dissection and the activities of 'resurrection men'. Doctors claimed that it was necessary to have a supply of corpses in order to teach anatomy and further medical research. Unfortunately, the supply was inadequate. The only bodies available legally were those of executed criminals, but the supply was supplemented by raids on churchyards. Such activities were highly illegal but the trade in bodies was a profitable one; it associated the medical profession with a group of unpleasant criminals. The eighteenth century may have been the Age of Reason for an educated minority but most people believed implicitly in the physical resurrection of the dead at the Last Day and were much concerned with ghosts and unquiet spirits. Midnight exhumations and breaking open of coffins were not merely distasteful, they were deeds which threatened the immortal souls of both the dead and the living. It was but a short step to seeing the medical profession as agents of the Devil and the whole atmosphere of dark lanterns, moonless nights and lookouts could easily suggest nameless rituals of Satanism.

Public confidence in the medical profession reached its nadir in 1828 with the trial in Edinburgh of William Burke and William Hare, suppliers of corpses to Dr Robert Knox. Burke and Hare realised that they could save themselves a lot of trouble if they simply murdered people and handed them over to Knox. Knox did not ask inconvenient questions but, if Burke's confession is to be believed, any doctor should have suspected foul play from the condition of the bodies.

The next was Mary Paterson, who was murdered in Burke's brother's house in the Canongate, in the month of April last, by Burke and Hare, in the forenoon. She was put into a tea-box, and carried to Dr Knox's dissecting-room in the afternoon of the same day; and got £8 for her body. She had twopence halfpenny which she held fast in her hand. Declares that the girl Paterson was only four hours dead till she was in Knox's dissecting rooms. She was warm when Burke cut the hair off her head; and Knox brought a Mr—— a painter to look at her, she was so handsome a figure, and well shaped in body and limbs.[5]

Burke actually confessed to sixteen murders. Somewhat surprisingly Knox was cleared of all blame, but as Burke mounted the scaffold, the crowd screamed 'Hang Knox'. Knox was burned in effigy in several parts of Edinburgh and his house in Newington Place was under almost constant attack. With the profession in such bad odour and its fees high, there was bound to be a good deal of reliance on folk remedies; the panacea against cramp was to wear a piece of brimstone, and a hop-filled pillow would always cure insomnia. One of the most widely read books of the century was John Wesley's *Advices with Respect of Health*; the book was reprinted many times and was often found in country cottages even at the end of the nineteenth century. Wesley's remedies relied on readily available herbs and foods. He declared that 'a poultice of boiled nettles' would cure pleurisy, and the quinsy; that erysipelas in the head or face will be remedied by applying 'warm treacle to the soles of the feet'.

Such remedies may have done no good but they probably did no harm. The same cannot be said of many patent medicines containing dangerous or even poisonous substances. The eighteenth century imposed virtually no restraint on the activities of the quack nor was there any compulsion for a manufacturer to reveal the contents of his 'sovereign remedies'. Patent medicines were closely linked with the newspaper trade. An astonishingly high proportion of advertisement revenue was derived from 'puffs' for patent medicines which were frequently sold by stationers rather than regular druggists. There was Madame Maintenon's Health and Beauty Cordial which would 'cure and relieve sick headaches, bilious attacks, nervousness and any other disorder and irregularity of the whole system'. Measam's Medicated Soap would deal with rheumatism and ringworm. Parr's Life Pills 'not only lengthens life but adds to its enjoyments'. Perhaps the most absurd was 'Insanity cured by the use of Padman's Powders'.

The most important medical development was in the field of preventive medicine. Until the middle of the eighteenth century, smallpox was virtually endemic, killing a high proportion of young children and accounting for over 10 per cent of all deaths. Even if medicine as a whole remained unchanged, any sharp reduction in the deaths from smallpox would result in a substantial increase in population. Inoculation against smallpox was introduced into England from Turkey by Lady Mary Wortley Montagu in 1721 and the technique of administering the serum by means of slight scratches on the arm was developed by the Sutton family of Framlington, Norfolk, in the 1760s. Woodforde's diaries abound in complications, serious illness and even deaths following inoculation. This picture is probably too gloomy and the Suttons claimed a death rate of no more than one in five thousand. At this time, however, the serum contained the smallpox virus itself and there was a considerable danger that those recently inoculated would infect others with a virulent form of the disease.

Inoculation certainly made progress and by 1780 perhaps 300,000 people had been treated. Women's fear of the disfigurement produced by smallpox probably played an important part. In *She Stoops to Conquer*, Mrs Hardcastle declares: 'I vow since Inoculation began, there has been no such thing as a plain woman.' In parishes where a deliberate programme of inoculation was undertaken, the results could be startling. At Maidstone in Kent there were ninety-one smallpox burials between 1781 and 1791 but only two in the next decade. But despite the best endeavours of charities, resistance to inoculation remained strong. It was not until a Cheltenham doctor, Edward Jenner, discovered that a serum derived from the much less dangerous cowpox also provided effective protection against smallpox, that most of the hostility disappeared. On 14 May 1796 Jenner vaccinated James Phipps, a boy of eight, with lymph taken from cow-pox pustules on the hand of a dairymaid, Sarah Nelmes. On 1 July 1796, Phipps was inoculated with smallpox. No sign of the disease appeared and Jenner's case was proved. A serious outbreak of the disease in Glasgow in 1801 encouraged the almost universal adoption of vaccination. Smallpox was certainly on the decline before the end of the eighteenth century but increasing natural resistance to the disease, probably similar to the increasing resistance against bubonic plague after 1665, was probably as important as inoculation.

Of course, many people who would have otherwise died of smallpox were now carried off by other diseases. It is frequently difficult to diagnose the precise disease involved in the frequent descriptions of 'malignant' or 'putrid' fever. Such outbreaks occurred in all parts of England. James Woodforde noted on 28 June 1781 that a 'raging fever' prevailed in much of Norfolk. Woodforde mentioned two local victims and added that, during the previous week, there had been fifty-three deaths in Norwich alone.

By the 1820s it was the general opinion of observers that things had improved and the change was usually attributed to increasing cleanliness among the poor. Francis Place rivalled Cobbett in his hostility to the Establishment but in 1824 Place was forced to admit that many things had changed for the better. It was unusual now to find children with lice in their hair, yet in the 1780s this had been virtually universal even among the children of well-off tradesmen and shopkeepers living in the Strand. Forty years later Place toured the back alleys of the same area yet 'I did not see a *scald head*, nor one with bandy legs called cheese cutters'. Ideas of cleanliness among adults had also changed. Until the close of the eighteenth century wives and daughters of London tradesmen wore quilted cambric petticoats stuffed with wool and horsehair. These petticoats were worn day in day out till they were literally rotten.[6]

Perhaps some of the improvements in health had been due to paving streets, constructing sewers and installing supplies of piped water, but Place believed that cheap cotton cloth, so hated by Cobbett, had done more than anything else for the health of English people in both town and country: 'These were found to be less expensive and as it was necessary to wash them, cleanliness followed almost as a matter of course. This very material change was not confined to the better sort of people as they were called; it descended, although rather slowly, to the very meanest of people, all of whom so far as respects females, wear washing clothes. Cleanliness in matters of dress was necessarily accompanied by cleanliness in other particulars.'[7]

In London the poorest areas tended to be just outside the limits of the City, in places like Southwark and St Giles, Holborn. Misguided attempts in the seventeenth and early eighteenth centuries to limit the growth of London encouraged overcrowding. Areas which had once been respectable, even elegant, declined in status; gardens were filled with cottages until they became a labyrinth of small courtyards. It was the courtyard, hidden from the main street, which provided the most typical housing for the eighteenth-century poor. Such courts may seem interesting, even romantic, compared to the grim regularity of Victorian back-to-back housing, but the disadvantages were formidable.

Most of the courts were approached through a doorway from the street and then along a passage three or four foot wide. The space between the houses was so narrow that overhanging top floors almost touched. The houses, built of boards tied together with iron hoops, were three or four stories tall; in many instances a different family lived in every room from the cellars to the garrets. Air could not circulate in such conditions, rubbish and filth were allowed to accumulate and, in retrospect, Francis Place considered that the London of the 1780s had been lucky to escape visitations of bubonic plague. At best, houses were 'shamefully propped up from time to time' and large parts of London were literally worn out. Even rather superior houses were made from bricks in which the clay had been mixed with 'the slop of the streets, ashes and scavengers' dirt'. In short, it was easy to paint a nightmarish picture of houses falling and the huge tradesmen's signs pulling away from the crumbling walls to dash out the brains of innocent passers-by.

Inside, acute overcrowding meant that scrupulous cleanliness was essential–but the usual practice was to change bed linen only three times a year. The rental of a cellar was about two shillings per week with other rooms costing more. There were important social distinctions within a tenement building; the families living on the first and second floors, particularly those occupying the front of the premises, thought themselves superior to the other tenants. But even their conditions were far from ideal. 'Many of the windows cannot be opened without admitting air apparently more noxious, certainly not less offensive than that already contained in the room; in other instances, the sashes have frequently been rendered by age or accident immovable; wood or paper has been substituted for broken panes of glass; every crevice is so carefully stuffed by woollen rags or some other fitting substance that as a means of admitting fresh air the windows are often totally useless.'[8]

In some areas conditions were actually getting worse. The last decades of the eighteenth century saw a large influx of Irish who took the worst jobs–or no jobs at all–and lived in the worst areas. In 1815 Montagu Burgoyne, Secretary of the Mendicity Society, claimed that he knew a court of twenty-four small houses with four Irish families in every room–a total of seven hundred people. If anything, the conditions in the barracks provided by the East India Company for Lascar sailors were even more deplorable. Notions of hygiene were primitive among many of the immigrants. The Irish saw no objection to sharing their cramped quarters with animals, especially with pigs which were particularly numerous in the Tottenham Court Road area. Irish burial customs were also highly inappropriate to city life. Whatever the cause of death, the body was not buried until large sums of money had been collected to pay for a wake. In 1817 a woman held no less than three wakes for her daughter; before the funeral 'a fever got into the house and there were six buried and eighteen or twenty ill.'

None the less, it could not be denied that London was expanding even more dramatically in area than in population. In theory, at least, there should have been more room for each Londoner. Cobbett was appalled at this parasitic growth of 'The Great Wen' and attributed it to the monstrous effects of the Pitt system, paper money and stock-jobbing. Much of this development was to the benefit of the *nouveaux riches* but there were also new suburbs for working men in Bethnal Green, Somers Town and Walworth. Some of these developments were started in the 1780s but war, by interrupting supplies of imported timber and by raising interest rates, put a stop to the housing boom. Unfinished streets and unoccupied, roofless dwellings were a common sight in the 1790s. There was a further period of expansion in the 1820s; small property speculators abounded and a journeyman earning thirty shillings a week often invested in a share of a cottage. Some of the speculators were dishonest; the infamous Hedger of The Dog and Duck in St George's Fields took a plot of land in 1789 from the Bridge House Estate. The lease included a £500 penalty if Hedger attempted to build. As soon as the lease was signed, Hedger paid the £500 and started building; his houses were so badly built that they had to be demolished in 1811.

Despite the enormities of men like Hedger, there seems little doubt that the new housing was more salubrious than the old. In the mid-1820s the creation of the London Docks provided an opportunity for the first big programme of slum clearance since the Great Fire. Francis Place noted in September 1824 after a visit to the East End, that despite the poverty and misery along the river from the Tower to the Isle of Dogs there had been considerable improvement. The change was particularly striking in places like Ratcliffe Highway and Cable Street where most of the old wooden houses had been demolished and replaced by brick.[9]

When Place visited Walworth in 1832 he was sure that back-to-back housing was a great improvement on the courts of earlier years. The streets were wider, cleaner and less evil-smelling. Even in areas of Lambeth, faced with economic difficulty as river fishing declined, there was a new spirit:

The window frames and door posts were perfectly black with soot and dirt, the rooms were neither painted nor whitewashed for many years together. No such thing as a curtain, unless it was a piece of old garment, was to be seen at any window. Now these same houses have nearly all of them sash windows, the frames of which are painted white and kept white and scarcely a window is to be seen without a white curtain. Formerly the women young and old were seen emptying their pails or pans at the doors or washing on stools in the street, in summer time without gowns on their backs or handkerchiefs on their necks, their leather stays half laced and as black as the door posts, their black coarse petticoats standing alone with dirt. No such things are seen now, compared with themselves at the two periods even these people are gentlefolks.[10]

Of course, housing conditions and living standards were closely bound up with economic prosperity. Despite Cobbett's belief that urbanisation brought poverty and degradation for the lower classes, most of the evidence for London seems to contradict him. Prosperity brought its own problems. There was a serious problem of industrial pollution. Sugar refining was heavily concentrated in Whitechapel, St George's in the East and Stepney after the West India Dock Company obtained a monopoly of the landing of raw sugar. What were described as 'noisesome trades' were heavily concentrated in this area—bone-boiling, glue-making, various chemical processes—and in Rotherhithe Street alone there were no less than nine factories manufacturing patent manures, 'nine sources of foetid gas'.

But traditional industries were often equally dangerous, particularly if they were carried on in the airless garrets and cellars which too frequently doubled as living quarters. Plumbers, painters and some glaziers were vulnerable to lead poisoning and in 1787 a glazier's apprentice complained that he was forced to sleep in the room where lead was melted. Refiners of gold, silver and the makers of looking glasses became paralytic from the use of mercury. In ill-ventilated rooms, the dust involved in baking, in flax-dressing and felt-making produced diseases of the lungs. The most unlikely trades were affected. The workmen employed by sugar bakers (confectioners) were exposed to intense heat and were often heavy drinkers. They were liable to rheumatism and diseases of the lungs. Those who remained in the job for any length of time became 'sallow, emaciated and dropsical' and usually died 'at an early period of life'.[11]

But it was the sheer labour of doing almost anything by hand which provides the greatest contrast with the future. For the one unfortunate and conspicuous freak whose hair had turned green after working in a brass works, there were thousands who were simply worn out by hard work. Although horses could be used in some heavy trades, the vast majority depended on the physical strength of the human frame. Adam Smith thought that heavy sawyers were lucky to last eight years before being forced to take lighter work. In 1842 it was estimated that at least 10 per cent of the labouring population of London suffered from hernias; the National Truss Society was founded in 1786, the Rupture Society in 1796 and the City Truss Society in 1807.

Yet even without the widespread adoption of machinery, things were gradually getting better. There was a clear trend towards shorter hours. In 1794 bookbinders worked two hours less each day than they had done at the beginning of the century–although shop assistants were lucky to be free before 10 pm. In times of exceptionally high demand, the hours were really punishing. In the boom of the early 1790s, Francis Place was making breeches for sixteen or eighteen hours a day, seven days a week. He worked so hard that he could not even find the time to shave; but sometimes he was overcome by sheer exhaustion. 'I do not know how to describe the sickening aversion which at times steals over the working man and utterly disables him for a longer or a shorter period from following his usual occupation and compels him to indulge in idleness. I have felt it, resisted it to the utmost of my power; but have been so completely subdued by it, that, spite of very pressing circumstances, I have been obliged to submit and run away from my work.'[12]

If labour was in such demand, it followed that there was a golden opportunity to increase wages. This seems to have happened in the case of men with a recognised skill. The traditional urban skilled crafts–printers, tailors, braziers, pewterers, cabinet-makers and saddlers–fared better than other workers during the Industrial Revolution. London was the centre of trades which were not yet affected by mechanisation. The increase in the wealthy and middle classes, so deplored by Cobbett, meant that there was more demand for their services. In such cases the Combination Laws, designed to prohibit trades unions, were far from completely effective. Place estimated that there were at least 100,000 members of trades clubs at the beginning of the nineteenth century. In these trades, wage rates were from eighteen to twenty-two shillings a week in the 1780s. Soon after the outbreak of war in France, prices began to rise very steeply. Successful strikes in 1795 and 1802 enabled the breeches makers to increase their wages and to keep pace with the rising cost of living. By the end of the Napoleonic wars average wages in the trade had reached thirty-six shillings; they remained at this level throughout the 1820s despite a marked fall in food prices. In other words, on the basis of wages, it is clear that this group was substantially better off in 1830 than it had been in 1780.

Yet it remained the overwhelming fact of life in early nineteenth-century England that, despite all improvements and better conditions, town life was much more unhealthy than existence in rural areas. As the proportion of the total population living in towns was rising, one might expect that the national death rate was actually *increasing*. Improvements were sufficient to prevent this outcome but the statistical evidence available from the 1820s suggests that the national death rate was virtually static. In other words, improvements and urbanisation cancelled each other out. In the Manchester of the 1820s, half the children born to lower-class parents died before reaching their fifth birthday. In industrial areas of Lancashire, life expectancy at birth was no more than twenty-five; in agricultural areas it was about forty.

## Teach Them to Spend Less

The standard explanation of poverty and suffering among the lower classes was that it was their own fault. Cobbett was prepared to admit that there were many of the poor who were idle and drunken. He was convinced, however, that this was not caused by any inherent viciousness but by a sense of hopelessness and shock at the destruction of old communities. Whatever the shortcomings of the old system, it had given a man a stake in life, something he could work for; now there was nothing. 'Go to an ale house in an old enclosed county and there you will see the origin of poverty and poor rates. For whom are they to be sober? For whom are they to save? For the Parish? If I am sober, shall I have land for a cow? If I am frugal, shall I have an acre of potatoes? You offer no motives; you have nothing but a parish officer and a workhouse–bring me another pot.'[13]

Many people believed that, during Enclosure, a little land should be set aside for use as allotments. The allotment garden would cushion the labourer against the effects of high prices and unemployment–as well as providing a counter-attraction to the ale house and 'rude sports' during leisure hours. For the tax-payer this was the powerful argument that such schemes were designed to reduce the poor rates. In 1799 the influential Arthur Young advocated the settlement of a million poor families on waste land. But the plan had powerful opponents. Cobbett suggested that each married labourer in the village of Bishops Waltham, Hampshire, should be given an acre of waste ground. The village vestry meeting, however, rejected these proposals because they would make the poor 'too saucy', 'want higher wages' and, significantly, 'breed more children'.[14] The allotment plan was similar to the situation in Ireland where population was growing faster than resources. In 1830, 42 per cent of English parishes operated some sort of allotment scheme; in most cases, however, the plots were very small. Malthusian fears of a population explosion based on the potato were to prove groundless.

For the upper classes, the most attractive solution to the problem of rural poverty was for the poor to reform their present improvident and extravagant way of life. Sir Frederick Eden, a sane, perceptive and well-meaning man, declared that he entirely agreed with those who regretted that the labourer did not get value for his shilling. There were some who claimed that the problem arose from poor men having to buy small quantities of food from hawkers and small shops when it would have been much cheaper to buy in bulk. But Eden had no time for such arguments; he believed that ignorance, outmoded custom and prejudice were responsible for improvidence in dress, diet and other aspects of private spending. It was no good for well-meaning writers to say that wages were not high enough for a labourer to live in tolerable comfort. It would be better if such people used their talents to point out to the labourers 'the best means of reducing their expenses without diminishing their comforts'.[15]

Eden stressed that low wages did not coincide with low living standards. When Eden was writing in the 1790s, wages were still higher in the south of England than in the north–although the position was soon to be reversed. The relatively well-paid labourer in the south lived on a monotonous diet of white bread and cheese with 'the deleterious produce of China' as the main drink. If a labouring family could afford meat, they actually took it to the bakehouse rather than cooking it themselves; above all, meat left over was never made into soup. Compared to this wasteful existence, Eden enthused on the variety, cheapness and nourishment of the food of the northern labourer. His favourite appears to be 'Hasty Pudding which is made of oatmeal, water and salt, about 13 oz. of meat to a quart of water which is sufficient for a meal for two labourers. It is eaten with a little milk or beer poured upon it, or with a little cold butter put into the middle, or with a little treacle. A good meal for one person, supposing the price of oats to be 20s. the quarter will not exceed 1d.'[16]

The general recommendation was that the southern labourer would be better fed if he gave up his attachment to expensive wheaten bread and abandoned his 'groundless prejudices' against potatoes and rye bread. Eden calculated that a Cumberland labourer with a wife and five children spent only £7 9s 2d per annum on oatmeal and barley, whereas a similar sized family in Berkshire spent £36 8s 0d on white bread alone. The southerner's taste in dress also came in for severe criticism. In the south, and particularly in the vicinity of London, labouring men usually dressed in clothes cast off by their betters–a coat, the most expensive item, cost about five shillings in 1798. Wives rarely made any clothes, except occasionally for the children. In the north, on the other hand, almost everything, except shoes and hats, were made at home. In many places the cloth itself, linen or felt, was home made. Although the clothes might be clumsy, they were warmer and lasted longer than shop goods. Money could also be saved by the Cumberland practice of wearing clogs, superior to shoes 'whether with respect to the price or to the utility'.

Attempts to convince the poor of the virtues of potatoes, black bread and wooden shoes fell on deaf ears. It was hard for them to believe that famine prices were caused by bad summers and expanding demand; the wickedness of profiteering corn merchants seemed nearer the mark. Cobbett was quick to point out that a large proportion of the trade was in the hands of Quakers. Some Jews worked, but not Quakers; they lived by buying and selling what others produced. In Cobbett's terms, they were parasites on the rest of the community. In the past, corn prices had been held down by the local magistrates who fixed maximum prices and prohibited the movement of grain from the area. Now such salutary legislation had been repealed in accordance with the dictates of 'Scotch Feelosophy'. Popular leaders refused to believe that the old legislation had gone; if magistrates did not do their duty, then the poor would do it for them. They would seize hoarded supplies and sell them at fair prices. Far from being rioters, they were, in their own eyes at least, enforcing the law. In 1795, one Sarah Rogers took the lead in seizing butter at Ipswich and sold it at a reduced price; at Bath, women boarded a grain barge and confiscated its cargo.

But it was not just hostility to corn merchants which made the labouring classes reluctant to take up Eden's suggestions. The reason for the superior nourishment of the northern diet was not the readiness to eat coarse grains but the availability of milk. It was a question of the type of farming practised in different areas. In counties largely devoted to pasture farming, milk was still plentiful. The south and east of the country was given over to corn growing. Once labourers there had had milk from their own cows but, after Enclosure, the situation changed. Such milk as did exist was carried off and, according to Cobbett, consumed by 'the idlers, the thieves, the prostitutes who are all taxeaters in the wens of London and Bath'. If milk and butter could be obtained, coarse bread might be fairly palatable; but without them the preference for white bread was understandable. Arthur Young was forced to admit: 'The quality of the bread that is eaten by those who have meat, and perhaps porter and port, is of little consequence indeed; but to the hardworking man who nearly lives on it the case is abundantly different'.[17]

Similarly, many of the nourishing meals recommended by Eden involved a pot being kept hot and simmering for several hours. One of the great problems of the southern labourer was a shortage of fuel. In the north coal was cheap and plentiful; in the south, particularly in areas not served by canals, it was expensive and, of course, Enclosure had reduced the amount of scrub land which previously had given the poor man his firewood. Eden recognised the problem and urged the poor to make their fuel go further by covering lumps of coal with clay. Fuel was wasted in the southern counties by constant boiling of the tea kettle; if the resources were properly applied there would be enough to cook a good soup. Cobbett and Eden disagreed about most things but they were both furious opponents of tea drinking among the lower classes. Eden's general level-headedness seems to desert him when talking about tea. It is striking that strong beer should be regarded as morally preferable to tea, an attitude which would have astounded Victorian temperance reformers. Cobbett was at his most rabid on the subject:

The drink which has come to supply the place of beer has, in general, been *tea*. It is notorious that tea has no *useful* strength in it; that it contains nothing *nutritious*; that it, besides being *good* for nothing has *badness* in it, because it is well known to produce want of sleep in many cases, and in all cases to shake and weaken the nerves. It is, in fact, a weaker kind of laudanum, which enlivens for the moment and deadens afterwards. Needs there any thing more to make us cease to wonder at seeing labourers' children with dirty linen and holes in the heels of their stockings? I view the tea drinking as a destroyer of health, an enfeebler of the frame, an engenderer of effeminacy and laziness, a debaucher of youth, and a maker of misery for old age. The tea drinking corrupts boys as soon as they are able to move from home and does little less for the girls, to whom gossip of the tea table is no bad preparatory school for the brothel.[18]

Cobbett, of course, was suspicious of anything new and Eden was inclined to disapprove of the poor adopting ways which had previously been the monopoly of the upper ranks of society. It was just not the poor man's *place* to drink tea. Eden had to admit that the hearth which boiled the tea kettle was not always suitable for a stockpot. The southern poor bought bread from the baker and brewed tea instead of beer because their cottages simply did not have proper cooking facilities. Enclosure was accompanied by the construction of new labourers' cottages; in many cases the design and quality of the building was extremely poor. On a Rural Ride in 1822 Cobbett came across some labourers near Cricklade: 'Their dwellings are little better than pig-beds, and their looks indicate that their food is not nearly equal to that of a pig. These wretched hovels are stuck upon little beds of ground on the roadside where the space has been wider than the road demanded. It seems as if they have been swept off the fields by a hurricane, and have dropped and found shelter under the banks of the roadside.'[19]

Although country life was healthier than in the new industrial towns, the bad conditions in many country cottages frequently led to serious epidemics. In 1813 one in ten people died in the Buckinghamshire village of Great Horwood during an outbreak of typhoid fever. In one cottage the floor covered a pit of stagnant water into which all kinds of filth oozed. All the people who slept in the room over this swamp were taken ill and three of the family died. The property belonged to the Warden and Fellows of New College, Oxford, who promised they would demolish it and erect something better. Perhaps the loss of a child in an epidemic was actually a blessing in disguise; there would be one less mouth to feed.

The most contentious issue in the debate on living standards was the effect of the old Poor Law. Many contemporaries not only blamed this system for encouraging rapid population growth, but also believed that it was impoverishing rich and poor alike. An increasing burden of poor rates seemed hard to reconcile with notions of national prosperity. In his *Letter to Parson Malthus* Cobbett pointed out: 'The Boroughmongers began to be alarmed at the increase of the *Poor-rates*. They boasted of the wonderful national prosperity; wonderful ease and happiness; wonderful improvements in agriculture; but still the poor rates *wonderfully increased*. Indeed they seemed to *increase* with the increase of the Boroughmongers *national* prosperity; which might, I think, very fairly be called the eighth wonder of the world.'[20]

Men like Eden were convinced that the obligation of the rich to preserve the poor from starvation was inherent in any idea of a civilised society. But he was equally sure that the system of outdoor relief was simply 'an encouragement to debauchery'. Reliance on 'charity' destroyed manly independence and self-respect. Eden believed that the heavy burden of taxation falling on the propertied classes meant that less money was available for men doing an honest day's work. It was the system of poor relief itself which reduced demand for labour, cut the 'going' rate of wages below the subsistence level and necessitated doles even to those in regular employment. Eden could foresee a terrible spiral of poverty which would culminate in everyone being a pauper. War and bad harvests in the mid-1790s had contributed to the difficult situation, but Eden still asserted that, but for the operation of the Poor Law, the demand for labour would have risen and increased wages even beyond the wants of the average labourer. The only way out of the situation was to make poverty a disgrace, a state which resulted from idleness and wickedness rather than from any trick or exploitation on the part of the rich. 'If the Poor do not prudently serve themselves, none can effectively assist them; if they are not their own friends, none can sufficiently befriend them. It is far more useful to teach them to spend less than to give them much more.'[21]

Cobbett, of course, could not accept such an analysis. He retorted angrily that it was all too convenient to believe that the cause of the increasing wretchedness of the people was to be found in the people themselves. The upper classes and the government were continually represented as the guide, the guardian, the nursing parent of the people; that was the justification of their privileges. It was curious, however, that when these guided, guarded and nursed children became half-starved, ragged and filthy, the fault was laid solely upon the children, and not upon the guide, guardian and nurse. In 1807 there were 1,200,000 paupers in England, or three times as many as in 1783. If increase in vice, and not increase in taxation, was the cause, then one had to assume that English people had become three times more vicious than when the celebrated William Pitt became Prime Minister.

Some felt that the solution was to be found in Scotland, where there was a wider spread of literacy which, it was claimed, helped the people to understand their misery and the way to escape from it. Cobbett denied that good would come from popular education. If poverty was indeed caused by a threefold increase in vice, then there was the uncomfortable fact that schools, books, pamphlets, reviews, magazines, reading rooms, circulating libraries, and Methodist and other meetings had increased tenfold. It did not seem to have occurred to Whitbread and William Wilberforce that when the poor had learned to read the Bible, they might want to read something else. Grub Street could give them ideas which would add to, rather than diminish, the fearful stock of vice which was assumed to exist already.

## Mansions of Putridity

By the 1820s it was obvious that hasty puddings, wooden shoes and even education could never provide the complete answer to the problem of poverty. If starvation on a wide scale was to be avoided, the poor had to be given money or food. Cobbett was convinced that the causes of pauperism were to be found in 'The Thing', the monstrous creature whose limbs were stock-jobbing, paper money, war taxation and borough mongering. The creature would ultimately destroy itself, but, until that glorious day, the poor were entitled to generous relief. Poor rates should be regarded as an essential charge on the land whose payment was in every way as binding as the tithe-charge. In the war years, the high profits enjoyed by agriculturalists meant that, despite complaints, the burden of the poor rates must have been tolerable. In his days at Botley, Cobbett had himself aspired to the role of a large farmer but he could not feel much sympathy with a group which complained of the cost of supporting the poor, yet according to Smollett:

They kept their footmen, their saddle horses and chaises; their wives and daughters appeared in their jewels, their silks and their satins, their negligees and trollopees; their clumsy shanks, like so many shins of beef were cased in silk hose and embroidered slippers, their raw red fingers, gross as the pipes of a chamber organ, which had been employed in milking the cows, in twirling the mop or churn staff, being adorned with diamonds, were taught to thrum the pandola, and even to touch the keys of the harpsichord.[22]

In the depressed 1820s, however, many farmers were forced into bankruptcy, and vestry meetings became more miserly in their attitude to the poor. Demands increased for a reduction in poor rates and informed opinion was becoming more hostile to 'outdoor relief'. Poverty was sin and must be punished by imprisonment in a workhouse. The workhouse must be the place of last resort, the shame of which men would do anything to avoid. To reinforce the point, it was essential that conditions inside the workhouse should be worse than in the most miserable cottage and the food more unappetising than that obtainable in the lowest-paid jobs. These were the principles applied on a national scale to the controversial new Poor Law of 1834. Cobbett thought the measure was certain to provoke a revolution: 'If the Scotch project be carried into effect, it will, in all probability, be the last act of the present system.'[23]

Yet attempts to establish 'Poor Law Bastilles' had been going on for over a century. In most workhouses, the master was paid little more

than the labourer; the temptation to profit at the expense of the inmates must have been very powerful. In many parishes the Overseers
of the Poor, often the local churchwardens, were so overawed by the
administrative problems that they simply turned the whole system
over to a contractor. The parish paid the contractor between three and
four shillings per week per pauper; the contractor ran the workhouse
and made what profit he could. According to John Scott, workhouses
were no more than 'mansions of putridity'[24] whose miserable inhabitants had little to expect but speedy death. Most workhouses were
originally built for other purposes and were terribly inadequate to the
demands made upon them. In many instances the workhouses simply
could not accommodate all of those who were entitled to relief; whatever the 'reformers' may have desired, a 'mixed' system of relief was
unavoidable. In rural areas, the poor houses were generally wretchedly
crowded and insanitary with the inevitable consequences of ill-health
and immorality. It was usual to expect three or four paupers to share
the same bed. The best solution appeared to be 'to set the Poor to work',
to compel those living in workhouses to produce things which could be
sold at a profit. The idea was that such activity would reduce the poor
rates and provide funds for the construction of more spacious and
sanitary poor houses. A Dr Trotter maintained that life in 'model'
workhouses could be positively delightful: 'As soon as they are removed
from their miserable cottages, and received into the hospitable mansion
they are stript of their filthy rags made perfectly clean and decently
habited, before they are admitted to join the family; and ever afterwards cleanliness is indispensably required. At breakfast, dinner and
supper they are all assembled by the ringing of a bell, in the common
hall, where they are provided with wholesome and well dressed food,
and proper to their station in life and in liberal abundance.'[25]

Despite such plenty, the returns on workhouse industry were lamen-
table. The poor at Beverley in Yorkshire were employed in 'Carding,
Knitting and spinning wool and yarn and the Infant Poor in Teasing
Oakum';[26] yet in 1772 the Beverley poor produced goods valued at
precisely six pounds. Of course many of those in the workhouse were
too old, too young or too sick to be able to do any work at all, but there
were frequent allegations that the poor deliberately sabotaged attempts
to make them into useful and industrious members of society. Materials
were spoiled or wasted at a quite scandalous rate. But it was not always
the fault of the poor, local tradesmen were liable to get themselves
elected as Poor Law Guardians in order to charge top prices for unsaleable produce. There were other sorts of abuse and at Leyton a
special resolution had to be forced through the vestry meeting that the

workhouse should not be used to accommodate the mistresses of the local guardians. Against this background it is easy to sympathise with the widespread antipathy to any form of 'public enterprise'. Frederick Eden complained that attempts to supply the poor with employment as well as the impotent with subsistence were fraught with serious disadvantages. It was impossible to provide work in any occupation without injuring those already engaged in that trade. If a parish workhouse began to manufacture mops and ropes the main sufferers would be those already making mops and ropes in private industry. There was no means by which the total demand for mops and ropes could be increased so someone was bound to be harmed by an increase in the supply.

Another widely canvassed means of alleviating the problem of poverty was for the parish to pay for pauper children to be apprenticed to a trade which would give them a steady income in later life. In the seventeenth century, almost all occupations, however humble, required a seven-year apprenticeship. By the end of the eighteenth century, however, the apprenticeship system had collapsed in many trades. In cases where real skill was to be acquired the master was likely to demand a higher premium than the parish authorities were prepared to pay. A respectable tradesman would probably be reluctant to take a child from an ignorant and possibly depraved home background. Pauper apprentices were therefore sent to masters in trades where the work was dangerous or where virtually no skill was required. Far from gaining the knowledge which would enable them to become independent in later life such children were exploited as cheap labour during the period of their 'apprenticeship' and then probably dismissed the moment they became eligible for full wages. There was scarcely any inspection of the conditions of work and occasionally public opinion was startled by revelations of a quite appalling kind. At the beginning of the nineteenth century Mrs Catherine Cappe tried to get something done. She drew attention to the fact that a Mr Jouvencaux worked his apprentices for sixteen hours a day and it seemed likely that five had actually died from lack of food. Action was made especially difficult because of the increasing demands for child labour in the factories of northern England; children were sometimes transported literally hundreds of miles from their native parish.

Those who abused their position as masters were rarely punished. A man who treated his apprentice 'in a manner exceeding the limits of true chastisement so that his life was despaired of' was fined a paltry 3s 4d.[27] Many apprentices simply ran away, some almost deliberately driven away by masters who had received their premiums–perhaps three or four pounds–from the parish and now had no further use for their charges. If the apprentice was useful to his master, however, advertisements offering rewards for information leading to the return of the miscreant were inserted in newspapers and warrants obtained from magistrates. Ralph Pearte, 'an idle dissolute fellow', absconded from his master, a butcher in Islington, and was run to earth at Wheat-hamstead in Hertfordshire. The Wheathamstead magistrate, Edward Wingate Esquire, ordered that Ralph Pearte should be whipped and kept in 'fetters or gyves' for a time before being returned to Islington.[28]

Perhaps the greatest defect of the Poor Law system was the provision that a pauper could obtain relief in only one specific parish–ideally that of his birth. This Law of Settlement dated from 1662, a time when society had been relatively static and when few labourers had any inclination to move from their native village. By the end of the eight-eenth century economic change meant that there was a serious over-population in parts of southern England yet something of a labour shortage in the north. The Poor Laws probably made the problem of poverty more acute by impeding desirable labour mobility. The notion that England was a free country needs the important qualification that a large proportion of the population simply could not move as it pleased. A man who occupied a house with a rental of under £10 per annum–that is, all labourers and most craftsmen–was considered liable to become a burden on the poor rates. Such a person was expected to notify the Overseers when he arrived in a new parish. The authorities then had forty days in which to decide whether he was to be ordered to leave or to be granted 'settlement'. In many areas the only way a labouring man could gain acceptance in another parish was to bring a certificate from the village of his birth acknowledging responsibility and promising to receive him if he ever became pauperised. It is not surprising that such certificates were not easy to come by.

The reluctance to receive poor strangers reflected the various aspects of parochial xenophobia. In some cases there was a genuine fear that new arrivals might bring in some fatal disease. The authorities at Tow-cester in Northamptonshire actually bribed diseased people to go away–'Gave a woman and two small children to Goe from Towne having the Small Pox upon them 6d.'[29] Similarly in villages built of wood, plaster and thatch, a careless drunken stranger could set the whole place on fire. Irish paupers–'Papists and other lewd persons disaffected to the government'–were regarded with particular suspicion. Some new arrivals might be criminals or semi-criminals but the main fear was for the pockets of rate-payers. Anyone who might become 'chargeable' had to be hustled on–what happened in the next parish was a problem for others to bother about. In the case of a pregnant woman with no visible means of support the need for despatch was especially acute; unless action was taken a child would be 'chargeable' to the parish, possibly for the whole of its life.

The poor who were unwilling, or perhaps unable, to move of their own accord were put into the parish cart and taken outside the parish boundaries as quickly as possible. Gradually arrangements became more complicated, particularly in the neighbourhood of big cities. The Mendicity Report of 1815 reveals a system operating in several counties and specifically designed for transporting paupers back to their parish of origin. Mr Davies, the 'vagrant contractor' for Middlesex, received £300 per annum and his organisation alone moved some 12,000 people back to their own parishes. Many people were shocked by the cruelty inherent in this system. Sir William Meredith declared in 1773: 'Coming up to town last Sunday I met with an instance shocking to humanity: a miserable object in the agonies of death crammed into a cart to be removed lest the parish should be at the expense of its funeral. Other instances every day met with and the removal of women with child and in labour, to the danger of both their lives, lest the child should be born in the parish.'[30]

Of course, the system was absurd. It is hard to generalise because, despite attempts to produce a more uniform system, there was an enormous variety in the competence, honesty and attitudes of those who operated the system of poor relief. The choice of the parish as the main administrative unit was no longer appropriate. Lack of effective control at the central, or even county level, meant that Overseers could be extraordinarily kind and indulgent or monsters of cruelty. Although kind Overseers did exist they are likely to have been exceptional. Reform was badly needed and despite Cobbett's protests it is possible that the new arrangements decided upon in 1834 were really an improvement on the chaos of previous years.

On the face of it, it is difficult to say much in favour of the old Poor Law, but it can be argued that contemporaries were wrong in thinking that existing arrangements actually damaged all sections of the community. Agricultural wages and the demand for labour in the countryside varied greatly from season to season. Robert Hughes told the 1833 Select Committee on Agriculture: 'There are no surplus labourers generally speaking in summer but unemployment commences very soon after harvest and they remain in that state until the spring work comes in, you may take it, from November to March.'[31] Yet the labour of such men was vital in August and September and some expedient was necessary to keep them alive during the rest of the year. Further, the

The major issues of 1830: Swing, reform and tithes. Cobbett was accused of advocating violence to destroy the threshing machine *The Mansell Collection*

Agricultural improvement. A prize cow inspected by Lord Somerville, President of the Board of Agriculture and patron of Arthur Young *Radio Times Hulton Picture Library*

The new gas lighting in Pall Mall, 1809. Obviously feared by the practitioners of 'prostitution and plunder' *The Mansell Collection*

Joseph Johnson, a black sailor with a model of the ship *Nelson* in his cap. One of the most famous of beggars *Radio Times Hulton Picture Library*

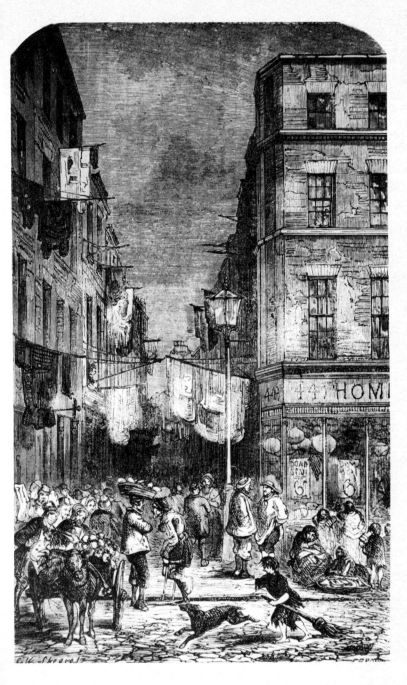

Slum housing old style, insanitary courts tucked away behind main
thoroughfares  *Radio Times Hulton Picture Library*

One of the more respectable 'Sovereign Remedies' so frequently advertised in newspapers, James's powders were actually used to 'cure' George III's insanity. Whatever patent the King may have issued, the powders only increased his suffering *Radio Times Hulton Picture Library*

The effects of vaccination according to Gillray. Opponents did claim that those treated developed bovine features, but female vanity and fear of disfigurement rapidly made vaccination popular *Radio Times Hulton Picture Library*

Dr James's Powder for FEVERS, And other Inflammatory Distempers. Publish'd by Virtue of His Majesty's Royal Letters Patent; WILL remove (as has been Experienced in many thousand Cases) any continual Acute Fever in a few Hours, though attended with Convulsions Light-headedness, and the worst Symptoms: But if taken in the Beginning of a Fever, one Dose is generally sufficient to perform a Cure. These POWDERS are Sold only by J. NEWBERY, at The Bible and Sun in S.t Paul's Church Yard, over against the North-Door of the Church, at 2.6.ᵈ the two Doses; with good Allowance to those who buy them for Charitable Uses or to Sell again

notion that the propertied classes suffered through the payment of unduly heavy poor rates is open to question. If a labourer received wages which were insufficient to keep up his strength then there could be a serious loss in productivity. There might be considerable advantage in terms of output in bringing him up to a tolerable level of biological efficiency–even at the cost of fairly lavish contributions to the poor rates. Neither of these points was appreciated by contemporaries. The fundamental problem was that the population of England was growing too rapidly to be supported by agriculture and traditional occupations. An entirely new range of job opportunities had to be created if the problem of poverty was to be alleviated. Although there were indeed great disparities between rich and poor it is unlikely that a more equal distribution of income would have helped matters. The numbers of very rich were insignificant compared to the numbers of very poor. Had this wealth been redistributed it would have produced only a marginal improvement in the living standards of the rural poor. For this group there was really only one consolation. As Dr Snape had declared in 1712: 'The wise providence has amply compensated the disadvantages of the poor and indigent, in wanting many of the conveniences of this life, by a more abundant provision for their happiness in the next.'[32]

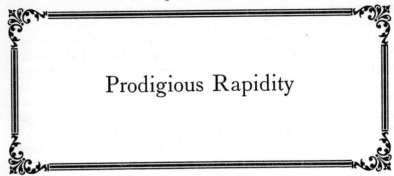

Chapter Six

# Prodigious Rapidity

## The Maximum Comfort which Circumstances Admit

Despite the many changes in agriculture, in population and in the life
style of existing towns, these developments were paralleled by similar
trends in other European countries. There were features, however, which
were virtually unique to Britain and it is to these that we must now turn.

One of the developments William Cobbett most deplored was in
transport–for him 'improvements' were a wicked way of stealing the
fruits of the earth from honest country-folk, in order to sustain the
'vermin' living in the Wens. The age of Cobbett saw dramatic developments in the road network, the creation of a national system of canals
and the beginnings of railways. All in all, the years between 1780 and
1830 witnessed the most profound transport revolution since the Romans.
Foreigners doubted whether all this travelling really reflected the
economic strength of Britain. Moralists deplored the vast amount of
unnecessary travel. The restlessness of the English was proverbial–
probably something to do with their notorious propensity for melancholy and suicide. Even so, it was hard to understand why so many
people should leave home and fireside to brave the perils of travel
simply because they wanted 'a change'. Wendeborn estimated that six
out of every ten travellers, some riding as if their lives depended upon
it, were trying to find a cure for boredom and depression:

The coaches are mostly filled with loungers of both sexes, who to get
rid of themselves, and to enjoy the fresh air, look at each other in
silence and have drawn up the glasses for protection against the dust
in summer and the cold in the winter. Even the stage coaches are continually crowded with passengers and the female ones make generally
the majority, most of whom travel to be absent from home, to pay some

74

unnecessary visit and to endeavour to get rid of ill humour and to go out of town that they may have an opportunity of returning to it again.[1]

By modern standards, the speed of travelling was very slow, yet the men of the early nineteenth century thought they were living in an age of speed. Certainly there had been a great acceleration during the previous decades. In the 1760s any coach which went faster than a walking pace unashamedly described itself as 'flying'. By 1830 there were regular mail services which averaged twelve miles per hour over considerable distances while chaises were capable of even greater speed. At a time when doctors solemnly believed that the human frame would disintegrate at speeds in excess of thirty miles per hour, nervous persons may have felt that the margin of safety was dangerously small.

For those who could afford to ride rather than walk, there were three options–the stage coach, the mail coach or the post chaise. The stage coach was the humblest and cheapest; one could travel on the *Highflyer* from London to York as an outside passenger for £1 5s 0d in 1790. Even a short journey 'outside' could be very unpleasant. In 1782 a Swiss visitor Carl Philip Moritz travelled the thirty-three miles from Leicester to Northampton in this way. It was an experience he would never forget. His companions were a farmer, a decently dressed young man and a 'blackamoor'. There was nothing to hold on to except a small handle on the roof and as soon as the coach set off, Moritz was sure that death awaited him. The coach travelled with 'prodigious rapidity' through the cobbled streets of Leicester, so fast that it seemed a miracle that the coach and horses did not simply take to the air and fly. Moritz was so frightened that he climbed down and got into the basket at the back, hoping to make himself comfortable among the trunks and parcels. It was all right going uphill but, when the coach started to go down, the parcels danced around him so that the basket seemed almost alive. For nearly an hour he was shaken to pieces and badly bruised. Eventually Moritz managed to climb back on to the roof; it was now pouring with rain, yet the decently dressed young man was sound asleep, rolling around and nearly pushing his neighbours from their seats.[2]

But things could have been much worse; in winter, cold was the greatest problem for the outside passenger. One day in March 1812 the people of Chippenham noticed that three outside passengers on the Bath coach were 'lying in a state of apparent insensibility'; it was found that they had died from cold and exposure several hours earlier. Apart from rugs and warm overcoats, there was little one could do about the cold; the 1820s, in particular, was a decade of exceptionally hard winters. For those who could not afford to travel inside, the only thing to do was to take the advice of the *Aylesbury News*: 'To attain the maximum comfort which circumstances admit, they should drink a tankard of good ale cold from the tap and rub their hands, ears and faces with snow immediately before they start. This will produce a more lasting and agreeable glow than any other artificial means is capable of producing.'

Inside passengers were charged more, about threepence per mile. There may have been greater comfort but against that one had to balance children threatening to be sick and rather hysterical women. Coach proprietors rarely made enormous profits but there were strong competitive pressures upon them to improve and accelerate their services. Races between coaches were frequent and the results sometimes unfortunate. In 1817 two rival coaches entered Leeds from York running neck and neck; the *True Briton*, in attempting to pass its rival, ran into a basket of dung and was overturned. One woman lost several fingers as a result.[3] The next year the Hemel Hempstead coach took a bend too quickly and two of the outside passengers were killed. Some accidents were caused by worn parts on the coach, others by unsuitable horses, appalling weather conditions or drunken coachmen. Everywhere the mania for excessive speed was blamed for causing ladies to faint and cattle in the surrounding fields to panic.

Parliament authorised local magistrates to levy on-the-spot fines on coachmen who drove carelessly, but more important, a man who worked his horses too hard would not be popular with his employers. Humanitarian considerations probably did not enter into their calculations but a good coach horse was an expensive item–at least fifty guineas–and some four years' work was expected in order to get a reasonable return on investment. The distance between stops–'the stage'–was determined by the horses' need for rest and water; there was usually a stop about every fifteen miles. In open country, a poor set of 'bokickers' and no inn for miles, a great deal of 'nursing' was required to complete the stage. A good coachman, like John Bayzand who was on the Oxford to Southampton run for thirty years, always insisted that some of his passengers walked up the hills in order to ease the strain on the horses.

Stage coaches rarely travelled after dark and, on a long journey, it was necessary to stay overnight at an inn. Standards varied enormously. After a tour of the west of England in 1781, John Byng decided that the innkeepers were insolent, the hostlers sulky, the chambermaids pert and the waiters impertinent; the meat was tough, the wine foul, the beer 'hard', the sheets wet, the linen dirty and the knives never cleaned. Occasionally the fastidious Byng did find a place to suit him. On 28 May 1792 he stayed at The Sun at Biggleswade where he enjoyed a well-cooked meal of spitchcock eel, roasted pigeons, a loin of pork, tarts, jellies and custards. After a day of strong winds, the evening brought heavy rain but Byng felt very snug. The Sun had good coffee and good wines; there was a polite clientele with whom a gentleman could safely play cards and backgammon. Seated in the window of The Sun, it seemed that only madmen would want to push on through the storm.[4]

For those in a greater hurry and with deeper pockets there were the smaller, lighter and faster mail coaches which made room for three or four passengers. The specially designed coaches with their red wheels and undercarriage, maroon bodies and black side panels, became objects of national pride. They represented, indeed, the first nationally organised system of transport. Although the coaches were owned by a number of private proprietors every detail of their operation and construction was minutely supervised by the Post Office. All of these 'patent' coaches were built and maintained by John Vidler of Millbank; each coach was 10 ft 8 in long and 7 ft 2 in high; the distance between the fore and hind axle was to be 6 ft 6 in and the width of the track 5 ft 1½in. Certain panels were to be covered with leather, oak used for the wheel spokes, elm for the stock and ash for the bars. Inside, the coach was to have drab lining with double crimson stripes, a matching carpet and cushions stuffed with the best horsehair.[5]

The mail contracts were awarded after investigation of the background and reliability of the various coaching firms who showed interest. Each coach carried an armed guard directly employed by the Post Office; coachmen were issued with a watch and firms whose services were consistently late found money deducted from their payments. Thomas Hasker, the Superintendent of Mail Coaches, did his best to ensure an efficient service; if a coach was delayed more than half an hour the guard was to ride ahead carrying the letters on horseback. The guard was armed with a blunderbuss and a brace of pistols so that few highwaymen cared to tangle with a mail coach. Horses were changed quickly–five minutes only allowed–and mail coaches had the right of way when meeting other traffic. On hearing the sound of the mail coach horn, turnpike keepers were obliged to throw open their gates so that the coach should not have to stop. Although there were accidents, the mail coaches were generally more reliable than the stage coach. The main problem seems to have been that the coachmen were notoriously short tempered and rude. Hasker sent out a circular: 'I am sorry to dismiss sober, honest men, but I must have civility also, and when you behave impertinently to passengers they find out some other error to couple the complaint with, that nothing less than dismissal can succeed.'[6]

For the rich, stage coaches, even mail coaches, were considered vulgar. The ownership of a private coach and horses gave a man a certain social status. *The Complete Servant* of 1825 believed that the sobriety, steady conduct and respectability of the coachman was the key factor in determining a family's standing in the eyes of its neighbours. Newspapers contained numerous advertisements for coachmen with good characters from their last places–although some employers made conditions that the man concerned must have had smallpox, be able to read and write, know how to deal with a cast shoe and be prepared to work in the gardens 'at leisure times'. In grand houses the coachman–probably dressed in low cocked hat, plush breeches and benjamin surtout–would have despised menial duties. He was the head of an important department, his standing and that of his master indicated by the number of footmen or 'outriders' who stood on the back of the coach. Some people, fearful of the well-established connection between knowledge of horses and sharp practice, went to great lengths to see that their stable servants were kept out of mischief. In the Roman Catholic household of Lady Petre the recommended routine was: 'Servants that are employed in the stables rise at 5 o'clock from which time till half past eight they find employment enough in cleansing their stables, dressing and feeding their horses; after which an hour or two is spent in watering and airing them. This being over the servants may be allowed an hour and the half to hear mass and eat their breakfast, after which they return to grease or clean their coaches, harness, bridles etc. as there is occasion.'[7]

Coaches were expensive, up to £225 for a good phaeton, while the cost of running a carriage, complete with appropriate coachmen and footmen, was about £200 a year. This figure included a licence fee of seven pounds for every four-wheeled vehicle; if the owner wished to emblazon his coach with arms, the government demanded a further two pounds. Those who wished to economise could always buy a coach second hand; but fashions were changing and after the invention of the elliptic spring in 1804 few can have wished to be seen in public in a coach which was obviously both old and uncomfortable. In any case, by the beginning of the nineteenth century, several large coach builders were prepared to accept 'deferred payments'; Maythorn & Son of Biggleswade offered landaus from 120 guineas cash or three annual payments of forty-two guineas.

Otherwise one could hire a post chaise and a 'post boy' to drive it on a mileage basis. The post boy wore a standard uniform of a bright yellow jacket and a large beaver hat; he would expect handsome tips on top of the usual one shilling per mile charged by the innkeeper who owned the chaise. But travellers in post chaises and private carriages were obvious targets for robbers; there were still highwaymen to worry about at the beginning of the nineteenth century. A father and son executed at Lancaster on 29 September 1827 had attacked their victims with large clubs used in 'a manner too shocking to describe'. A gang of highwaymen 'infested the Essex Road' in the 1780s and prospered for many years before being brought to justice. But not all highwaymen were so lucky; armed guards were sometimes a little trigger happy. In 1812 a coach carrying a representative of Gurney's Bank of Norwich was stopped on Thetford Heath; the highwayman was immediately shot dead. When examined, the would-be robber was found to be clutching a brass candlestick which he had hoped would pass for a pistol.[8] The presence of a 'defenceless woman' in the coach sometimes made it seem wiser to give in to the highwayman's demands; on these occasions there could even be an exchange of pleasantries. Horace Walpole recounted:

I heard a voice say 'stop' and the figure came back to the chaise. I had the presence of mind, before letting down the glass, to take out my watch and stuff it within my waistcoat under my arm. He said 'Your purses and watches.' I replied 'I have no watch.' 'Then your purse.' I gave it to him; it had nine guineas. It was so dark that I could not see his hand but I felt him take it. He then asked for Lady Browne's purse and said 'Don't be frightened, I will not hurt you.' I said 'No you won't frighten the Lady.' 'No, I give you my word I will do you no hurt.' Lady Browne gave him her purse and was about to hold her watch but he said 'I am obliged to you, I wish you good night.'[9]

Improvements to carriage design could have done little to accelerate travellers, had English roads remained in the same state as they had been in the early eighteenth century. In 1795 Thomas Hasker complained of the deep holes in the Great North Road which forced coachmen to drive slowly and so lose time on their schedules; even worse, if the driver did not see the hole the coach could be overturned. In 1830 things were far from ideal but they had improved enormously owing to the efforts of the Turnpike Trusts. The system whereby each parish was responsible for the repair of the roads within its boundaries had been criticised for many years. Groups of individuals believed they could make improvements to sections of road whose users would be prepared to pay tolls. Ideally, tolls would be used to maintain and further improve the turnpike–and still leave some profit for the promoters. But even if there was no profit, better transport would increase the pace of economic activity in the surrounding area. Although a landowner who invested money with a turnpike might never get a proper return on his money, he might well find any losses more than outweighed by the increased sales of his farm produce.

Once sufficient support had been promised for a turnpike, an Act of Parliament had to be obtained setting out details of the road improvements to be undertaken, the maximum tolls that could be levied, and giving exemptions to various kinds of travellers. The Act of 1791 for the improvement of the highway from Buckingham to Banbury via Brackley exempted a good deal of local farm traffic, military men and their baggage, anyone going to or from his place of worship on Sunday or attending a funeral, and clergymen travelling on their parochial duties.[10] There were differing views on the best means of highway improvement. John McAdam preferred a soft foundation whereas Thomas Telford preferred a solid stone base. MacAdam's roads were designed to allow water to run off easily and were about three inches higher at the centre than at the sides. Stones were to be of uniform size and were intended to bind together to form a hard surface. The final task was to stop up side roads in order to force travellers to use the turnpike and then to build the toll houses–many of them in the fashionable 'rustic' style. In order to get an immediate return on their investment, the turnpike company auctioned the right of collecting tolls to a contractor; thus, the toll had to find a profit for two different organisations. Complicated lists of rates were drawn up; heavy wagons with narrow wheels, which were particularly damaging to the road surface, were charged higher rates.

The main problem faced by the turnpikes was evasion of tolls. The sort of Englishman Cobbett admired did not take kindly to demands of payment for driving his cart a few hundred yards down the road which had previously been free to all comers; he could see no reason why he should pay for macadamised surfaces and toll houses built in the most refined taste. Some drove their wagons and coaches into fields to avoid the toll gate, and bolder spirits–like the Shrewsbury wagoner at Bryngwilch–forced their teams through the toll bar, used abusive language and threatened the gate keeper with violence.

To some people the toll gate symbolised improved transport and progress, to others it was a sign of oppression. Obviously the manufacturer or tradesman wanted to make the most efficient use of his horses. Better road surfaces meant that loads could be heavier and–

even allowing for the tolls–transport costs lowered. A wagon, however crude, was a great improvement on a pack horse, but at the end of the eighteenth century large tracts of the north of England were served by causeways, just wide enough for one animal. Although a horse could pull ten times the weight on wheels as he could carry on his back, there was not enough traffic to justify the construction of a proper road. But cheaper transport was not all gain. Areas of high cost production would find that the protection they had previously enjoyed would disappear and their former markets would be flooded with cheaper goods from outside. Similarly, cheaper transport would encourage the movement of food out of a low price area and might well result, not in the fall of urban food prices, but in the rise of rural food prices to the same level as in the towns.

When these sort of considerations seemed operative, antagonism to turnpikes could go beyond mere evasion of tolls. The toll gates were the main targets of the 'Rebecca Riots' in South Wales in 1842–3. As on similar occasions, popular protest took a religious colouring; the way for an all-out attack was clear when it was discovered that toll gates had been mentioned in the Book of Genesis: 'And they blessed Rebecca and said unto her, thou art our sister, be thou mother of thousands and let thy seed possess the gate of those that hate them.'[11] Encouraged by Primitive Methodist preachers, the rioters broke down gates, forced keepers out, and burned down toll houses. Soon there was not a toll gate standing in Pembroke or Cardiganshire. As the trustees charged an incredible 12s 6d for a market cart going a dozen miles, there was some justification for the popular fury. Overweight loads were subjected to heavy surcharges and this led to questioning of the reliability of the weighing machines installed at some of the toll gates.

Faced with evasions, riots, inadequate traffic and defaulting contractors, it is not surprising that many turnpikes got into financial difficulties. In all, about 20,000 miles of road, or about one-fifth of the total, were affected by Turnpike Acts by 1830; the gross income from tolls was over £1,500,000 per annum. But there were too many small trusts–1116 in 1838–some controlling only a couple of miles of road. A traveller came across a stretch of good road, then reverted to a cart track, before coming into the territory of another trust. There were numerous bottlenecks and no attempt at a national system. Road transport had some advantage of flexibility over its rivals but its organisational and administrative failings were an important factor in bringing about its sudden eclipse in the 1840s. After a brief glory, the splendid mail coach of the 1820s was lucky to find employment as a hen coop in a farmyard.

## The Calm Element

Although substantial volumes of goods traffic were carried by road, the most remarkable feature of the Age of Cobbett was the development of canals. The advantages of this system of transport were summarised by James Phillips in his *General History of Inland Navigation*, published in 1792. Phillips claimed that canals damaged the prosperity of coastal shipping but goods were certainly safer travelling on inland waterways than on the open sea during periods of bad weather and in time of war when coastal shipping was exposed to privateers. Although bargees were not ideal material for the Royal Navy, Phillips could assert: 'But however little inland navigation may be supposed to form navigators for the sea, no lives are lost in the calm element on which they are employed; the diseases of hot countries, so destructive of our seamen are also unknown to them; and there is no danger of their defection, either in peace or war, to the service of foreign states, our rivals and enemies.'[12]

Above all, the cheaper transport provided by waterways enabled the manufacturer to obtain his materials, fuel and food for his workmen at a lower rate, to convey his goods to market at less expense and consequently to sell cheaper than his competitors. The main reason for the cheapness of water transport as compared to the roads arose from the fact that a pack animal could scarcely carry more than a couple of hundredweight, a cart horse would be strong indeed to manage more than a ton but a single horse could pull as much as thirty tons on water. Of course, some of the advantages of canals could also apply to river navigation but the effort to drag boats upstream, against the current, was considerably greater than that required on the calm element (or stagnant water) of a canal. Further, rivers did not always take the most convenient course, or link the centres with complementary economies; in many parts of the country, rivers were either too shallow or too fast-running to be of much use for boats.

The first burst of canal building followed the Seven Years War and witnessed the completion of the pioneer Bridgewater Canal. This work astonished travellers by its impressive aqueduct over the River Irwell, its long underground sections going into the heart of the Duke of Bridgewater's coal mines, and its extraordinary hydraulic cranes. A new wave of activity began as Britain recovered from the depression coinciding with the American War of Independence. The main river systems of England–the Severn, Thames, Great Ouse, Trent, Humber and Mersey–were linked by trunk canals. Construction reached levels which justify the description of 'The Canal Mania' often given to the 1790s. Although construction fell off in the 1820s, there were over 4000 miles of canal and improved river navigation open for traffic in 1830.

The essential alliance of the Industrial Revolution was between canals and coal. Cheap coal was essential if the country was to overcome the fuel crisis which had seriously hampered progress in the first half of the eighteenth century. The construction of the Bridgewater Canal halved the price of coal in Manchester and was an important factor in the phenomenal growth of the town at the end of the eighteenth century. The canals thrived on bulk loads; artificial waterways in coal mining areas were markedly more profitable than in other parts of the country and James Phillips noted that ninety of the 165 Acts obtained for canals since 1758 had been to serve collieries and another forty-seven on account of iron, lead or copper mines.

Work on canal construction dramatically increased employment–and thus spending power–precisely at the time when industry was first beginning to look for mass markets. But the social effects of the arrival of hundreds of 'navigators' were even more dramatic than the economic. To villages with long memories and little contact with the outside world, the experience must have seemed similar to the enforced billeting of soldiers during the Civil War. In the early days, there were attempts at an almost military discipline; labourers were still 'bound' to their work and threatened with legal action if they absconded. The 'navigator' worked hard for his employer, usually a small contractor or 'hag-master', who was responsible for a few miles of the construction work. All digging was done with ordinary spades while wheelbarrows on planks were the usual way of removing spoil. Canals passing through porous rock had to be lined with 'puddle clay' in order to keep the water in. In clay areas, temporary brick works were set up to provide building material for locksides, bridges and tunnel linings. In the early canals, construction costs had to be kept to a minimum and lavish engineering works were avoided–even at the cost of long detours. Canal engineers were inclined to follow a contour line as long as possible, however winding, until it became absolutely necessary to insert a lock. The navigators might stay for several years in one area if they were building a massive embankment, an aqueduct or a tunnel; the 2880-yard Harecastle Tunnel on the Trent and Mersey Canal took eight years to build.[13]

The work was dangerous, the 'navvies' seemed to delight in unnecessary risks, and accidents were frequent. Many were killed or injured in the tunnels by falls of rock and sudden rushes of water. In most cases there was no compensation, although sometimes the contractors, often former 'navvies' themselves, would contribute a guinea to funeral expenses. In many ways, the canal navvies were the pioneer corps of the Industrial Revolution, moving on to another canal when the work was finished rather than going back to work on the land. But the break with the past was not complete–the harvest continued to dominate all else and, in September, many navvies returned to the fields for a fortnight. In 1794 the start of work on the Peak Forest canal was delayed until after the harvest was in.

Perhaps the canals provide a key to the new spirit which was appearing in both scientific and cultural activity. If nature was to be vanquished, nature must be better understood. Cartography and geology were the obvious beneficiaries of canal building but the enterprise also produced a great interest in nature as such–not in the carefully contrived 'natural' landscapes of Capability Brown, but nature in a more challenging mood of the kind encountered by the canal builders in the Peak Forest. The traditional explanation of the Romantic Movement, as exemplified in Wordsworth, is of cultivated men recoiling from the horrors of the Industrial Revolution; yet the Romantic's obsession with nature owed a great deal to the spirit contained in poems like Erasmus Darwin's *The Botanic Garden*, published in 1791. In Canto III, the poet discusses canals and the genius of James Brindley:

> *So with strong arm immortal* Brindley *leads*
> *His long canals and parts the velvet meads;*
> *Winding in lucid lines, the watery mass*
> *Mines the rock firm, or loads the deep morass,*
> *With rising locks a thousand hills alarms*
> *Flings o'er a thousand streams its silver arms,*
> *Feeds the long vale, the nodding woodland lanes*
> *And Plenty, Arts and Commerce freight the waves.*[14]

From an interest in nature, there followed an admiration for the men who challenged it successfully. Long before the appearance of Samuel Smiles's *Lives of the Engineers*, James Brindley was a cult figure. The great thing about Brindley was that he had come up in the world. He was presented as the progeny of peasants who dissipated away the little freehold they possessed and totally neglected their son's education. Yet young Brindley's application and zeal as an apprentice to a millwright near Macclesfield soon meant that he was left in charge of his employer's works for weeks on end. His acute observation and quick intelligence enabled him to devise improvements, while his thirst for knowledge made him think nothing of walking fifty miles to see a new piece of machinery.[15] At first, Brindley's plans were dismissed as chimeras, his suggestions thwarted by the envy of his ungrateful superiors and his original solutions crushed by the weight of prejudice in the engineering establishment. But in the end, his talents were recognised by Francis Egerton, 3rd Duke of Bridgewater. Under Bridgewater's patronage, Brindley became a national hero, with an appropriately large income.

Figures like Brindley, Telford, Arkwright and later George Stephenson were constantly cited as proof that working men could rise in the world–not by marrying above their station or by a prize in a State Lottery–but by ability and unstinting endeavour. Of course, for every Brindley or Stephenson, there would be thousands of failures; but if the success of a tiny minority produced a spirit of emulation in others the results would be dramatic. If invention in engineering brought social recognition and financial rewards then there would be more inventions. For the moment, invention was in partnership with the nobility, but the constant emphasis on the Brindley story hints at the beginnings of a belief in meritocracy. There was an increasing ambivalence in attitudes to the poor. They were told to be contented with their lot, yet they were also urged to constant endeavours to rise in the world. If the lot of the poor had been tolerable, Cobbett would have been in favour of the first argument; he could never accept parvenus. In other words, the heroes of the Industrial Revolution, as exemplified by James Brindley, could no longer be accommodated into a traditional social structure.

Although Phillips claimed that a mile of canal could be made for less expense than a mile of turnpike, this assertion was true only in exceptionally favourable circumstances. The resources of the Bridgewater estates had been barely sufficient to pay for the building of the Duke's canal. It was obvious that larger projects were beyond the pocket of any individual, however wealthy. The ideal solution was for a large number of people to invest in the scheme. Some men invested in a canal company because they believed that it would improve the value of their land or benefit their business; their interest was personal and local. It is easy to see why Josiah Wedgwood invested in the Trent and Mersey Canal. Water carriage was not only cheaper but plates, cups and saucers were less likely to be broken if they were carried on barges than in carts over uneven roads.

Canals could be very profitable; few railways were ever to rival them in this respect. In good years the Birmingham Canal and the Loughborough Navigation declared a dividend of 100 per cent, the Trent and Mersey 75 and the Oxford Canal about 35 per cent.[16] Wide sections of society were interested. The shareholders of the Stratford upon Avon

Canal included a plumber, a mealman, a perukemaker, an innkeeper, two coopers and a joiner.[17]

Like the Turnpike Trusts, canal companies derived their income from tolls levied on traffic passing through the locks; only a few actually operated their own barges. Canal companies rarely farmed their tolls; perhaps the reason for this important difference compared to the Turnpikes was that maintenance had to be of a much higher standard. A deep rut in a road might cause inconvenience but it would not render the turnpike impassable; a serious breach in a canal embankment might well paralyse a whole system. In other industries, family control meant that management was usually in the hands of partners but, in the canals, one can see the beginnings of a new element in English society–a salaried managerial class. The canals needed general managers, clerks, treasurers, accountants and engineers. Of these the general manager was the most important, the man who set the tone for the whole organisation. Thomas Brewer of the Dudley Canal received a substantial £400 per annum. At a lower level there were office staff, lock-keepers, toll collectors, masons, carpenters and labourers. John Brown, a toll collector on the Oxford Canal, received eighteen shillings per week in 1790 but was expected to provide his own firearms. Most canals had an official molecatcher devoted to an all-out war on the little creatures who posed a serious threat to the embankments.

The most common type of barge was the type developed by Brindley to fit the 74 ft $\times$ 7 ft lock walls in the middle sections of the Trent and Mersey. The barges were built of wood, although a few canals used iron boats for ice breaking in winter. Companies did their best to prevent inexperienced boatmen causing delays and the Birmingham Canal used to insist that no barge should enter a lock except in the company of 'an able horse and able and experienced hands'. Boatmen disliked companies which did not maintain their tow paths properly; these were liable to collapse, sending both horse and man into the 'cut'. The motive power on most canals was the horse, but a few canals had sailing barges; on canals lacking a tow path it was sometimes necessary to employ gangs of men known as bow hauliers to drag the barges along. Few tunnels had tow paths and the usual way of passing through was for two or three men (leggers) to lie on boards across the barge and push against the side of the tunnel with their feet.

As traffic built up there were backlogs of goods on the wharfs. Annual licences were introduced to remove the ritual of toll paying at each lock, saving both time and a toll collector's wages. In some places, the peace of the canal was broken by the arrival of steam paddle tugs, to tow barges through the tunnel and throw the leggers out of work. But despite these improvements, there were signs of trouble in the 1820s. Almost none of the canals were suited to the successful application of steam power. The canals made a tremendous contribution to the Industrial Revolution but their basic technology was primitive; when the fruits of the Industrial Revolution were applied to transport, the canals could not accept the challenge. England was too hilly for canals to provide a long-term answer; boats could only go uphill by means of the pound lock which was both expensive to construct and time-consuming in operation. A glance at the canal map of England will underline this point. London is the centre both of the system of Roman roads and of Victorian railways; Birmingham is the canal capital of England. The canal was at its best in the flat lands in the triangle bounded by Birmingham, Liverpool and Manchester; the chalk and limestone ridges which separate southern England from the midland plain, were perhaps the main reason for the essentially provincial character of the canals.

But one could not blame it all on nature. Theoretically the proliferation of companies should have meant that there was a healthy competition; but in practice the canal user lost rather than gained. The companies squabbled over rights to fill their canals from rivers and reservoirs and took positive delight in seeing a rival's canal run dry. Negotiations to offer a 'through toll' for the journey from London to Birmingham did not succeed until the very end of the nineteenth century! Perhaps the saddest story is that of the Bridgewater Canal itself. After the Duke's death the canal was run by a body known as the Bridgewater Trustees. Partly from inclination and partly because of the orders of the Duke's legatees, the Trustees followed a policy of maximising present income regardless of long-term considerations. Maintenance work was neglected yet the tolls were increased. Manchester's attitude to the canal changed from enthusiasm to fury; warehousing was inadequate and pilferage was rife. Cotton manufacturers swopped stories of consignments which took months to get from Liverpool to Manchester and were utterly ruined when they did arrive.[18] It is ironic that discontent with the first major canal should have produced the first major railway.

Yet in 1830 the threat still seemed pretty remote. Short colliery railways operated by horses and a few cumbersome steam engines were operating in the north-east. Most people, however, regarded railways as frightening and dangerous but still no more than a curious mechanical novelty. On 14 November 1829 Thomas Creevey wrote to his step-daughter:

# The Price of Progress

Today we have had a lark of a very high order. Lady Wilton sent over yesterday from Knowsley to say that the Loco Motive machine was to be upon the railway at such a place at 12 o'clock for the Knowsley party to ride in if they liked. I had the satisfaction, for I can't call it *pleasure* of taking a trip of five miles in it, which we did in just a quarter of an hour–that is 20 miles an hour. But the quickest motion is to me *frightful*: it is really flying, and it is impossible to divest yourself of the notion of instant death to all upon the least accident happening. It gave me a headache which has not left me yet. Sefton is convinced that some damnable thing must come of it.[19]

For stage coaches, mail coaches, even the proprietors of canal shares, the results were indeed damnable.

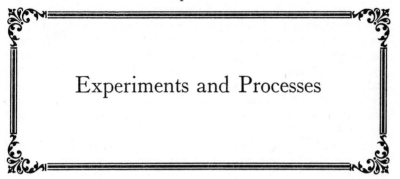

Chapter Seven

# Experiments and Processes

## Books Have Been Used to Light the Fires

To later generations the Age of Cobbett was remarkable for its rapid technological change. There were spinning jennies, water frames, self-acting mules, power looms, steam engines and pumping gear, iron bridges, railway engines and hosts of other inventions which transformed England into the first genuinely industrial nation. The most obvious explanation of this spate of inventions is that people were better educated and more scientifically inclined, yet even the education of the children of the rich left much to be desired. An amateur interest in scientific subjects was permissible but there was a widespread view that the practice of applied science was incompatible with gentility.

Fortunately, this attitude was less general in Scotland and some students were sent to the universities of 'North Britain' after completing their studies at Oxford. Scottish universities attracted students from England for a variety of reasons, anything from an interest in the 'Romantic' Scotland of the Waverley novels to a desire to imbibe Political Economy (Scotch Feelosophy to Cobbett) from its fountainhead at Glasgow University. More important, Glasgow and Edinburgh placed greater emphasis on scientific studies than was found anywhere in England. Hugo Arnot's *History of Edinburgh*, published in 1770, described lectures given by Joseph Black, the professor of 'Chymistry'; not only did Dr Black try to explain 'many of the most extensive operations' and curious 'phaenomena of nature' but also set out to 'adapt them to the use of arts, particularly of pharmacy, illustrating the whole with a great number of experiments and processes'.[1]

Of the mechanical geniuses of the Age of Cobbett, the one most closely linked with a university was James Watt. Through his relation,

TPP—D                                89

George Muirhead, Professor of Oriental Languages at Glasgow University, Watt came to know many of the great intellects in the Scotland of the 1760s, and was appointed as official mathematical instrument maker to Glasgow University at the early age of twenty. While occupying this position, Watt made his most important invention, the steam condenser. Although Glasgow University protected Watt when other craftsmen tried to get him dismissed because he had not served a proper apprenticeship, this support represents almost the total university patronage of mechanical inventors throughout the eighteenth century.[2]

The situation was worse south of the border. In Tudor and Stuart times the English grammar school had been an important force for social mobility but there had been a marked deterioration since 1660. The reports of the Municipal Commissioners in the 1830s reveal a widespread misapplication of legacies and endowments, particularly when the school was administered by the local aldermen. The quality of instruction was deplorable. The Free Grammar School in Coventry had been endowed with former monastic and guild lands. In the 1820s this property produced a healthy £908 per annum, but the money was merely divided between two octogenarian schoolmasters. In the 1790s there had been some thirty pupils; by the time the Commissioners came to Coventry, there was only one. Classrooms had been locked up for years and a blue mould covered the rotting desks. The Commissioners declared that the state of the school was discreditable to all concerned in its management; the fate of the library founded in 1602, was disgraceful: 'The books were formerly placed in a room on the south side of the school, which was taken down to widen the street in 1791, and afterwards removed to a small damp room on the north side of the school. Here (with the exception of a manuscript copy of Lydgate's poems, which the headmaster removed to his own house) the books seem to have been entirely neglected and exposed to destruction. From the evidence of a person who had been a pupil of the under master, the books appear at the time he was at school, to have been used to light the fires.'[3]

The deficiencies of grammar and public schools were partially offset by Dissenting academies. These institutions placed greater emphasis on the practical and scientific and the schools at Warrington and Daventry enjoyed a high reputation. Joseph Priestley, the first serious investigator of combustion, was educated at Daventry and later praised the school as being 'peculiarly favourable to the pursuit of truth, as the students were about equally divided upon every question of much importance'. But it would be unwise to exaggerate the 'scientific' aspect of Dissenting education. The questions Priestley referred to were more theological than scientific; the school was bitterly divided over atonement, predestination, free will and the validity of St Paul's dialectics. It was an intellectual climate which belonged more to the seventeenth than the eighteenth century. Many of Priestley's theories were absurd and Cobbett had little difficulty in combining ridicule of his experiments with derision of his eccentric theology:

> He preached up a kind of *deism* which nobody understood, and which it was thought the Doctor understood full as well as his neighbours. This doctrine afterwards assumed the name of Unitarianism. The sect never rose into consequence and the founder had the mortification of seeing his darling Unitarianism growing quite out of date with himself... But the strangest part of the story remains to be told; for when this bustle was all over and settled and everybody thought the perverse fellow was going to get his living in an honest way, what did he do but set to work bottling up his own farts, and selling them for superfine inflammable air, and what's still worse, had the impudence to want a patent for his discovery.[4]

Priestley was apologetic in his advocacy of scientific education, and his *Essay on a Course of Liberal Education* placed greater emphasis on the study of 'civil policy'. It is true that Dissenters were prominent in societies founded to strengthen the ties between science and industry. The most important was the Lunar Society of Birmingham whose membership included Priestley and Josiah Wedgwood. The Society was unfortunate in its name which to popular imagination carried undertones of mystery, alchemy, pantheism and freemasonry. In fact, the Society met to discuss scientific papers on nights when there was a full moon because members needed light as a protection against the perils of footpads and open sewers. Public opinion still regarded scientists with suspicion and hostility. It was widely believed that the French Revolution was the first step of an international conspiracy organised by the Freemasons, who with their emphasis on 'natural' magic figured prominently in scientific circles. In July 1794 a Birmingham mob destroyed the Unitarian Chapel–'this temple of sedition and infidelity'–and then turned their attention to Priestley's house and laboratory, smashing and burning everything they could find under the slogan of 'no philosophers'.

Was it scientific progress that made England unique? In fact one is constantly faced with the question of why the Industrial Revolution did not take place in France rather than in England. The greatest mechanical genius of the eighteenth century was a Frenchman named

Vaucauson; no one in England could have invented the mechanical duck designed by Vaucauson and later described by Andrew Ure, the former professor of Chemistry at Glasgow University. The clockwork automaton was so perfect that it reproduced almost every bodily function. Like its original, the machine swallowed its food hastily; the grain was ground in the gizzard as 'preparatory to digestion' and 'finally subjected to excrementitious actions'. It is remarkable that until the middle of the eighteenth century, mechanical toys, musical boxes and elaborate theatrical machinery represented the greatest achievements of human ingenuity. Vaucauson also invented more practical devices such as silk-winding machines and tapestry looms. But it was England, not France, that led the world and we are forced to accept Ure's conclusion that mechanical invention was 'not of itself sufficient to found a successful manufacture'.[5]

What mattered was not the date of an invention but the date when it was adopted for commercial use. The adoption of new techniques was forced on England because materials used in traditional processes became scarce and prohibitively expensive. Enclosures and increasing population pressure meant a drastic reduction of acreage under timber– previously vital both for fuel and construction. Timber could be imported from Scandinavia but transport costs were high and the supply at risk in wartime. The answer was found underground, in coal and in iron ore. The increasing use of coal was noticed even in the seventeenth century when John Stowe noted that the shortage of timber meant that fires of 'seacoal' were to be found 'even in the chambers of honourable personages'.

The use of coal for domestic and industrial purposes grew so rapidly that seams close to the surface became exhausted. Providence had endowed England with coal sufficient to last for centuries, but the problem was to get at it. Water constantly flooded out deep workings and a perceptive writer declared 'Were it not for water, a colliery might be called a gold mine to purpose.' Attempts were made to drain mines by means of a bucket chain powered by a horse, and by the use of water wheels and windmills. But neither wind nor water could be relied upon, while buckets were only effective in fairly shallow mines. In fact, it was the necessity to open up deep coal mines which produced the first practical steam engines and pumping gear. In other words, it was *adverse* circumstances which played an important part in deciding that an Industrial Revolution should occur in England rather than elsewhere.

Of course, the knowledge that certain inventions were needed and could be relied upon to bring handsome rewards concentrated attention on annoying 'blockages' in the production process. The inventions required were often simple and did not depend upon an extensive scientific education. The men who invented the processes that made the Industrial Revolution–Compton, Arkwright and even Josiah Wedgwood–were intelligent craftsmen, able to rearrange a cog here and there, to render machinery simpler and cheaper to make, rather than abstract scientists. But it was up to the entrepreneurs whether or not to take up new inventions. It is interesting to put oneself in the position of a man thinking of setting up a cotton factory. There were many jobs which could be done either by steam or by horses: which should he choose?

A steam engine would consume coal and a horse would consume fodder; the cheaper coal became in relation to horse fodder, the more compelling the argument in favour of steam. In terms of actual work done, one engine horse-power is equal to one and a half times the strength of even the most powerful dray horse in peak condition. Moreover, a horse does not stay in peak condition for very long. Animals need rest and horses cannot work efficiently for more than eight hours per day, whereas a steam engine requires far less time out of action. Thus, a man who decided to use horses would buy several relays to work at different times of the day. These two factors meant that the real equivalent of an engine rated at sixty horse-power was no less than 270 dray horses! In the 1820s the cost of keeping a horse was about 1s 2d per day, £15 15s 0d for 270 horses and, assuming a six-day week, the annual bill would be in the region of £4800. The annual cost of a sixty-horse-power steam engine, using about 180 bushels of coal per day, would be less than £1500. Although a steam engine might need expensive repairs, if properly maintained it would last for fifty years or more; a horse would be completely worn out after ten.[6] Faced with calculations like these, it is not surprising that steam engines and inventions in general ceased to be regarded as toys, and were investigated very carefully indeed by merchants and businessmen.

## Golden Chains of Folly

There was little point in installing machinery to increase production unless one could be sure of a market for one's products. Inventions and cheap transport were important, but the essential requisite of an Industrial Revolution was the existence of purchasing power sufficiently widespread to justify a manufacturer moving over to a system of mass production. The demand did not have to come from British consumers; as far as the manufacturer was concerned, the same considerations applied if foreigners wanted to buy his goods. A large export trade has always been an obsession with British governments; spokesmen constantly asserted that a large import and export trade was 'essential to the vital interests of this country'. The relatively high incomes of ordinary people in North America provided a market for British goods. The industry which was changing most dramatically was cotton and, in some years, as much as 70 per cent of the cotton cloth produced in Lancashire was sent abroad.

The greatest monument to the importance of foreign trade was Liverpool. New docks were constantly being constructed to accommodate ships bringing sugar from the West Indies. Outward cargoes included cotton cloth from the mills of south Lancashire and metal ware from the forges of the Black Country. Liverpool was a town of great opportunity, a place where enterprising young men, particularly those interested in sugar, cotton, slaves and shipping, could make enormous fortunes. In the space of a few years John Gladstone, father of the Prime Minister, rose from a humble immigrant from Leith to become a great merchant prince. Even at the beginning of the eighteenth century, Daniel Defoe had realised that Liverpool would soon wrest control of the American trade from its rival Bristol. The growth of the town was phenomenal–60,000 in 1791 and 120,000 in 1821. Yet the very basis of it all was foreign trade; how could anyone but a madman desire that trade should be no more?

William Cobbett did; between 1806 and 1808 he published a number of articles in the *Political Register* under the arresting title of 'Perish Commerce'. Many commentators had argued that the government's revenue depended on import duties: the East India Company made huge payments to the Exchequer on account of its tea imports. Cobbett denied that these payments justified the privileges of the Company, in fact they were not payments at all; the duty was simply passed on to the consumer and thus paid out of the produce of labour in this country. The vaunted advantages of the Indian Empire were illusory.[7] Despite these self-evident truths, the 'shallow-headed Pitt' had actually asserted that the overthrow of Tipoo Sultan and the extension of the Indian Empire had added more to England's security than if the British army had subdued the whole of France. In the name of commerce there had been wars in Egypt, wars in India, wars in South America–'Oh! what English blood and English labour and English happiness and English honour has not this commerce cost!'[8]

Many writers shared Cobbett's distaste for the corrupting tendencies of brandy, tea and tobacco. But, it seemed, great as she was, England could not afford to offend other countries; there were some imports, particularly naval stores, that she simply could not do without. A greater danger, however, was that foreign nations would exclude exports from Britain, thousands of people in the textile trades would be thrown out of work and great manufacturers would be 'ruined men'. By 1807 the coast of Europe from St Petersburg to Constantinople did not contain a single port friendly to British commerce, and there was a possibility that the United States would impose a similar ban. The French were convinced that England would soon seek peace on any terms and there was panic among the Spinning Jenny Baronets. Cobbett was undismayed; the Americans bought British goods because they needed them–not from a sense of Christian charity: 'God preserve the country I love from a dependence upon American generosity, charity, or even American Justice. To hear some men talk upon this subject one would imagine that to *get rid* of goods, the produce of sheep's backs and of our mines and of the work of our hands was a positive good that nothing could counterbalance.'[9]

Although individuals might be injured by the end of such a trade, Cobbett thought that the community in general would actually benefit. The first effect would be that cloth and wool would become cheaper in England; fewer sheep would be raised but the land concerned would be used for food crops and new occupations would soon be found for the displaced textile workers. In all probability they would return to the land, which 'always calls for labour and which never fails to yield a grateful return'. Even Cobbett had to admit the difficulty of turning factory workers into expert ploughmen, but he believed there would be no long-term problem of unemployment. The reduction in foreign trade would mean that fewer naval vessels would be needed for escort and convoy duties. In turn, taxation could be reduced, leaving consumers with more to spend on goods made in this country. Many commodities like hemp which had previously been imported could be grown here. England was unique in being self-sufficient in almost everything she really needed, yet her muddle-headed rulers trembled at the idea of a collapse of overseas trade.

Cobbett was prepared to welcome any development, however unpleasant its side effects, which could result in a return to the land. He gravely underestimated the numbers of people who would suffer if there was a serious disruption of foreign trade. Yet his argument contained one important element of truth: he recognised that foreign trade was less important than domestic demand. He pointed out that taxes on malt and beer alone produced more revenue than all shipping and foreign commerce put together; the value of the trade to America was actually less than that of the porter consumed in the City of Westminster. In other words, one must see home demand as the most crucial factor in persuading enterprising men that money could be made by increasing their output and experimenting with machinery.

To some observers the high level of domestic demand was simply an indication of the corruption of English manners and society. The luxury of London was only a reflection of a nationwide passion for worthless trifles. Frederick Wendeborn was astonished by the large number of elegant print shops. He noticed hundreds of fine prints, many with superb frames, hung up and exhibited in windows. Passers-by might glance at a new print but it seemed that no one ever went in to buy. The costs of running such an establishment were obviously considerable, the income tiny; how could the owner possibly avoid bankruptcy? The mystery was only cleared up when a print seller, obviously a rich man, told Wendeborn that as much as £500 per week was taken on prints sent into the country.[10]

Wendeborn was astonished at the visual signs of wealth but disapproved of the attitudes that lay behind it. Wendeborn hinted that the English were not really richer than other nations; they simply spent more freely. The proverb 'A short life and a merry one' was widely quoted and far too many people actually put it into practice. They spent and spent and when the creditors finally closed in, they made their last choice—between razor, rope or river. The listlessness of English people made them tire of everything after a few months; it needed little salesmanship to persuade them to buy whatever happened to be the latest craze. The turnover was so rapid that it did not matter if the goods were badly made; they were simply discarded long before they were worn out. Yet Wendeborn had the insight to perceive that these attitudes had actually promoted British commercial and industrial greatness:

In former times, people of some consequence and fortune, thought themselves to appear very decently, if they had every year a new suit of cloaths, but at present three and more are annually required by a man in a middling station of life, who wishes to make what is called only a decent appearance...Frequent changes of fashion, in regard to dress and furniture, are a great support of British manufacturers; they promote trade, and keep all sorts of tradesmen employed; they are beneficial to government by imposts and taxes; they are the principal links in those golden chains of folly, by which men suffer themselves to be bound and to renounce, insensibly their natural liberty and independence.[11]

There were ways of increasing consumer demand where it did not exist already; beneath the scandalised eyes of Cobbett and Wendeborn, the modern art of salesmanship was emerging. Josiah Wedgwood has many claims to fame but it was in this sphere that he made his greatest contributions to the future. Wedgwood realised that the craze for tea drinking had created an opportunity for enterprising potters. At first the trade showed little sign of rising to the challenge; earthenware cups and plates were made in various parts of the country and sold to the local community. Wedgwood saw that earthenware, despite its cheapness, was too coarse and heavy for the taste of such a refined age. On the other hand, porcelain was too fragile and expensive to gain a large share of the market. A man who produced a cup and saucer which was both elegant and cheap was well on the way to a fortune. After many experiments Wedgwood found that he could meet the vital requirements by using a ball clay from Devonshire. The new pottery was covered with a tough lead glaze and named Creamware.[12] Later Wedgwood introduced Jasperware for use in ornaments.

Wedgwood had to persuade people to throw away their earthenware cups and plates and buy Creamware services. Although Creamware had real advantages, Wedgwood added a new dimension. He set out to create an impression that earthenware was to be equated with ignorance and vulgarity while the purchase of a Wedgwood tea service conferred instant gentility and social status. The promotion of a product by its associations rather than by its intrinsic merits is the most striking feature of modern salesmanship. Such techniques could actually persuade people that they 'ought' to buy something for which they felt absolutely no need before they looked into the shop window.

Wedgwood based his sales techniques on that most inveterate of English vices–snobbery. The receipt of an unexpected order from Queen Charlotte produced an immediate realisation of the advantage of aristocratic and royal patronage. Assiduous cultivation of the Queen resulted in Wedgwood's appointment as 'Potter to Her Majesty' and this legend figured prominently in all literature connected with the firm. Perhaps the greatest coup was the order for the magnificent 'Frog Service' consisting of 952 items which, after a well-advertised exhibition in Wedgwood's London showrooms, was despatched to Russia for the use of Catherine the Great. In the early days of a new line Wedgwood was careful to limit sales and to keep prices high. The craftsmanship was so superb, the design so exquisite that only the cream of society deserved such masterpieces. It was sacrilege to suggest that *objets d'art* like this would ever be contaminated by sale in an ordinary shop, or subjected to the ignominy of being advertised by handbills.

Wedgwood knew that products which were expensive, scarce and 'exclusive to the nobility' had an especial appeal to ordinary people. In fact, the line had never been scarce at all. The warehouses were bulging with crates of it. Suddenly the rush was released and prices cut while thousands of ordinary people were informed that, for a very modest outlay, they could dine off plates identical to the ones used by the Queen of England and the Empress of Russia. Even for those who had not been considering the purchase of dinner plates, cups and saucers, this chance of a lifetime was too good to miss. This was the crucial moment; in the case of Jasperware ornaments Wedgwood declared: 'The great people have had these vases in their Palaces long enough for them to be seen and admired by the Middling sort of People, which class we know are vastly, infinitely superior, in number to the Great, and though a great Price was, I believe at first necessary to make the vases esteemed Ornament for Palaces that reason no longer exists. Their character is established and the middling People would probably buy quantities of them at a reduced price.'[13]

Kings and queens, lords and ladies had been a charade, a mere loss leader. It was the mass market, supposedly despised by Wedgwood, that brought the real profits. The plates and cups on sale in Birmingham and Manchester were indeed similar to those used by Queen Charlotte but they were not quite the same. The clay, pattern and firing might be identical but infinitely greater pains would be taken in the decoration of the items intended for royal use. Wedgwood himself decorated the plates for Queen Charlotte; powdered gold was mixed with honey and the honey later washed away. It was a tricky process and Wedgwood thought he was lucky because none of the gold was wasted on plates which were subsequently rejected.

But manufacturers did have more solid reasons to increase their output than mere English recklessness exploited by effective sales techniques. England was unique in Europe in the high proportion of its people who were neither poor nor rich. As early as 1700 there were nearly a million people living in families with incomes of between £50 and £400 per annum. In other words about 12 per cent of the population was above the poverty line and had a small surplus to spend or save after paying for the basic necessities of life. Only in England was there anything like the potential purchasing power to justify mass production.[14] As the eighteenth century progressed the size of this consumer group continued to expand–perhaps to three million by 1800. Of course, some of the demand for industrial goods was caused by increasing urbanisation. Cobbett considered it no improvement for a family to move to a town, cease brewing their own beer in order to buy adulterated poison from a common brewer and stop making their own home-spun cloth in order to buy factory-made rubbish which would not last for more than a few months. Yet, there were others, like

Andrew Ure, who declared that it was not only the 'middling sort' but also the working classes themselves which were buying the products of the Industrial Revolution and improving their living standards as a result. Ure was astonished by the consumer goods to be seen in the cottages attached to Mr Ashton's works at Hyde in Cheshire. He wrote in 1835:

The rent for a good lodging, containing an improved kitchen-grate with boiler and oven is only £8 per annum, and good fuel may be had for 9s. a ton. I looked into several of the houses, and found them more richly furnished than any common work-people's dwellings which I had ever seen before. In one I saw a couple of sofas with good chairs, an eight day clock in a handsome mahogany case, several pictures in oil on the walls...In another house I observed a neat wheel barometer with its attached thermometer, suspended against the snow-white wall. In a third there was a piano with a little girl learning to play upon it.[15]

## War and Peace

Demand for goods, probably the most important cause of the economic changes of the Age of Cobbett, did not have to come from individuals. In 1790 the total expenditure of the central government amounted to about £15 million per annum; by 1810 the Chancellor of the Exchequer was asking for £52 million in taxation and expecting to spend still more. Government spending was largely concerned with the armed forces and, in wartime, the sums involved increased dramatically. As England was at war for precisely twenty-five of the fifty years between 1780 and 1830, the role of government in causing economic and social change deserves attention. The expenditure of over £20 million on the army alone in 1810 would have appalled almost everyone before 1793. Fears of despotism and arbitrary government kept military budgets low for most of the eighteenth century. In 1790 the old attitudes still flourished; Wendeborn declared: 'The English are very justly of opinion that standing armies are the grave diggers of the liberty of a nation, whenever a despotically inclined prince can make use of them to bury the rights of mankind.'[16]

Concern for freedom was combined with reluctance to pay taxes, and the main victim of this attitude was the ordinary soldier. Perhaps hardship and privation was inevitable on active service, but life in barracks was scarcely much better. Government money certainly did not 'go to waste' in providing creature comforts for the men in the ranks. Cobbett could speak with some authority in these matters. After leaving Farnham he was sent to work in a lawyer's office in London–'an understrapping quill driver perched on a high stool in a dark corner of Gray's Inn'.[17] He could not stand the life, and, in the spring of 1784, he was attracted by an advertisement, inviting all loyal young men, who wanted to achieve riches and fame, to enlist in the Royal Marines. Cobbett left his employer and sneaked off to Chatham where, instead of the Marines, he found himself in the 54th Regiment of Foot. Cobbett took the shilling to drink King George's health and 'his further bounty was ready for my reception'.

Things did not turn out to be too bountiful. Carrying heavy packs and muskets, the soldiers were drilled for six or eight hours each day. Pay was sixpence a day, before deductions for laundry, hair powder and pipe clay to meet the exacting standards of dress. Only then could the soldier think of what he could afford to eat. Cobbett was kept awake at night listening to young recruits from Norfolk crying from sheer hunger. Cobbett thought he was stronger and tougher than most of his comrades but, one miserable Friday night in 1784, discovering he had lost a halfpenny–carefully set aside to buy a herring for Saturday–he too buried his head under the tattered covers and cried like a child.[18]

In dealings with common soldiers the official attitude was one of remorseless penny pinching. The bitterness which resulted sometimes came close to mutiny. In July 1809 the local militia at Ely objected to deductions from their pay in order to purchase new knapsacks. Some of the men gathered round their officers and demanded payment of 'arrears'. That was all it amounted to and no one could claim that Ely was exactly in the front line. Yet four squadrons of German Legion Cavalry were sent from Bury St Edmunds to suppress 'this mutinous spirit'. The ringleaders were court-martialled and sentenced to *five hundred* lashes each. Even the navy could not compete with that sort of punishment. Cobbett was infuriated by the employment of German troops to discipline English soldiers: 'Five hundred lashes each! Aye that's right! Flog them; flog them! They deserve it and a great deal more. They deserve a flogging at every meal time. Lash them daily, lash them duly. What, shall these rascals dare to *mutiny* and that too when the German legion is so near at hand! Lash them; lash them; lash them! They *deserve* it. Oh yes; they merit a double-tailed cat. Base dogs! What, mutiny for the sake of the price of a knapsack and then on the appearance of the *German* soldiers, they take a flogging as so many trunks of trees.'[19]

Cobbett seemed to be implying that the Ely militia should have taken its 'mutiny' a good deal further. Of course, Wellington's view that the lower ranks of the British army consisted of 'the scum of the earth–all enlisted for drink' could provide some justification for this parsimony.

Popular opinion held the Royal Navy in much higher regard than the army, and it was felt that the 'Jolly Jack Tar' was altogether more deserving than 'Tommy Atkins'. In the past the navy had certainly been of more use, it was 'the best bulwark of the British Empire' and as such subjected to far fewer restrictions than the army. But this did not make the life of a sailor an enviable one.

The lashings, the maggot-ridden food, the disease and cramped conditions meant that, despite the bounty, there were few volunteers in the Royal Navy. Most of the sailors were literally prisoners, captured by force. Bands of armed sailors, led by an officer, roamed the streets of port towns. Any stratagem was considered fair–including the use of prostitutes–to lure the unsuspecting into their clutches. Drunks were obvious targets. The 'press gang' met with fierce resistance, particularly when they boarded merchant ships and tried to take the crew away. Violent battles and even murder were common on these occasions.

It was hard to reconcile the press gang with the much-vaunted English liberty. Wendeborn felt that some excuse could be made if only idle people and perhaps single men were impressed and exposed to injury and death for the good of the country. There could be no justification, however, when industrious fathers were torn away from their wives and families, perhaps reducing three or four children to starvation and forcing them to go begging on the streets. 'How can a nation pride itself on the rights and liberty of the meanest of its individuals, when, in times of war, such things happen so frequently? The cries of the oppressed are loud; complaints of patriots on this subject are made before the publick; friends to mankind propose plans to remedy this evil; but it continues notwithstanding.'[20]

The expenditure of public money on comforts for soldiers and sailors was not a major government outlay. What really mattered was the level of orders for ships and guns. In other words, as private demand stimulated change in industries like textiles and pottery, so government demand was of vital importance to heavy industry. The government itself was a substantial employer and the naval dockyards at Chatham and Deptford were among the largest units of industry. The war against Revolutionary France had a dramatic effect on Chatham, making it into one of the 'Wens' Cobbett so hated. Before 1793 the dockyard already covered some sixty-eight acres and employed nearly 2000 people. In the next twenty years two million pounds were spent on improvements; new machine shops and storehouses were built and, significantly, five dry docks with cast-iron water gates.

At first sight the government seems to have been in the forefront of innovation and progress. Careful regulations were laid down to ensure high standards of workmanship. The security of England could be endangered by a few defective castings. Unlike the army, where generals were rarely in danger, life at sea exposed everyone from cabinboy to admiral to an equal chance of drowning. The exacting standards imposed at Chatham and Deptford were supposed to ensure that ships built in royal dockyards lasted ten years longer than those purchased from commercial yards. Other modern features included a highly paid and somewhat truculent work force. The shipwright's skills were in great demand and the men concerned knew how to exploit the situation to their advantage. During the War of American Independence there was a concerted strike in all naval dockyards which was settled only when the Navy Board conceded most of the men's demands. In 1812 an officer at Deptford noted that the workers there were 'very boisterous and unruly in time of war'.

But the naval dockyards were not really examples of progress. The quality of management was deplorable and the many regulations largely ignored. The most important officials were often appointed through political influence rather than because they were the best men for the jobs. Despite all the controls suppliers were able to demand top prices for inferior materials, and pilferage reached fantastic proportions. Patrick Colquhoun claimed that supplies worth one million pounds per year were stolen at Portsmouth alone. In 1803 it was discovered that two men at Deptford had obtained £2413 from the pay office; they had actually completed work valued at £235. The atmosphere and problems had not changed markedly since the days of Charles II and Pepys.[21]

Yet there was one man, connected with the royal dockyards, who made a great contribution to the future. Henry Gort, an illegitimate son of a Mayor of Kendal, married Elizabeth Heysham, the niece of an official in the Portsmouth dockyard, in 1770. Gort set up in business on his own and by 1780 was supplying ironwork for the Victualling Board. In 1784 Gort bought a job lot of surplus pig-iron ballast from the Navy Board and by application of the puddling process he was able to convert it into acceptable wrought-iron bars. When rolling mills were introduced, the time taken to make wrought iron was drastically reduced.[22] Before the introduction of Gort's process it took twelve hours to make one ton of iron bars; now up to fifteen tons could be made in the same time. The output of iron in 1796 was about 125,000 tons per annum, but by 1815 production reached 340,000 tons.

It is hard to know to what extent this increase was caused by government purchases of armaments. Certainly, one of the most important firms, the Carron Company of Falkirk, concentrated on the production of cannons. In 1805–6 this one firm cast over 5000 cannons, mostly for sale to the British government. The small arms trade was centred on Birmingham and enormous quantities of muskets were produced there–some three million between 1804 and 1815. The new large iron works of South Wales and the continued expansion of Coalbrookdale produced changes in the physical environment far more dramatic than anything to be found elsewhere. Even Cobbett, who usually loathed industry, was impressed by the grandeur and 'horrible splendour' of the furnaces around Sheffield. Carlo Castrone, an Italian visitor to Coalbrookdale, declared: 'The approach to Coalbrookdale appeared to be a veritable descent to the infernal regions. A dense column of smoke arose from the earth; volumes of steam were ejected from the fire engines; a blacker cloud issued from a tower in which was a forge; and smoke arose from a mountain of burning coals which burst out into turpid flame...The scene could only be compared to the regions so powerfully described by Virgil.'[23]

Even lost wars could be beneficial. In 1786 Lord Sheffield claimed that the improvements in iron working which had appeared during the American War of Independence would ultimately prove far more beneficial to England than the possession of the Thirteen Colonies.[24] In such a world enormous fortunes could be made. The Fereday family had been in the Black Country for generations, enjoying modest prosperity as nailmakers. The tremendous expansion of the iron trade turned Samuel Fereday into one of the most important men in Staffordshire. By 1815 he was the owner of blast furnaces at Priestfield and Bradley and the employer of 1500 workmen.[25] It is curious that a trade so closely linked to war should have contained so many men dedicated to peace. The great Coalbrookdale Ironworks was owned by the Darby family who were staunch Quakers. Government orders for cannons to coerce colonists or to destroy Jacobinism were adamantly refused.

Cobbett frequently jibed at the hypocrisy and 'the chafferings and the cheapenings, the lyings and roguish cant'[26] displayed by the Quakers; it is true that the temptation to profit from war was too much for some Friends. Samuel Galton, a leading Birmingham Quaker, started to produce guns after 1793 but Galton was not allowed to get away with it; in 1795 he and his son were disowned by the Quaker community. The London Yearly Meeting still enjoined that: 'When warlike preparations are making, Friends be watchful lest any be drawn into loans, arming, or letting out their ships or vessels, or otherwise promoting the destruction of the human species.'[27]

Of course, as extensive government spending on armaments stimulated many industries, so its sudden reduction after 1815 produced grave difficulties. In 1821 Cobbett described the effects of the rundown of the dockyards and arsenals at Portsmouth:

Whole streets are deserted and the eyes of the houses knocked out by the boys that remain. The jack-daws, as much as to say 'Our turn to be inspired and to teach is come', are beginning to take possession of the Methodist chapels. A gentleman told me that he had been down to Portsea to sell half a street of houses, left him by a relation; and that no-body would give him anything for them further than as very cheap fuel and rubbish! We shall see the whole of these wens abandoned by the inhabitants and, at last, the cannons on the fortifications may be of some use in battering down the buildings.[28]

The effects of peace were almost as serious in the 'iron districts'. By the end of 1816, forge pig-iron was selling for half its wartime price and twenty-four blast furnaces were idle in Shropshire alone. In such a climate iron masters who used old-fashioned processes were particularly hard hit. Thomas Butler, who visited Coalbrookdale soon after the end of the Napoleonic wars, was far less enthusiastic than most eighteenth-century visitors had been. What had once been universally acclaimed as 'a spectacle horribly sublime' was to Butler simply an old-fashioned and inefficient iron works with ill-designed and clumsy machinery and a general air of being forty years out of date.[29] In 1817 the neighbouring Ketley iron works, complete with wagon ways, a branch canal and spacious offices, could find no purchasers when it was put up for sale. The works were closed, three hundred men were thrown out of work and spending on poor relief in the parish rose to £9600. In some places the works were never reopened and one begins to find examples of the now familiar story of industrial dereliction. A few years later John Randall described the miserable prospect at Broseley in Shropshire:

Grimy ruins, chimney stacks looking gloomily conscious of their uselessness, and disjointed masses of masonry, give a singular aspect to scenes formerly characterised by manufacturing activity. Grasslands occupy the place of forge and furnace; old pit banks have had their angles lowered and vegetation year after year has bequeathed so much of its remains, that they look like some Celtic or ancient British barrows. Cottages have been built over shafts long forgotten, and the inmates have even now been surprised to find the floor give way, as if by the effects of some engulfing earthquake.[30]

Examples of the same thing were repeated all over Britain and even the newer and more efficient iron areas like South Wales encountered

The new Poor Law of 1834–before and after. Advocates believed that in the past the authorities had been over-indulgent *Radio Times Hulton Picture Library*

The orderly docility which supporters of the 1834 law believed their measure would produce *Radio Times Hulton Picture Library*

The Stage Coach. A traditional English scene, but in town or country there were always beggars *Radio Times Hulton Picture Library*

A toll gate. To some a symbol of transport improvements, to others like the Rebecca rioters, one of tyranny and oppression *The Museum of London*

The Liverpool and Manchester railway, 1830. The line was constructed to undercut the high rates charged on the Bridgewater Canal *Photo: Science Museum, London*

Josiah Wedgwood, potter and pioneer of modern marketing *National Portrait Gallery, London*

Another attempt by Gillray to portray Cobbett as a Republican and a traitor.
There was no truth in either charge  *Radio Times Hulton Picture Library*

considerable difficulty. Although there was a brief recovery in the mid-1820s, the iron trade did not enjoy great prosperity again until the arrival of massive orders from the new railways. In their attempts to keep up prices the iron masters produced countless schemes for reducing output. Even if adopted, these self-denying ordinances usually collapsed after a few months. The smaller producers, particularly those in Staffordshire, were heavily indebted and had frequently taken mineral leases from the local landowners at very high annual rentals. They found themselves in a position where it was impossible to reduce their expenses and many of them responded to a depression by actually increasing their output in a vain attempt to keep up their earnings. This behaviour, which only made things worse, infuriated larger producers like John Guest of Dowlais; in general the South Wales masters came to the sad conclusion that Staffordshire was 'a millstone hung around the neck of the iron trade and from which it cannot extricate itself'.[31]

Although the iron trades did depend heavily on contracts from the government, it did not follow that there were no 'civilian' uses for the material. Iron probably found its salvation on a more humble scale—in the middle-class market. After 1815 many firms in Birmingham and the Black Country turned to the production of domestic hardware while the Carron Company expanded and improved its range of elegant fire grates and kitchen stoves. Quite a lot of the iron used was not visible to the casual observer. It can be argued that the numerous Improvement Acts which passed through Parliament in the 1820s had little effect on public health, but the Acts certainly helped the iron masters. As early as the 1780s John Wilkinson had decided that the best way to respond to the depression following the end of the American War of Independence was to make iron water pipes. Wilkinson was a vigorous exporter and soon gained contracts to send water pipes to both New York and Paris. The improvement of water supplies was often the main purpose of an Improvement Act; the second was to improve lighting. Better lighting meant gas and gas meant pipes. Firms like Newton Chambers & Co were able to exploit this market with great success.

But perhaps the greatest contribution made by the iron industry to the townscape of England were railings and bollards. The dramatic change from war to peace is exemplified in London's cast-iron bollards; many of them are simply cannon blanks which were surplus to requirements in 1815. Today it is difficult to appreciate just how much the squares, crescents and terraces of polite society in London, Liverpool, Edinburgh and Bath were dominated by iron railings; most of them were removed during the great 'scrap' drive of the Second World War.

Houses with basements needed to have some sort of fencing around the 'area' but, in time, very elaborate iron balconies were added to first-floor windows for essentially decorative purposes. Isaac Wave's *The Complete Body of Architecture* was published as early as 1756 but in its eulogy of cast iron it exactly catches the mood of ostentation on the cheap which Cobbett found so typical of the Regency period: 'Cast iron is very serviceable to the builder and a vast expense is saved in many cases by using it; in railings and balusters it makes a rich and massy appearance when it costs very little and when wrought iron, much less substantial, would cost a vast sum.'[32]

The heavy industries had their ups and downs; perhaps without the Napoleonic wars their expansion would have been slower but in their exploitation of the opportunities offered to them both in war and in peace it is hard not to see commercial genius which stands comparison with any Spinning Jenny Baronet.

Chapter Eight

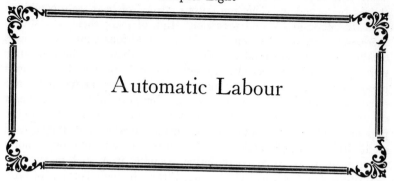

# Automatic Labour

## Establishments To Boast Of

In terms of national income and purchasing power, England was certainly in an excellent position to launch herself into a period of rapid economic expansion. But in order to understand life in the early nineteenth century we must investigate the impact of economic and technical change on people at all levels of society. Although confined to a few areas the large factory, employing hundreds, even thousands, of workers, was the most significant development for the future. There can be little doubt that people did not relish the idea of working in a factory and in some places it was difficult to fill all the vacancies. Mr John Wyllie, the proprietor of the Tan-Field Factory in Edinburgh, claimed that the average power-loom weaver employed at his mill earned about twelve shillings a week and that without unduly hard work or long hours. The wages of the hand-loom weaver were much worse than this and the hours required even to obtain the lowest subsistence considerably longer. Wyllie's firm posted up advertisements in the streets of Edinburgh asking for workers, but very few came forward. Of the eighteen workers produced by this recruitment drive, five left voluntarily in less than a month.[1]

Was it the physical conditions inside the cotton factories that caused this reluctance? Cobbett and others had plenty of evidence to support this explanation; to him the life of a factory operative was one of 'misery and slavery'. Cobbett portrayed a scene where the temperature in the cotton mill was over 80° Fahr., where factory workers had no cool room to retreat to, not a moment to wipe off the sweat and no breath of fresh air to bring relief. They were literally locked in for hours and not allowed to send for water to assuage their terrible thirst; in many establishments the masters even ordered that the rain water should be locked up! The 'murderous effects' of heat were combined with 'the abominable and pernicious stink of gas'; there was steam, there was dust and 'cotton fuz'. It was notorious that under these conditions men were rendered old and past labour by the time they were forty; children became decrepit and deformed and 'thousands upon thousands of them are slaughtered before they arrive at the age of sixteen'. Cobbett demanded: 'And are these establishments to boast of? If we were to admit the fact that they compose an addition to the population of the country; if we were further to admit that they caused an addition to the pecuniary resources of the Government, ought not a government to be ashamed to derive resources from such means?'[2]

Writers whose political views ranged from the high Toryism of Lord Shaftesbury to the revolutionary socialism of Friedrich Engels joined Cobbett in their indignation at the sufferings of the factory children. Engels believed that factory labour produced deformities in growing children; their 'unnatural' position, performing the same task thousands of times a day, led some to be knock-kneed and others to have the spinal column bent forward or sideways. Mr Edward Tuffnell, one of the Commissioners of the 1833 Factories Enquiry, conducted a survey of various streets in Macclesfield, concentrating on 'some of the cleanest and prettiest in the town'. He discovered there were ten cripples in Townley Street, five in George Street, four in Charlotte Street, four in Watercots, three in Bank Top, seven in Lord Street, twelve in Mill Lane, two in Great George Street, two in the workhouse, one in Park Green and two in Pickford Street.[3] The relations of these cripples claimed that their deformities were caused by factory work. If one is to believe Engels a factory child was extremely fortunate if he did not suffer from pains in the back, hips and legs–and probably from swollen joints, varicose veins and deep-seated abscesses in the thighs and shins as well.

More dramatically, critics of the factory system pointed to the accidents caused by a hand or arm being trapped in the fast-moving powered machinery. The loss of a finger was regarded as a fairly minor matter but even this could lead to death from blood-poisoning or lock-jaw. In Manchester it was not unusual to come across workers who had lost part or whole of an arm, leg or foot. The most dangerous part of the machinery in a cotton factory was the belt which conveyed power from the overhead shafting to the individual looms. A worker caught in this belt would be thrown up to the ceiling and then hurled down to the floor with such force that every bone in his body would be broken and he would be killed instantly.[4]

Apologists for the factory owners blamed accidents on the 'culpable temerity' of their work force and claimed that many safety precautions were ignored. The critics replied that it was unreasonable to expect children of six or seven to appreciate the dangers of fast-moving machinery; when a wheel was moving at a tremendous speed it might appear stationary and its spokes 'disappear'. How many children could be expected to resist the temptation to put out a finger to see if the spokes were still there? Even in the case of adult workers the almost universal system of payments by piece-rate was a serious disincentive to safety precautions. Above all, the practice of cleaning machinery when it was in motion–obviously lethal–was the result of the insistence of mill proprietors that the machinery should be stopped and cleaned only during official meal breaks.

Even when the factory worker returned home conditions were scarcely any better. Cobbett pointed out that the factory master was often the owner of the cottages 'or rather holes' which the work people rented. Cottages of 'exceedingly small dimensions' were let to workmen at £9 a year and the money deducted from their wages. If a workman decided not live in a cottage owned by the factory master he was still liable to find the 'rent' deducted from his meagre earnings. Effectively, therefore, he was compelled to live where his employer chose; any attempt to find work elsewhere, to escape from the factory, would result in eviction.

The coming of steam driven machinery meant that industry had to be located near to coalfields. New towns mushroomed in Lancashire and there was a dramatic shift in the economic 'centre of gravity' of the country away from the south to the north. The new towns of the north were populated by a mixture of immigrants from the surrounding agricultural areas and a substantial minority of Irish. Cobbett always did his best to be fair to the Irish but he believed that the presence of a large number of Irish workers in Lancashire was a major cause of low wages in the cotton factories. Cobbett was being uncharacteristically moderate but others were more blunt. In 1839 Thomas Carlyle wrote that in the past England had behaved abominably to Ireland and now she was reaping the full reward of fifteen generations of wrongdoing. Vengeance was coming at fourpence a time–the price of a ticket on a steam boat from Dublin to Liverpool. Already 'wild Milesian features, looking false ingenuity, restlessness, unreason, misery and mockery' could be seen on every highway. The Irish immigrant was the sorest evil this country had to bear; in his rags and laughing savagery he was prepared to take any work and be satisfied with wages that would buy him a few potatoes; for him even a pig-sty was an acceptable dwelling.

The Irish labourer in squalor and unreason, in falsity and drunken violence was a terrifying prophesy of what could happen to the working men of England.[5]

Quarrels and gang fights between English and Irish, Protestants and Catholics, were a feature of Lancashire life for generations. Engels found 'a total indifference to religion' in the vast majority of Lancashire workers, but 'No Popery' remained a powerful cry. As late as 1852 two Catholic chapels in Stockport were sacked and desecrated by a mob of working men. The hostility between English and Irish may have directed working-class energy away from the organisation of really effective means for improving their common lot–and the division was occasionally fomented by unscrupulous employers.

Whether in amity or hostility, the English and the Irish had to live together in Manchester, the greatest of the new factory towns. By the 1830s Manchester and its townships had a population of nearly 400,000, mostly working people. Yet it was possible to live in the town for years without ever seeing a factory worker. Working-class and upper-class districts were becoming clear-cut; as one moved away from the smart shops of the centre the streets became dirtier and taverns and gin palaces more and more frequent. This segregation was the real purpose behind all the humbug about 'town planning'. In the older areas, housing was on the old 'courtyard' system but further from the centre the newer system of 'back-to-back' began to appear. On the face of it this represented a substantial improvement. A closer inspection, how-ever, would reveal that walls were only half a brick thick; forty years would be a very optimistic estimate of the life span of such housing. In the last ten years the decline was likely to be particularly rapid; by then the cottage would have sunk so low that only the Irish would consider living there and their usual practice was to use the remaining woodwork for fires.

Such housing, coupled with non-existent drainage and tainted water supplies, surrounded by dung hills and stagnant ponds, was ideal for the spread of cholera. It was the terror inspired by the epidemic of this disease in 1832 that compelled the authorities in Manchester to take the first tentative steps towards improvement. Public health was not improved by the lower-class practice of buying food late on Saturday night when the shopkeeper or hawker was anxious to sell his goods at reduced prices. Obviously, if the food were kept over Sunday it might become completely unsaleable but even on the Saturday night it was likely to be long past its first freshness. Fines imposed by the courts on butchers who sold tainted meat were ridiculously low and all sorts of practices resulting in the dangerous adulteration of groceries went completely unpunished.

Pounded rice and other cheap materials are mixed in sugar and sold at full monopoly prices. A chemical substance–the refuse of the soap manufactories–is also mixed with other substances and sold as sugar… Cocoa is extensively adulterated with fine brown earth, wrought up with mutton fat, so as to amalgamate with portions of the real article. The leaves of tea are mingled with sloe leaves and other abominations, to swindle the public. Used leaves are also re-dried, and re-coloured on hot copper plates and sold as tea.[6]

## Lively Elves

But by no means all writers thought that factories and steam power had been an unmitigated disaster. The motives of critics were analysed in a most unflattering way by Andrew Ure; distaste for factories was simply another brand of the envy and obscurantist prejudice which idle aristocrats had always shown towards men of more humble origin who had 'bettered' themselves by their own efforts. The critics did not like 'progress' and its social implications of giving greater power to the middle classes; they were prepared to use any argument, however unscrupulous, to damage the reputation of the factory owners. There was something sinister about Robert Southey who dared describe the advances of recent years as 'tumours' and 'fungous excrescences'. Ure remarked sharply that Southey ought to recollect that the manu-facturers were the chief patrons of literature. The demand for books fluctuated with the prosperity of manufacturing industry; agricultural fluctuations had no noticeable effect.[7] Ure set out to stem 'this torrent of falsehood and defamation' which was being directed against the factory owners; above all he believed that the lot of the factory children was far from unpleasant:

I have visited many factories both in Manchester and in the surround-ing districts and I never saw a single instance of corporal chastisement inflicted on a child, nor indeed did I ever see children in ill-humour. They seemed to be always cheerful and alert, taking pleasure in the light play of their muscles. It was delightful to observe the nimbleness with which they pieced the broken ends, as the mule-carriage began to recede from the fixed rollerbeam, and to see them at leisure, after a few seconds' exercise of their tiny fingers to amuse themselves in any attitude they chose till the stretch and winding on were once more completed. The work of these lively elves seemed to resemble a sport in which habit gave them a pleasing dexterity.[8]

According to Ure the 'lively elves' enjoyed far healthier conditions in well-designed factories than they found at home. A twelve-hour day might sound excessive for small children, but it had to be appreciated that they had nothing to do when the loom carriage moved away from them. In cotton spinning, a child could be idle for 'three-quarters of a minute or more' before performing his task again. Thus what appeared to be a twelve-hour day was, in reality, no more than three hours of actual work. The Mr Tufnell who counted the cripples in Macclesfield certainly did not subscribe to the view that factory workers suffered from foul air and inadequate ventilation: 'It would be an outrageous falsehood to assert that any part of a cotton mill is one tenth part as crowded, or the air in it one tenth part as impure, as the House of Commons with a moderate attendance of Members.'9

Similarly there were doctors who denied that the factory children were prone to illness. A Dr Harrison from Preston said that factory children were ill for an average of four days a year, and he had met with very few children who had been injured by machinery. In his evidence to the 1833 Factory Commission, Sir David Barry described the 'fine grown girls' he had seen in the factories and Dr Hutton of Stayley Bridge asserted that fever had become less common since the erection of factories. Ure admitted that the diet of many factory workers was unsuitable; the bacon on sale in Manchester was 'much more rank' than the bacon in London. But it seemed the factory operatives actually liked 'rank' bacon because it suited 'vitiated palates accustomed to the fiery impressions of tobacco and gin'. These stimulants were used far too widely and were to blame for the prevalent disorders of the stomach and liver; compared to this, the alleged evils of factory conditions were unimportant.

Such arguments are difficult to resolve but there can be no doubt that the supporters of the factory system did have a good case as far as money wages were concerned. The gradual introduction of improved machinery produced a steady lowering of prices–which in turn meant an increased demand and more opportunities for employment. In a sense wages did not keep pace with gains in productivity but earnings per hour certainly did increase. There was no aspect of the spinning or weaving process which called for the 'same solicitude in the workman's mind and the same labour of his arms as were requisite to earn the same wages twenty years ago'. Despite occasional difficulties factory employment was more reliable than many other occupations. When Ure visited the mills owned by Messrs Strutt at Belper in Derbyshire he commented: 'The cotton factories of this eminent family have for half a century furnished steady employment and comfortable subsistence to a population of many thousand individuals. During this long period, the skill, prudence and capital of the proprietors have maintained their business in a state of progressive improvement, and nearly exempt from those fluctuations which have so often spread seasons of distress among agricultural workers.'[10]

Belper was the ideal factory town, a handsome place of hewn stone with flagged streets and operatives' houses built on 'the most commodious plans'. The mills themselves, driven by eighteen magnificent water wheels, were 'plainly elegant'. In all, the impression was of a picturesque Italian scene–a beautiful village against a background of a river, overhanging woods and distant hills. In the works a 'neat refectory' had been fitted out where work people could buy a pint of hot tea or coffee, including milk and sugar, for one halfpenny. Those who attended the refectory regularly were entitled to free medical treatment while the management had actually provided a 'dancing room' for the recreation of the young.

If Belper was anything to go by then the motives of men like Southey were highly questionable. Ure had no doubt that the attack on the factory system was simply a smoke screen to distract attention from the terrible state of affairs in the purely agricultural counties. Many factory owners believed that the evidence published by the 1833 Factory Commission was distorted; the question had been subjected to a process of 'medical mystification'. Eminent London physicians produced dogmas about the inevitable results of factory labour without ever visiting a cotton mill. Dr Carbutt of the Royal Manchester Infirmary was astounded by the widespread view of his London colleagues that factory labour produced scrofula; in Carbutt's experience the incidence of the disease was noticeably lower among factory workers than in the population as a whole. The Commissioners visited Manchester but took no evidence from any doctors, clergymen or manufacturers. One witness was a yarn dresser, later sent to London by a 'combination' to promote the Ten Hours Bill. This man was a close associate of the militant union leader Thomas Doherty who originally came to Manchester with a 'forged character and who was subsequently imprisoned for two years for a gross assault upon a woman'. A second witness kept a small public house and the third was an atheist whose evidence filled no less than nine large pages in the Commission's Report yet whose charges were shown to refer to events which occurred over twenty years earlier.

There were two main dangers arising from this irresponsible behaviour; it would 'justify' the resentment which some misguided factory workers felt against their employers and it would provide ammunition for those who demanded government action to reduce the length of the working day. The most likely outcome of increasing resentment would be strikes:

The factory operative little versant in the great operations of political economy, currency and trade and actuated too often by an invidious feeling towards the capitalist who animates his otherwise torpid talents, is easily persuaded by artful demagogues, that his sacrifice of time and skill is beyond the proportion of his recompense, or that fewer hours of industry would be an ample equivalent for his wages. Instead of repining as they have done at the prosperity of their employers and concerting odious measures to blast it, the factory operatives should, on every principle of gratitude and self interest, have rejoiced at the success resulting from their labours.[11]

Monied men would set up more factories if only they could be sure of a loyal work force. Thus, there would be more employment, higher wages and the way would be open for particularly diligent workers to become foremen, managers and even partners; without 'violent collisions and interruptions' the factory system would have brought much greater benefits to all concerned. Yet instead of seeing that the real way to higher wages was through cooperation with the mill owners, far too many factory workers spent a considerable part of their earnings on 'the fomentors of misrule, the functionaries of their Unions'. Such behaviour is scarcely comprehensible when it is realised that in the early 1830s the wages of a cotton spinner in a factory rarely dropped below thirty shillings per week at any time of the year–an income nearly three times that of the average farm labourer or hand weaver for no longer hours and much easier work.

When factory workers went on strike, they suffered 'merely' the loss of their wages whereas the manufacturer lost the interest on his capital, his rent and his taxes 'as well as injury to the delicate moving parts of metallic mechanisms by inaction in our humid climate'. Yet what most angered contemporaries was the power of intimidation used by the unions. There were men who actually boasted of their ability to bring ruin on the employer who had given them work for many years. Those who resisted their designs were liable to be attacked 'sometimes with weapons fit only for demons to wield' and there were frightful stories of oil of vitriol being thrown in the faces of blacklegs and managers– 'with the effect of disfiguring their persons and burning their eyes out of their sockets with dreadful agony'. In some factories there were serious attempts to enforce a closed shop while in Glasgow the cotton spinners carefully regulated the number of 'piecers' who were permitted to become spinners; in fact it was impossible for a piecer to obtain a better job unless he was related to a spinner.

But strikes in which the workers succeeded were probably fewer than the ones in which they failed. The spinners employed by G. R. Chappel of Manchester went on strike in October 1830; they did so on instructions from their union and not out of any specific grievances against Chappel. Pickets were posted on all roads leading to the mill and the men remaining in work 'persuaded' to join the strike. At one stage Chappel was so desperate that he tried to sell his mill at almost any price; there were no buyers. At the end of twenty-three weeks, however, the strikers gave in and asked to be taken back at their old rates of pay–£2 13s 5d per week–and explaining that the union organised by Doherty had forced them to leave their work.

Strikers were bad enough but government interference could prove even more damaging. Factory Acts containing regulations about hours of work had been passed in 1818, 1825 and 1831, but far from reducing 'turmoils and complaints' the Acts seemed to encourage them. The Acts were denounced because they discriminated against the law-abiding employer; those who were unscrupulous had little difficulty in evading the provisions. The simple fact was that factory workers wanted high wages and were quite prepared to work long hours in order to obtain them. Cotton manufacturers knew only too well that if they stopped their mills half an hour earlier than their competitors they would soon lose the best part of their work force. The children who worked in the factories often came from very poor families and their exclusion from work would result in a sharp fall in their living standards. A reduction of working hours would be a tremendous boon to Britain's foreign competitors; exports would decline and large numbers would be thrown out of work. Thus, so far from being a benefit to poor people, factory legislation was one of the greatest injuries that could be inflicted on the manufacturing population. On 5 July 1833 Lord Ashley's Bill for a ten-hour working day for adults and eight hours for children under fourteen was discussed in Parliament. The proposals for adult workers were defeated by 238 votes to ninety-three. Ure declared:

It will certainly appear surprising to every dispassionate mind, that ninety-three members of the British House of Commons should be found capable of voting that any class of grown up artisans should not be suffered to labour more than ten hours a day–an interference with the freedom of the subject which no other legislature in Christendom would have countenanced for a moment. The Gloucestershire manufacturers justly characterized the proposal as 'worthy of the darkest ages'.[12]

Although there was some support for factory legislation among the Lancashire factory workers, few were particularly concerned about the welfare of children. There was a widespread view that shorter hours would mean lower production, higher prices and higher wages; Ure believed that if the working-class advocates realised that the Ten Hours Bill would not mean higher wages then they would lose interest in the measure. As children in cotton mills were not injured by their labours nor, in general, were they overworked, it was absurd that the industry should be clogged with legislative restrictions. If factory life was intolerable, then how could 'persons of the utmost respectability in private life' send their children to work in cotton factories? Yet Mr Rowbotham, the superintendent of nearly 400 workmen in Mr Birley's mills, a man of equal respectability to any London shopkeeper, had brought up all his children in cotton factories; three of them were actually employed in the carding room which was supposed to be the most unhealthy part of the factory.

Was one to suppose that Mr Rowbotham, and hundreds like him, was such a hard-hearted parent that he was prepared to see his children become deformed and diseased? Was it likely that Rowbotham would fail to notice if his children came home completely exhausted from their day's work? There could be only two explanations; either the tales of hardship were unfounded or Lancashire people were utterly devoid of humanity and parental tenderness. If even those advocates of legislation who actually knew the factory districts did not base their arguments on pleas for humanity then the whole case against the factories collapsed:

It neutralises, nay annihilates all other evidence of any kind that sophistry can adduce. Were it contradicted by all the physicians of London the physicians must be wrong; if returns of sick societies or mortality tables say otherwise, they must be false–all the testimony that can be raked together from other sources cannot overlay this evidence, without leading to the absurd conclusion that the whole population of the said districts are void of sense and feeling.[13]

## Annulling the Institution of Domestic Life

The argument about the effects of the coming of industry on the lower classes started in the 1820s and shows little sign of abating today. As far as physical well-being is concerned the most likely conclusion is that some groups suffered while others benefited. But contemporaries were not concerned only with material questions; they wanted to know about the social, psychological and even spiritual implications of industry. The defenders of the factory system only half appreciated that for many of their critics the issues of wages, the length of the working day, illness, accidents and cruelty were of secondary importance. Many workers objected to the factories because they resembled prisons and workhouses and robbed a man of his dignity and independence. In his attack on factories, Cobbett reproduced a table of offences for which fines were deducted from a man's wages:

| | |
|---|---|
| Any Spinner found with his window open | 1s 0d |
| Any Spinner found washing himself | 1s 0d |
| Any Spinner leaving his oil-can out of its place | 0s 6d |
| Any Spinner putting his gas out too soon | 1s 0d |
| Any Spinner spinning with his gaslight too long in the morning | 2s 0d |
| Any Spinner heard whistling | 1s 0d |
| Any Spinner being five minutes after the last bell rings | 2s 0d |
| Any Spinner being sick and cannot find another spinner to give satisfaction | 0s 6d |
| Any two Spinners found together in the necessary, each man[14] | 1s 0d |

How could any worker who agreed to labour subject to such pains and penalties still regard himself as a man? Only a base and cool hypocrite could look you in the face and call England a free country when he knew that such things went on. It was this threatened loss of independence and fear of regimentation, symbolised by the factory, which caused many hand-loom weavers to cling to their old way of life–even when economic considerations suggested the need for change. The Commissioners of 1840 found that hand-loom weaving gratified the universal human love of independence and left the workman as complete master of his own time and the sole guide of his actions. He could play or idle, as feeling or inclination led him; he could rise early or late, apply himself assiduously or carelessly as he pleased and work up to any time to make good the hours previously sacrificed to indulgence or recreation.[15]

Factory labour was entirely incompatible with such attitudes. Powered machinery demanded a standard working day, regular changes of shifts and the employer knowing what every one of his workers was doing at any particular moment. In such a world there could be no place for men who delighted in 'Saint Monday' (certainly not 'Saint Tuesday') and then worked almost non-stop on Thursdays and Fridays. Every minute mattered and 'the clock' became an obsession with factory owners. The search for the perfect clock was regarded as a matter of public concern and by 1810 John Tibbot of Newtown, Monmouthshire, claimed to have perfected a clock which would not vary more than one second in two years. There could be no clearer evidence of a worker's respectability and high moral character than a clock on his mantelshelf or a watch in his pocket.[16]

Many of the penalties imposed on factory workers were obviously designed to promote regular times of coming to work. In some establishments fines were supplemented by a time-sheet, a time-keeper and the recruitment of reliable workers to inform on latecomers. A number of manufacturers saw the value of the 'carrot' approach and gave bonuses to men who always came to work on time. Some who had doubts about the value of education for the masses were converted by the arguments that schools would inculcate habits of regularity. In some places the object seems to have been to produce almost zombie-like automata. In the Methodist Sunday Schools in York there was a rule for every moment of the lesson: 'The Superintendent shall again ring,–when on a motion of his hand the whole School rise at once from their seats:–and on a second motion the Scholars turn;–on a third, slowly and silently move to the place appointed to repeat their lessons,– he then pronounces the word "Begin".'

It is hard to estimate the success of this propaganda campaign but there can be no doubt that many employers found it difficult to secure that regularity of work without which the whole idea of a factory became absurd. More than any other factor, the reluctance of employees to come to work at a specific time six days a week was the reason why so many mills had a turnover of over half of their work force every year. The attitudes of those who had grown up in a world where regularity was less important were so slow to change that employers were forced to look elsewhere for their labour. Andrew Ure declared:

To devise and administer a successful code of factory discipline, suited to the necessities of factory diligence was the Herculean enterprise, the noble achievement of Arkwright. Even at the present day when the system is perfectly organized and its labour lightened to the utmost, it is found nearly impossible to convert persons past the age of puberty, whether drawn from rural or from handicraft occupations, into useful factory hands. After struggling for a while to conquer their listless or restive habits, they either renounce the employment spontaneously, or are dismissed by the overlookers on account of inattention.[17]

As a general rule, one could say that the more skilful the workman, the more he was likely to be truculent, self-willed, unreliable and intractable in his dealings with his employer. Highly skilled craftsmen just did not fit into the factory. In fact it is probably true that the object of much technological change was not *labour saving* but *labour substitution*, the replacement of skilled by unskilled workers. Obviously such unskilled workers, probably children, were cheaper to hire than skilled craftsmen but, perhaps more important, the child workers were likely to be more docile and reliable. Andrew Ure not only believed that the physical well-being of the factory children compared favourably with children in other stations of society, but he also claimed that the same was true of their mental powers. Long apprenticeship in a particular trade only cramped the mind; abolition of the outmoded notion of 'the division of labour' enabled the worker to be moved from one machine to another: 'He varies his task and enlarges his views by thinking on those general combinations which result from his and his companions' labours. Thus that cramping of faculties, that narrowing of the mind, that stinting of the frame, which were ascribed, not unjustly, by moral writers to the division of labour, cannot, in common circumstances, occur under the equable distribution of industry.'[18]

Ure believed that the very nature of their work would convince factory children of the fundamental truths of 'the philosophy of manufacturers'. Other writers, however, thought that it was unlikely that the unthinking work of the cotton factory would give rise to 'philosophy'; some sort of erotic day dreaming seemed much more probable. A north country doctor, Philip Gaskell, was the author of *Artisans and Machinery*, published in 1836–a year after Ure's book– and Gaskell examined this question in some detail. The mind of an impressionable child or adolescent could be warped by what he saw in the factory:

The mind is but little engaged–there is no variety for it to feed upon, and it has none of the pure excitements which home affords. It becomes crowded with images of the very opposite quality and no opportunity is given for the growth of modesty. The mind does not keep equal pace with the body, though in some respects its faculties are precocious. Its better qualities are destroyed by the preponderance of animal sensations; it is a period when, even under the most favourable auspices, it is vacillating and uncertain in its determinations–now dreaming of sensual indulgence and now devoting itself to better purposes–but hurried away by external associations and forming itself in the model of whatever is near it.[19]

Philip Gaskell advanced a number of explanations for immorality and general degradation in the cotton factories. While Cobbett denounced the high temperatures of the cotton factories as damaging the physical health of the work force, Gaskell seemed convinced that the higher the temperature, the more immoral people were likely to become. Above all he argued that the excessive heat of the cotton factories produced unnaturally early puberty, particularly in girls. The *North of England Medical and Surgical Journal* quoted the example of a girl working in a cotton factory who had become pregnant at the age of ten. Such circumstances encouraged early marriages and girls became mothers when in many ways they were still children themselves. However unfortunate the consequences of early puberty, one has to admit that it was probably the result of good nourishment rather than excessive heat.[20] If Gaskell's theory had any truth in it one would imagine that people living in extremely cold climates would be paragons of morality, yet in later editions of his book Gaskell was forced to concede that 'in no country is prostitution carried to a greater extent than among the Esquimaux–no people are more libidinous and dissolute'. Gaskell was well aware of the temptations:

> Man cannot be taught to forget that he is a man, or that the breathing and blushing being before him is a woman; that she is endowed like himself with an ardent temperament–a desire for gratification; that she has within and around her a world of delights which he is framed for and destined to enjoy; and that she has passions which if roused into activity, would overwhelm all sense of shame or propriety. Neither can he forget that he has a fire within his own breast, which, if freed from the asbestos coating of moral decency, would overthrow all obstacles standing between him and the object of his desires.[21]

But why was the 'asbestos coating' so feeble in factories? Gaskell's explanation was simple–the effects of industry on the family. Whatever the economic disadvantages of cottage industry it did help to reinforce the moral obligations felt by members of a family to each other and to protect children and mothers from dangerous outside influences. Now family ties and even the domestic circle were under severe strain. When the members of a family were dispersed in different factories for twelve or fourteen hours per day, there could be no real home life. The cottage which had previously symbolised love and family affection was transformed into a mere shelter where meals were hastily swallowed and a few hours of sleep snatched. Even if the overseers and factory masters did not actually maltreat the children under their charge, they were bound to look upon them in an impersonal way–the human beings who crowded into their mills from five o'clock in the morning to seven o'clock in the evening were to them just so many accessories to the machinery. Indulgence or punishment were simply alternative policies for the achievement of the one thing that really mattered, the maximum production for the minimum cost. In such a world a concern for a child's mental, moral and spiritual health was likely to be a very low priority.

If anything, the evils of the employment of married women in factories were even greater than those of child labour. How could a wife and mother possibly carry out the duties assigned to her by Providence when she spent her working life in a factory? The general impression of factory women was that they were untidy, slovenly, dirty, ignorant of the most basic skills of needlework, neglectful of their house-work, careless of their children, incapable of managing a household budget and prone to perpetual waste and extravagance. The high wages were thus of no real advantage.[22] Women who returned to work soon after giving birth and long before their babies had been weaned suffered severely. There were women who returned to work within ten days of confinement and then complained of acute pains in their breasts caused by long absence from their babies. Thus babies were not only deprived of the food that they most needed but also left in the care of child minders. Undernourished babies are apt to cry and be generally difficult to manage: some of the child minders found an ideal answer in the form of Godfrey's cordial. Godfrey's cordial was an opium-based medicine which certainly kept the babies quiet. It was alleged that the quantity of this pernicious product sold in factory districts would 'stagger belief' and that many children became virtually opium addicts while they were still in the cradle.

If mothers neglected their children they were also liable to forget their proper obedience to their husbands. Many Evangelicals believed that the greatest evil of the factory system was that it undermined the teaching of St Paul: 'But I would have you know that the head of every man is Christ; and the head of the woman is the man. For the man is not of the woman; but the woman of the man. Neither was the man created for the woman but the woman for the man.'

The deplorable results of women receiving high wages could be easily observed in Manchester. Work was tiring and thirsty; for a woman with money in her pocket, the gin shop might seem more at-tractive than the miseries of a back-to-back workman's cottage con-taining screaming children and a husband demanding his supper. In some Manchester gin shops well over 6o per cent of the customers were women. The factory women seemed to be becoming more and more masculine; while, as adult male labour was less and less in demand, the husband wielded correspondingly less authority. Women were setting up clubs where they could drink, smoke and sing and 'use the lowest, most brutal language imaginable'. Lord Ashley gave an example of this strange perversion of roles:

A man came into one of these club rooms with a child in his arms; 'Come lass,' said he, addressing one of the women. 'Come home, for I cannot keep this bairn quiet and the other I left crying at home.' 'I won't go home, idle devil,' she replied, 'I have thee to keep and the bairns too and if I can't get a pint of ale quietly, it is tiresome. This is only the second pint that Bess and me have had between us; thou may sup if thou likes and sit thee down, but I won't go home.'[23]

In some families the disintegration had gone even further and neither parent could preserve any vestige of authority over children on whose wages they depended. Children used foul language and if corrected were liable to turn round and say '—— you, we have you to keep.' One poor woman begged her husband not to remonstrate with their daughters for going to the public house. He did so but the girls immediately replied that they would not be dictated to when they provided their parents with the only money that was coming into the family. These young women said they had been insulted; they had now no compunction about leaving their parents in absolute poverty. Everywhere the story was the same; children of thirteen could claim that their parents had no right to interfere or control them since, without their earnings, those parents would be utterly destitute.[24]

The implications for the future were hideous. The 'ferocity of character' to be observed in the 'great mass of the female population of the manufacturing towns' was demonstrated in the increasing role of women in strikes and in the general erosion of belief and authority. There were women who said plainly that churches and chapels were utterly useless and all the talk about education so much humbug. Sir Charles Shaw, Superintendent of the Manchester Police, summed up the situation: 'Women by being employed in a factory lose the station ordained them by Providence and become similar to the female followers of an Army, wearing the garb of women but actuated by the worst passions of men. While they are in themselves demoralized, they contaminate all that comes within their reach.'[25]

Philip Gaskell did not question Ure's picture of the excellent state of affairs in various 'model' factories owned by men like Henry Ashworth, but he came to the conclusion that the influence of Ure's writing was bound to be harmful. The theory that economic development must lead to the establishment of order and morality within the walls of a factory overlooked one essential point. Before the 'palladium' of British industry could be reached, the number of workers employed in the factories would have been reduced to a tiny fragment of the present labour force and this fragment would consist almost entirely of women and girls. Ure completely ignored the question of whether enforced idleness would lead to greater depravity among the 'male part of the community', which was surely the most important question of all. By his careful choice of examples, his partial presentation of statistics and his ability to side-track difficult points, Ure had presented a powerful case. Gaskell was convinced, however, that despite Ure's sophistry, 'reasoning and observation lead to an inference fatal to the opinion of those who advocate the moral and industrial advantages of the factory system'.

The arguments of most writers on the factory question have one important defect; they tend to come from middle-class commentators who had views on the 'best interests' of the lower orders. The concern for morality, perhaps even for life expectancy, is pre-eminently a middle-class preoccupation. The real question is what the factory workers thought themselves–not whether they were moral or long-lived but whether they were happy. This is the question which Cobbett had the breadth of sympathy to tackle in the case of people in the countryside but, as far as factory life is concerned, there is really no writer on whom one can rely. Of course there are volumes of evidence of what working men said to the members of the Royal Commissions but there is a strong possibility that such witnesses were likely to say different things or–equally important–couch their language in different terms when they were talking among themselves than when they were being interviewed by gentlemen from London. In many cases middle-class writers found it hard to account for the happiness of working girls who by all the 'right' standards should have been among the most miserable creatures in the world. There were the girls who shovelled coal in South Wales: 'One of these girls, in her coarse great-coat, with her hands in her side pockets, presents a picture of rude jovial independence of life...They drive coal carts, ride astride upon horses–sometimes two or three together upon a large long backed horse–drink, swear, fight, smoke, whistle and sing, and care for nobody. Being very happy, they are certainly no objects for pity, but surely their circumstances are of a kind in which girls should never be placed.'[26]

There was a strong presumption in middle-class observers that the lower orders were 'coarse' and that 'coarseness' was a major obstacle to a 'reformation of manners'. Even in industrial society there was an infinite number of subtle social distinctions which middle-class writers were unaware of. Many craftsmen and factory workers would have been extremely surprised to hear themselves described as coarse; they did not consider themselves so. Standards differed but perhaps the most puzzling and annoying thing about the lower classes was that even their 'friends' were never quite sure how they would react. There is a strong case for believing that, during the Age of Cobbett, the mind of the working man, as distinct from his physical condition, was virtually *terra incognita* for the upper classes. Those who sympathised with working people believed that factory operatives disliked machinery because it somehow deprived a man of the dignity of his labour. But the men who broke machinery were not the factory workers themselves –as one might expect–but the handicraft workers whose earnings had been reduced by competition from machine-made products. In fact there often seems to have been a strange affection and loyalty to 'their' loom among many cotton workers. The almost fanatical devotion which, from the very beginning, locomotive men felt for their engines was incomprehensible to romantics who could see in the railways only smoke, dirt, ugliness and the destruction of the relationship between the mail coach driver and his horses.

Chapter Nine

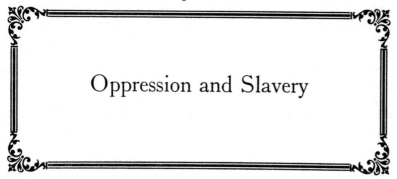

# Oppression and Slavery

## The Afflicted Poor

The condition of factory workers attracted much attention, yet there were other groups in some ways even more deserving of concern. One of William Cobbett's reasons for disapproving of the 'lords of the loom' and 'horrible establishments called manufactories' was the effect of the new technology on handicraft industries. The moral implications were obvious. Once, dutiful wives and daughters had spent their time making cloth, but the arrival of cheap factory-made cloth meant that girls had nothing to do, or at least nothing suitable to their age and sex. Country girls had once boasted that they had made their own clothes but now the poor creatures were decked out in tawdry cottons, hardly remembering that linen was made from flax or broad cloth from wool. The cheap cottons symbolised the whole spirit of the times–'a glaring show, a tawdry show; but at bottom, weakness and worthlessness'.[1]

Cobbett also deplored the effects of factory production on handicraft workers who produced goods for the market. Cobbett and Engels painted an attractive picture of the life of an average family making cloth in years before the factories came. Wives and daughters spun the yarn while the men wove under the direction of the father of the family. The weavers are presented as living in the country, marketing their cloth in a neighbouring town and earning enough to live on. Engels wrote in 1845:

In the circumstances the workers enjoyed a comfortable and peaceful existence. They were righteous, God-fearing and honest. Their standard of life was much better than that of the factory worker to-day. They were not forced to work excessive hours; they themselves fixed the length of their working day and still earned enough for their needs. Children grew up in the open air of the countryside and if they were old enough to help their parents work, this was only an occasional employment and there was no question of an eight or twelve hour day.[2]

Even at the best of times, this picture needs qualification. Many weavers lived in towns, in filthy 'courts' of the kind described by Francis Place. Few could afford to rent a small holding and the vast majority were dependent on the earnings of their loom. Houses were crowded, poorly ventilated and insanitary–and not improved by continual irritation of cotton dust and fluff in the atmosphere. Although weavers could work when they liked, there was much less freedom than Engels suggested. Work was certainly irregular but unless a man put in over sixty hours a week he could not feed his family. Engels's suggestion that children were not expected to undertake hard work will not bear serious examination. Children started work in the old-fashioned cottage industries at even earlier ages than in factories. In 1721, well before the situation was affected by technological change, Daniel Defoe praised the East Anglian textile districts where children started work at the age of three.

The change away from cottage industry was very gradual. In fact it can be argued that the golden age of the system was not in some remote past, nor even during Cobbett's childhood but during the 1790s. During this period cotton spinning jennies were spreading rapidly and increasing the production of cotton thread. The early cotton jennies were hand-operated and were cheap enough for many ordinary families to install in their cottages. Gradually the jennies grew larger and could be worked only with the assistance of water or steam power. The cotton factory was about to appear on the scene. By 1780, about twenty water-powered spinning and carding factories were in operation but the real expansion did not begin until 1785 when the restrictive patents owned by the Arkwright family were rescinded. The new factories subjected their work force to tighter control than had been possible under the domestic system but there was still considerable flexibility. A high proportion of the unskilled workers were not engaged by the owner directly but were taken on by the spinners themselves. Thus it was possible for an adult spinner to employ his own children and retain control over his family. Although groups might be under a bigger roof, the basic relationship was similar to the days of cottage industry. Above all, the increasing output of cotton thread meant that in the absence of an effective power loom, the hand-loom weaver had a strong bargaining position. There was a blockage in the process of technical change which was advantageous to the hand-loom weaver. The increased opportunities in weaving more than absorbed any labour displaced by changes in the spinning and carding process.

In 1802 James Ramsbottom was paying his women nankeen weavers as much as fifty shillings a week for five days' work, while the piece-rate payments to the weavers employed by Samuel Oldknow of Stockport rose by 25 per cent between 1790 and 1800. In 1834 a Bolton manufacturer told a Parliamentary committee that, in his youth, weaving had been the trade of a gentleman. There were weavers who wore top boots and ruffled shirts; some owned a swagger cane and reminded one of army officers when they appeared in public. In Scotland most weavers had 'enough cash by them in October to lay in all the meal, potatoes, cheese, butter, salt meat and coals they would need to last them until the Spring'.[3]

This picture of affluence was probably exaggerated but there can be no doubt that things took a turn for the worse in the early years of the new century. Weaving was a craft which could be acquired easily and the remaining apprenticeship regulations were largely ignored, so thousands of extra people decided to become hand-loom weavers. Soon there were too many and the weavers were forced to compete with each other in order to obtain work. Thus there were clear signs of difficulty even before the appearance of the power loom. Improved looms, designed by William Radcliffe, were patented in 1802 and 1803 but the steam-powered loom did not gain widespread acceptance until the 1820s. As late as 1830 it was estimated that there were still 240,000 hand looms as against 60,000 power looms. Machine-made cloth was cheaper and its advocates claimed that its quality was superior to that produced on a hand loom. It was only the readiness of the hand-loom weavers to work longer hours and accept lower rates of pay that prevented a more rapid expansion of the power loom. The hand-loom weavers did not accept their deteriorating conditions without protest while their distaste for the new machinery was shared by traditionalists of many shades of opinion. In 1790 Wendeborn thought that the old prejudices against machinery had disappeared: 'It is not many years since the English have recovered from those prejudices which could not but obstruct the progress of manufacturers. It was thought that poor people were deprived by them of employment to gain their bread and that it would be better to get numbers to work than one person, by means of a machine, should do with ease the work of many, who were to be left idle. At present, as I have been informed the people are so well convinced of the usefulness of machines, that perhaps, riots would ensue if an attempt were made to prohibit them.'[4]

In 1830, however, these 'prejudices' were still flourishing. Cobbett, although claiming to have an open mind whether machinery was good or bad, was quite sure that it could be 'carried to excess'.[5] Cobbett had a strong following among the hand-loom weavers and this group figured prominently in outbreaks of machine breaking. The same outlook was found among the stocking frame knitters of Nottinghamshire who formed the core of the Luddite movement. As in the case of the agricultural labourers in 1830, Cobbett was accused of using the *Political Register* as a means of stirring up discontent and undermining confidence in 'progress'. In fact Cobbett never encouraged machine breaking; he told the Nottinghamshire men that the true cause of their misery was the funding system rather than machinery. He believed that machine breaking–'acts which admit of no justification either in law or in equity'[6]–simply played into the hands of 'the God save the King party'. It actually enabled them to declare that a woman who stole some potatoes in Manchester was guilty of a 'treasonable design' against the government.

Cobbett was right in claiming that the threat to society from weavers and from stockingers was exaggerated. Even so, the presence of 12,000 troops in Nottinghamshire–as many as in the Peninsula–was not sufficient to prevent substantial destruction of machinery.[7] The upsurge of violence came as no surprise to the government. Men who had grown up in the eighteenth century knew what to expect when falling wages coincided with rising food prices. In February 1812, the Prime Minister declared that the decline in trade, falling wages and bitter disputes between masters and workmen were sure to result in violence. There could be no doubting the severity of the workers' distress; an address presented to Parliament in 1811 on behalf of the inhabitants of Bolton spoke of 'the frightful situation of that valuable part of the people the Cotton Weavers'.[8] The following year a Manchester businessman had to admit that honest and industrious workers could not get bread, much less clothes for themselves and their children; things were getting to 'the point which human nature cannot bear'.[9]

In February 1812 stockingers living at Arnold, near Nottingham, entered the workshops of employers making cheap and inferior hosiery and swiftly immobilised the frames by the removal of jack wires. The general population was clearly on the stockingers' side and prepared to make things difficult for the authorities. Despite the arrival of regular troops, the movement spread rapidly. The 'Luddites' were well organised; bands of fifty or sixty met nightly and set about their pre-arranged task. Once the workshop to be attacked had been agreed upon, a group went ahead armed with hammers and muskets and guards were placed to give the alarm. Every man had his appointed task—to smash the doors, or to destroy the frames or to intimidate the owner and his family. By the end of 1812 substantial funds had been collected and a sophisticated protection system established. A typical note read: 'Gentlemen all, Ned Ludd's Compliments and hopes you will give a trifle towards supporting his Army as he well understands the art of breaking obnoxious Frames. If you comply with this it will be well, if not I shall call upon you myself. Edward Ludd.'[10]

The Luddite movement did not begin to falter until 1816. By that time stocking frames and lace-making machinery worth at least £30,000 had been destroyed in the east Midlands. In Lancashire and Cheshire the equipment was more complicated and expensive and the damage amounted to over £50,000. On the face of it, the Luddites were remarkably successful and under the threat of force some employers actually agreed to increase wages and cease using labour-saving 'long' stocking frames. Many small employers gave in readily. Some felt threatened by large factories and were in no position to install expensive new machinery. They had almost as much interest in a return to the old system of domestic industry as the stockingers, lace-makers and hand-loom weavers. Although never proved, there were allegations that the smaller employers actually fomented the attack on Heathcote and Boden's modern lace-making factory at Loughborough on 28 June 1816.[11]

It was impossible to control the Luddites without an efficient police force. Such forces as did exist were not always considered reliable; the two regular constables at Oldham were both 'Methodistical' and 'Jacobinical'. There were never enough policemen to disperse a determined crowd and, in the absence of telegraphs and railways, troops took a long time to come. In most cases, Ned Ludd's men had plenty of time to do their work. The regular army went about its task of putting down the Luddites with little enthusiasm. As there was never any declaration of martial law, the army had to act under severe restraints and some magistrates were to accuse its commander, General Maitland, of being far too cautious. In 1812 there were some officers who refused to act without a magistrate's warrant, even when they could actually hear machines being smashed. But there was one aspect of army operations against the Luddites which was far from restrained: Maitland was authorised by the Home Office to hire informers and spies amongst the Luddites to reveal the whereabouts of ringleaders and the location of the next workshops to be attacked.

If one examines the conditions of the displaced handicraft workers it is not surprising that some should turn to violence. Economic conditions were so unfavourable to the stockingers and hand-loom weavers that strikes were almost certain to be defeated. It was difficult to achieve any concerted action with the weavers working in cottages spread over a very wide area. The weavers of south Lancashire did go on strike in the summer of 1818 in an attempt to increase their wages from five shillings to nine shillings per week. The strike was defeated, although there was some machine breaking again in 1826. On the whole, however, the weavers were astonishingly docile, so much so that the Vicar of Blackburn could write: 'The demeanour of the afflicted poor at this time of unparalleled distress has been such as to recommend them effectually to our respectful consideration and continued bounty. To their praise be it spoken, that there have been no symptoms of discontent, disaffection, or sedition. They have trusted in Providence; and God's servants will not desert them.'[12]

The relatively minor outbreaks of 1826 represented the last spark of the old militancy; although some hand-loom weavers played an important part in Chartism the general attitude was one of demoralised acceptance of economic doom. There was nothing romantic about the poverty of the hand-loom weavers; as their wages fell–Mary Taggart of Glasgow was earning 2s 6d per week in 1840–so did their conditions of work become more squalid. Poor conditions produced disease and conditions for cotton weaving seem to have been worse than for the other handicraft trades. Most of the hand-loom weavers worked in cellars which rarely saw the sun. The reason for this strange choice was that the ideal atmosphere for cotton weaving was cool and damp. Some of the cellars seemed to have been dug out of an undrained swamp. There was rarely any drainage in the surrounding streets and in periods of heavy rain the cellars must have resembled sewers. The Commissioners of 1840 occasionally descended a broken step-ladder into the underground gloom. They found the floor rarely boarded or paved; such a place might be suitable for storing coal but it was scarcely fit for a dog to live in and was far less suitable for use as a workshop than the worst kind of Irish hovel.

Although there was sympathy for the handicraft workers, some observers could not refrain from implying that their distress was the reward of wickedness. The sobriety of the handicraft workers varied from village to village but the state of affairs among the silk weavers at Foleshill near Coventry was particularly deplorable. 'It is not a population which has gone down into ignorance, it has never emerged from it. There is more profanity, more Sabbath-breaking and more immorality than formerly. Their language is awfully depraved. Bastardy is greater than ever and at any little holiday there, the public houses will be thronged with girls ready for the lowest excesses. Both sexes are great drinkers, chiefly of ale.[13]

It is interesting that witnesses blamed this state of affairs not on poverty but the fact that so many men from the Coventry area had joined the army during the Napoleonic wars. Young lads had gone away fools; they returned as rogues.

Hand-loom weavers, silk weavers and frame-knitters all received extensive publicity but the group of workers whose conditions were most miserable received almost no notice. The girls working in the dressmaking and millinery workshops in London had a higher death rate than coal miners! The elegant fashions of Regency England depended on a degree of exploitation unrivalled by other industries. In the 'best regulated establishments' the hours of work during the London season were 8 am to midnight but in emergencies this limit was exceeded. When orders for mourning dresses poured in after the death of William IV, one girl was forced to work without rest from four o'clock on the Thursday morning until 10.30 am on the Sunday. Food was poor, conditions were cramped and there was a heavy mortality from consumption. Without a constant accession of 'fresh hands' from the country the trade could not have functioned. At best constant application to close work produced red and swollen eyes. The conclusion was inescapable. 'There is no class of person in this country living by his labour whose happiness, health and lives are so unscrupulously sacrificed as those of the young dress makers. It unfortunately happens that they begin the business about the age of fourteen to sixteen, when the most important change in the female constitution takes place; and thus the injurious effects produced by protracted labour in an unwholesome atmosphere and want of rest often extend to their whole future existence.'[14]

## Living Like Fighting Cocks

Some workers managed to avoid a deterioration in their earnings without entering the dreaded factories. Although one cannot describe miners as handicraft workers in the strictest sense, the coal mine had more in common with the domestic system of industry than with the cotton factory. Conditions in mines varied but it is hard to prove that things got worse during the Age of Cobbett. There is no denying that conditions were most appalling in areas where mining was carried on in traditional ways. The various reports of the 1830s and 1840s leave one in no doubt that the worst coalfield in Britain was in Midlothian. Yet it was in Midlothian that the relationship between miners and masters most clearly approximated to Cobbett's idealised medieval feudalism. Long after most traces of feudalism had disappeared in England, many Scottish coal miners were literally serfs, legally bound to serve a particular master; only a few miles from the aggressively modern brilliance of Glasgow and Edinburgh there were creatures described as *adscripti gleboe*. Cobbett had good reason for thinking that it was presumptuous of 'Scotch Feelosophers' to tell England what to do when living standards were so appalling north of the Border. His description of a miner's cottage in Scotland was not far wrong: 'A cabin built of mud and thatch, having no floor but the earth, having no window of glass, but a hole to let in light, stopped occasionally with a board; a hole through one end of the roof to let out the smoke, and a division by a hurdle, to separate the family from the cow, or pig, where either happens to be kept. The bed is made of heath, placed the stems downwards and cut off smooth at the top, the elasticity of which renders it less galling to the body.'[15]

Throughout northern England there were colliers known as 'bondsmen' who contracted with the colliery owners to receive a sum of money and then work until the debt was repaid. The 'bondage' system was becoming increasingly unpopular in the 1820s and several areas went on strike in an unsuccessful attempt to change 'bondage' into more conventional wages. But the feature of coal mining which enlightened opinion found most distasteful was the employment of women and children in arduous and dangerous work below ground. In this respect, the Midland coalfields emerged as islands of civilisation and humanity but east Scotland was disgraceful–even by the standards of colliery owners elsewhere. In most other coalfields at least some attempt was made to minimise labour by the installation of tramways and winches; in Scotland coal was moved from one part of the mine to another on the backs of women and girls.

A little girl in East Lothian was called Ellison Jack. In 1842 she was eleven years old and had worked in the mine since she was six. She had to carry coals in a creel, a type of basket shaped to fit her back, rather resembling a cockleshell flattened towards the neck so as to allow lumps of coal to rest on the back of the neck and shoulders. The creel was secured by straps passing over Ellison's forehead. When carrying coal children were bent almost double; not infrequently the tags securing the creel would break and the coals would fall on to the girl who was following. Coals were brought to the surface by a complex of ladders and it was calculated that each journey to the surface involved an ascent equal to the height of St Paul's Cathedral.[16] The weights of coal varied but there were plenty of adult colliers who had ruptured themselves from straining to lift a laden creel on to a child's back. Well might a woman in the Fife collieries declare: 'Oh Sir, this is sore, sore, sore work. I wish to God that the first woman who tried to bear coals had broke her neck and none would have tried again.'[17]

It was not always easy to estimate the number of accidents which had occurred in coal mines. Many miners were reckless and regarded the use of the safety lamp to indicate the presence of coal damp as a decidedly 'cissy' practice. Only the best organised pits in the Midlands kept an accurate record of serious accidents and in Scotland there was no one to correspond to the English coroner to enquire into fatalities. One girl declared: 'My two sisters were sair horrible crushed by stones falling from the roof; their bowels were forced out and their legs broken.'[18]

Apparently no enquiry was made. The plight of women, utterly exhausted, drenched in sweat and doing work which should have been done by horses was terrible enough, but perhaps the most appalling life was that of the little children, scarcely able to walk, who were employed to open and shut the ventilation doors. The 'trappers' sat in a little hole scooped out for them by the side of the trap door; all the time they held a string attached to the door and opened it when they heard a rattle of wagons. Immediately the wagons had passed the door had to be shut again, otherwise there could be an explosion. The trappers had nothing else to do but they were also the first to arrive at the pit and the last to leave–well over twelve hours a day for children of five. Many of the trappers were terrified of the dark yet in the dark they had to stay, squatting on a damp floor and exposed to cold rushes of ventilation draught. Most colliery owners refused to allow the trappers to have light; once in a while a good-natured collier would bestow a little bit of candle on them as a treat.[19]

Under the circumstances it is astonishing that the coal mining communities enjoyed relatively good health. Colliers earned very much higher wages than hand-loom weavers; an able-bodied young man would receive about twenty-five shillings a week. To some extent the value of this money was eroded by the widespread use of the truck system whereby the men were payed in tokens only accepted in a particular shop controlled by the owners. Parliament tried to insist that all workmen should be paid regularly in coin-of-the-realm; but such measures seem to have had little effect until the 1840s. Before then the truck system enabled prices at the colliery stores to be at least one-quarter higher than those obtainable on the open market.[20]

But the degree of exploitation could not be taken too far. Coal mining required physical strength and, in order to do their work effectively, it was essential for the colliers to have plenty of nourishing food. The Leicestershire miners enjoyed better health than the agricultural workers, despite the obvious disadvantages of their working conditions. The Warwickshire colliers were described as a tall, athletic and powerful race of men who lived all their lives 'like fighting cocks'. In the Midlands it was possible to find colliers who reached a good old age and there were men in their early sixties who were doing the same work as miners forty years their junior. The prosperity of some coal miners drew sour comments from upper-class observers; there were some who actually blamed the collier's typical ailments on 'ridiculous and excessive living'.[21]

In general, however, the picture was less attractive. It was true that young miners were healthy and strong but most of them were showing signs of declining strength by the time they were thirty. Difficulty in breathing began to trouble them and many succumbed to fever and inflammation of the lungs, probably caused by over-exertion, exposure to cold and wet, insufficient clothing and foul air. Before he reached middle age the average miner found himself coughing frequently with a great deal of expectoration of frothy yellowish mucous fluid containing blackish particles. He would still be capable of work for a few more years–but not for long: 'This difficulty of breathing increases and expectoration becomes very abundant, effusion of water takes place in the chest, the feet swell and the urine is secreted in small quantity, the general health breaks up and the patient after premature old age, slips into the grave at a comparatively early period.'[22]

Middle-class observers were concerned about the working conditions in coal mines but, as so often, their first priority was the religious and moral condition of the mining community. There was good reason to believe that the miners and their families had been less influenced by the general 'reformation of manners' than any section of society. The presence of women and children in dark recesses of coal mines was bad enough but in many mines ventilation was so inadequate and the heat so intolerable that male and female workers were almost naked. To make matters worse, the colliery owners often had no control over what went on below ground. In most areas the women and children were hired by the individual collier. There was a terrible danger that colliers would use their power over the young children in order to gratify their sexual desires. There were horrifying estimates of the number of bastards conceived in the darkness but it is hard to avoid the impression that some respectable commentators liked to dwell on the salacious aspects of the situation which would have been regarded as perfectly natural by the ordinary miners. The Children's Employment Commissioners found a gem in Ebeneezer Healey, aged thirteen, who worked in a colliery near Huddersfield. Ebeneezer told the gentlemen about the interesting effects of pulling coal tubs by means of a leather belt and chains passing between the legs. 'I hurry (pull coal tubs) now with a belt and chain in the broad gates. There are girls that hurry in the same way with belt and chain. Our breeches are often torn between the legs with the chain. The girl's breeches are torn as often as ours; they are torn many a time and when they are going along we can see them all between the legs naked. I have often and that girl Mary Holmes, was to-day; she denies it but it is true for all that.'[23]

The Commissioners dutifully recorded that they could not imagine a sight more disgusting, indecent or revolting. They were of the opinion that 'no brothel can beat it'; although they did not reveal from what sources they derived their knowledge of brothels. The colliers seemed no more influenced by moral improvements when they came above ground. They were particularly prone to heavy drinking and cruel sports. The general 'viciousness' of the mining population was attributed to ignorance and irreligion. The provision of schooling was poor in every mining area in Britain and at least in east Scotland some observers believed that ignorance was actually increasing; they were convinced that educational and religious facilities had not kept pace with either 'the advancing population or the growing degeneracy'.

The trouble was that children were sent down the pit before they had acquired even the rudiments of learning. It is true that there were Night Schools and Sunday Schools but the quality of teaching in these institutions was often very low. In the 1820s some Ministers believed that there was a danger of Sabbath-breaking if reading and writing were taught on Sundays; they therefore insisted that their Sunday Schools should confine themselves to providing religious instruction. In any case many teachers were well aware of the problems of getting the colliery children into the classroom at all. Attendance was irregular and when they did come after working for ten or twelve hours in the mines, the children were too tired to pay attention. Appeals to parents to send their children to Chapel Sunday Schools were not well received. In winter mothers replied that when the boys had been beaten, knocked about and covered with sludge all week, they deserved to be able to rest all day in bed on Sunday. In summer, parents said that the fresh air of the moors would do their children more good than reading in stuffy classrooms.

Thus many colliery children were able to 'lake' about on Sunday, and middle-class observers were able to find examples of horrifying ignorance. There was a little boy in Derbyshire who had attended a Baptist

Sunday School for five years yet could not spell 'horse' or 'cow', while the Children's Employment Commission was convinced that the youthful population of the Yorkshire coalfield was in a state of 'mental imbecility'. Illiteracy was bad enough but the Commissioners were even more scandalised by the children's ignorance of the basic truths of the Christian faith. Some children claimed that they had never heard of Jesus Christ, but there is a possibility that they were trying to make fun of the Commissioners and seeing what paroxysms of moral indignation their ignorance would produce. The Commissioners reported that they had been told that 'The Lord sent Adam and Eve on earth to save sinners' and that 'Jesus Christ came to earth to commit sin'. One of the Commissioners went into a Sunday School class near Sheffield and asked what sort of people the Apostles were. He was met with complete silence and apparent incomprehension until a sharp-looking little boy put up his hand and cried with great glee, 'Please, Sir, they were the lepers.'[24] Some of the replies were so shocking that it was impossible to print them, but it was widely rumoured that a Commissioner had asked a little boy where he would go when he died. The child had thought for a while and then replied 'buggery'. He had heard his father say that some miners killed in an underground explosion had been 'blown to buggery'.

Yet even in this nightmare there were faint glimmerings of hope. The general consensus of opinion was that colliery children were less ill-used than in the past and some owners were beginning to enquire more closely into what went on underground. Coal mines which did not admit women or young children seemed to be altogether more respectable and even more efficient. There were some signs of 'moral improvement'. The colliers of south Gloucestershire had once been 'the terror of the surrounding neighbourhoods and for gross ignorance, rudeness and irreligion were almost without parallels in any Christian community'. In the Forest of Dean 'concubinage' had been a prevalent substitute for marriage and illegitimate births so common as to attract no notice. On the 'Sacred Day' no one thought of going to church, but rather of rural games and 'vicious revelry'.

The Forest was 'extra-parochial' and there had been virtually no churches. Yet in a few years the miners of the Forest of Dean had become as remarkable for their attendance on religious worship as they were for their 'former desecration of the Sabbath by trespasses, outrages and savage amusements and revels'. There was no denying that the Dissenters deserved the main credit for this remarkable transformation. For thirty years they had worked almost as missionaries in a heathen land. An enormous number of chapels had been built and the miners themselves were giving handsome contributions to put up more

Zions and Bathsedas. The Anglican Church was falling far behind but there were some signs of revival. In the Forest of Dean, the Wesleyans and Baptists were the strongest denominations; the Baptists were particularly strong at Coleford–'several of the most opulent coal-owners being of that persuasion'. A Mr Waring gave a graphic description of the differences between south Gloucestershire in 1800 and the same area in 1840: 'You could not ride through some of the villages and hamlets without being insulted by the boys, who would throw stones at both the horse and rider without provocation. "The Kingswood colliers" was then a phrase that conveyed every idea offensive to civilization, order and religion. At the present period there is, perhaps, as much decorum in the manners of the population as is witnessed in the generality of rural districts.'[25]

Religion probably did fill a genuine need. Despite his brutal exterior, no miner could ignore the fact that his job was dangerous and he could be blown to pieces at any moment. The miner was a strange mixture of cynicism, superstition and the capacity for moods of religious enthusiasm. This was particularly true of the miners of Cornwall and South Wales who were liable to indulge in 'paroxysms' of enthusiasm. It was hoped that this would be a temporary phase; a degree of religious hysteria was probably natural during the period between the first communication of religious truth and the prevalence, among the body of the people, of a sober and settled faith. On the other hand the enthusiasm of the miners in Cornwall and Wales might be more permanent; in that case 'their Celtic origin may in part account for this disposition'.

Perhaps the miner's life was more tolerable than that of the hand-loom weaver. There might be years of depression but the fundamental fact of the Industrial Revolution was that more coal would be required. It was a tough life and a brutal one but it retained a vigour, even glamour, that other trades completely lacked.

## Honest, Industrious and Sober

One of the most mystifying features of the lower classes was their reluctance to take to the occupation which their sympathisers regarded as most appropriate for them. The Commissions which examined the moral conditions of the factory workers were concerned at the ignorance of the basic skills of house management among 'female factory operatives'. Mr Joseph Corbett told the 1843 Commissioners that on the basis of his own experience he had concluded that if women could be given instruction in the work of a house and taught to produce 'cheerfulness and comfort at the fireside' much misery and crime could be prevented. There would be fewer drunken husbands and fewer disobedient children. Although there were a few enlightened employers who tried to instruct their women workers in sewing and cookery, it was generally believed that these skills were best acquired through employment in domestic service.

There was more to it than that; traditionalists like Ashley believed in the moral virtues of domestic service. Servants fitted into a hierarchical pattern of society and were more likely to 'know their place' than factory workers. Under the constant supervision of their social superiors, they were unlikely to stray from deference and morality, or become contaminated with notions of Radicalism and Equality. Women in domestic service would have the opportunity of observing the respect for decency and sobriety which now characterised the behaviour of polite society. After marriage they could perform the valuable service of introducing these ideas to their husbands and families. In other words, it was hoped that working-class wives would be a powerful force for respectability and the adoption of middle-class values by the labouring poor.

One of the main motives of the factory reformers was to get women and children out of the factory and into domestic service. There was certainly a need for such servants; as the middle classes grew in numbers and opulence so their demand for servants increased proportionately. Domestic service was every bit as much of a growth industry as the manufacture of cotton cloth; in fact, in 1835, the year of Cobbett's death, there were far more people employed in 'service' than in factories. The Commissioners of 1843 gave a number of hopeful examples of women who gave up their employment in mines or factories in order to enter gentlemen's service. But these cases were exceptional and the woman who preferred the gentility of service to the coarseness of factory life was rare. In fact, despite all the talk of 'surplus population' and its resultant unemployment there was always a shortage of good indoor servants.

Why were 'oppressed' and degraded factory workers so reluctant to become servants? We shall never know the whole story; as Sir John Clapham observed, governments were ready enough to set up enquiries into the conditions of hand-loom weavers, nailers, frame-knitters, canal navvies and a host of other occupations, but never once was there a commission on domestic service. It might be in the public interest to send Members of Parliament into cotton factories and down coal mines but no one dared to suggest that they should intrude into that bastion of freedom, the matrimonial home of the upper-class Englishman.

Such evidence as is available gives some explanation of the general distaste for domestic service. In a large country house the number of servants required was enormous; at Stowe, the house of the understandably impecunious Dukes of Buckingham, the 'below stairs' section included the steward's room, the housekeeper's room, the tenants' hall, the 'evidence room', the servants' hall, the pantry and strong room, the still room, the kitchen, the great kitchen, the confectionery, sculleries, larders, the cold room and general storerooms, six beer and wine cellars, the coal bunker, the brushing room, two sitting rooms for housemaids, the butler's room and bedroom adjoining, six footmen's rooms, pages' rooms, the housekeeper's bedroom, the cook's room, the laundrymaids' room, the ladies' maids' room, the housemaids' dormitories and accommodation for the servants of visitors–quite apart from the servants attached to the dairy and the gardens who had separate living quarters. Awe-inspiring figures like the butler and the housekeeper at Stowe, waited upon by their 'own' servants, enjoyed a life style which has its attractions even today, but the same can hardly be said for the 'lower servants' who formed the great majority. In London houses, in particular, the servants' accommodation was extremely cramped. Footmen lived in dark and ill-ventilated basements and, even in royal palaces, were expected to share a narrow and uncomfortable truckle bed.

Work was hard, frequently unpleasant and the hours long. For servants, the absence of central heating and electric light meant attending to vast numbers of candles and lamps and carrying heavy coal scuttles up long flights of stairs. Even in the best of houses sanitation was primitive and as late as 1844 no less than fifty-three overflowing cesspits were discovered at Windsor Castle. In such a situation it is not surprising that the occupation of many servants was simply to empty the chamber-pots used by their betters. In many eighteenth-century houses, cupboards were installed behind the shutter recesses of the dining-room windows to contain chamber-pots for the convenience of gentlemen who drank long and deep. Even the cult of greater cleanliness among the upper classes meant extra work for the servants. The Duke of Wellington for the Tories and Lord John Russell for the Whigs set the fashion of the daily bath. It is true that this development was admirable and also that the bath water was expected to be cold–hot baths were considered effeminate and immoral at least until the 1860s–but, in a world where the only water tap was likely to be in the basement, the amount of fetching and carrying must have been prodigious.

It is hard to present an attractive picture of the life of the average servant. It is true that there were always servants who could intimidate and cheat their employers. Cockney servants were notorious for their impertinence, and the works of Charles Dickens, taken from the author's observations in the 1820s, tend to confirm this view. When Susan Nipper, a servant in *Sketches by Boz*, heard her mistress complain that she had seen better days, Susan replied tartly that she 'pitied the better days which had seen Mrs Pipchin'. But such flashes of revolt must have been rare. The fundamental fact about girls in service was that a 'slavey' would be lucky to receive £10 per year. A woman working in a factory, for all its physical and moral evils, would earn more than twice as much. Picturesque as the custom may seem to later generations, the annual hiring fair must have been a rather humiliating experience for many young people. Servants of the 'lesser order' were hired for a year at a time; if an employer had no longer any need for the services of his cook, housemaid or milkmaid the girl concerned would go to the hiring fair in search of a new master. Different types of servants were clearly distinguishable by their appearance—cooks usually wore a red ribbon and carried a basting ladle, housemaids wore a blue ribbon and carried a broom while milkmaids carried a pail.

Despite such humiliations, there was no guarantee that domestic service would provide a suitable training in the domestic skills required by a working-class housewife. The waste in large kitchens was enormous and the methods of cooking utterly inappropriate to the needs of those who lived on small incomes. Even when attempts were made to teach cookery, the results were not much better; girls were brought into classrooms and made to learn about 'carbonaceous and nitrogenous' foods yet they were utterly ignorant of how to boil a potato. Recipe books were produced in the hope of overcoming working-class resistance to 'nourishing soups', but a wife who presented her husband with such food would be lucky to escape a beating.

Under the circumstances it is not surprising that there were always 'places' vacant and that some servants should prove most unsatisfactory. Particularly in middle-class houses servants and employers were in close physical proximity; the urban villa was designed vertically rather than horizontally with accommodation for the servants in the basements and the attics and the family living in between. In such a situation the foibles of servants could scarcely escape notice—the designs of a pert maid on the son of the house, the drinking of one servant, the dishonesty of another or the slovenliness of another. Of course such people could be dismissed but it was often a problem to find someone better. The only solution was yet another 'reformation of manners' with various societies founded to improve religion and morality among the servant classes. The ideal servant was already being described as a 'treasure' to whom a certain amount of consideration had to be afforded. Henry Mayhew described the ideal–a respectable middle-aged woman who would work for £10 a year and find her own tea and sugar. The woman concerned would have 'A ten years excellent character from her last situation which had been with a clergyman in the country. She was cleanly, even tempered, an early riser, a good plain cook, and a decent Christian; she was honest, industrious and sober; in fact she had just taken the pledge.'[26]

Although these words were written in 1847 they accord very well with the picture of what the lower orders ought to be like held by the politer sections of society in the 1830s. With servants, as with factory workers, there could be no escaping from Andrew Ure's conclusion; godliness was, indeed, a great gain.

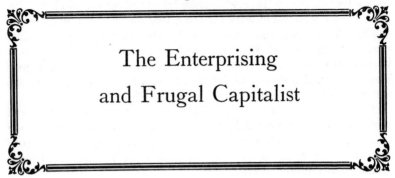

# Chapter Ten

# The Enterprising
# and Frugal Capitalist

## A Man Made Out of Coarse Material

The work force of Cobbett's England whether in farm, workshop, mine or factory were certainly undergoing enormous changes. Yet the same is true of the men who employed them. The social structure of England was changing in the middle and upper levels as well as in the lower. It is easy to portray 'the capitalists' as cruel and brutal. Many of them were, but it is also essential to explore the forces working upon them, their hopes and fears, in order to understand why they behaved in the ways they did and why so many of them opposed factory reform, the case for which seems so irrefutable to modern observers.

Out of sheer humanity Cobbett supported the demand that the hours of labour in the cotton factories should be reduced; it was a case of 'mammon against mercy'. On 19 July 1833 a Mr Bolling told Parliament that a reduction in the hours of children's labour would be a 'suicide act' which would inflict a blow to the prosperity of Britain from which the country might never recover. Cobbett's irony was superb:

*Mr Cobbett* said a new discovery had been made in the House that night, which would, doubtless, excite great astonishment in many parts. It had formerly been said that the Navy was the great support of England; at another time that our maritime commerce was the great bulwark of the country...but now it was admitted, that our great stay and bulwark was to be found in three hundred thousand little girls, or rather in one-eighth of that number. Yes; for it was asserted, that if these little girls worked two hours less per day our manufacturing superiority would depart from us.[1]

One of the main problems of the factory system was ignorance–the vice from which all other evils flowed. In 1833 Ashley's Factories Regulation Bill included a clause designed to ensure that children under the age of twelve received two hours of teaching every day. This clause was an act of despotism towards trade; unless there was a school close to the factory it required owners to go to the expense of setting up classrooms within the mill. Rather than comply with this absurd Act many proprietors were forced to dismiss their child workers. These poor children were thus deprived of their light and profitable labour and, instead of receiving the sort of education promised by the Act, they got none at all. They were thrown out of their warm spinning-rooms upon the cold world to exist by beggary or plunder, in idleness and vice. Andrew Ure recognised that it was in the owners' interests to have an educated workforce: 'Persons not trained up in moral and religious nurture necessarily become from the evil bent of human nature the slaves of prejudice and vice. They are readily moved to outrage by crafty demagogues, and they are apt to regard their best benefactor, the enterprising and frugal capitalist who employs them, with jealous and hostile eye.'[2]

A great convulsion and uprising of the factory workers would indeed produce national bankruptcy and beggary, but Ure had no fears of such an outcome. He was convinced that the Sunday Schools and evening classes which were springing up on the work people's own initiative all over the factory districts were more than adequate to deal with the problem. Ure exhorted all friends of humanity not to miss the chance of visiting the town of Stockport on a Sunday when they would witness the 'sublime spectacle' of crowds of factory children drawn up in their classes.

Stockport Sunday School was built in 1805. It was a large, plain and lofty building which had a magnificent hall for examinations and public worship. This hall could hold 3000 people and there were no less than forty other apartments–classrooms, committee rooms and library rooms. By 1833 the school could boast that 40,850 children had received instruction there; it was no coincidence that Stockport was known for 'the general decorum that pervades the town' and the regard for the liberties, lives and property of others which was in such sharp contrast with conditions in other towns. 'I witnessed the very gratifying sight of about 1500 boys and as many girls, regularly seated upon separate benches, the one set on the right side and the other on the left. They were becomingly attired, decorous in deportment, and of healthy, even blooming complexions. Their hymn singing thrilled through the hall like the festival chorus of Westminster.'[3]

But the best way to ensure a respect for morality and religion was through the example of the owners and managers themselves. Ure believed that in every instance of a factory being notorious for dissolute manners the owner or manager would be found to be licentious and immoral himself. Ure's slogan was 'godliness is the great gain' and he constantly asserted that this 'gospel truth' was particularly applicable to large factories. A mill owner who combined genuine concern for the physical and moral welfare of his work force, together with a proper understanding of his own long-term interests, would do everything in his power to improve the moral standards of his employees. An employer who was lax in his own principles would never enjoy the genuine respect of the men who worked for him:

Let us figure to ourselves a proprietor of extensive factories, a man of old experience, an unwearied worshipper of Mammon, and, of course, a stranger to the self-denying graces of the gospel. Such a man knows himself to be entitled to nothing but eye-service and will therefore exercise the most irksome vigilance, but in vain, to prevent his being overreached by his operatives–the whole of whom, by natural instincts as it were, conspire against such a master. Whatever pains he may take, he can never command superior workmanship, he will find the character of his goods to be second rate in the market.[4]

In fact it was in the factory owner's interest to 'organise his moral machinery on equally sound principles with his mechanical'. The work of the factory needed steady hands and clear eyes whereas improvident work people were apt to be reckless and the dissolute workers likely to be unhealthy and diseased. A factory with low standards of moral discipline was obvious at a glance. There was no sense of order, machinery was in poor repair, and time and raw material grossly squandered. In the factories of New England, proprietors paid the salary of the local preacher and officiated themselves at an evening service. Many were strict teetotallers and would not employ workers who drank spirits. The moral structure of the Lancashire cotton workers certainly fell short of these exacting standards but Ure hinted that an improvement was vital if Lancashire was going to meet the challenge of American competition.

Philip Gaskell took a less sanguine view of the incentives for factory owners to set a good example and he produced an impressive list of reasons to explain their depravity. The successful mill owner was liable to be ignorant and his earlier life best described as 'animal'; the sudden acquisition of wealth was unlikely to produce a corresponding improvement in his moral and social character. He was probably a vain man who attributed his wealth entirely to his own superior merits and was thus unrepentant in his vulgarity. Gaskell believed that most of the early factory owners were 'of coarse habits, sensual in their enjoyments and partaking in the revelry of their dependants'. Everything about the factory encouraged the owner to gratify his appetites. 'The facilities for lascivious indulgence afforded them by the number of females brought under their immediate control–the herding together of work-men, more especially multitudes of boys and girls from ten to sixteen years of age–the separation of man and wife during the hours of labour– the dependence which naturally grew up on the part of the labourers.'[5]

Certainly the successful manufacturer was likely to encounter criticism, and Cobbett, Gaskell and Engels regarded the type with extreme distaste. Dickens's Mr Bounderby is a caricature but the essential features are there. Bounderby talked endlessly of his terrible childhood–without shoes or stockings, passing days in a ditch and nights in a pig-sty, abandoned by his mother and beaten by his grand-mother, who drank fourteen glasses of spirits before breakfast. But Bounderby had pulled through, though no one had ever given him a helping hand. His career had been one of steady improvement– vaga-bond, errand boy, labourer, porter, clerk, chief manager, small partner and finally Josiah Bounderby of Coketown:

He was a rich man: banker, manufacturer, and what not. A big, loud man with a stare, and a metallic laugh. A man made out of coarse material, which seemed to have been stretched to make so much of him. A man with a great puffed head and forehead, swelled veins in his temples, and such a strained skin to his face that it seemed to hold his eyes open and lift his eyebrows up...A man who could never sufficiently vaunt himself as a self-made man. A man who was always proclaiming, through that brassy speaking trumpet of a voice of his, his old ignorance and his old poverty.

In a more attractive and sympathetic guise the rags to riches story can be traced in the pages of Samuel Smiles and Andrew Ure. Bounderby's toadies might make him out to be the Royal Arms, the Union Jack, Magna Carta, John Bull, the Bill of Rights, an English-man's home is his castle, Church and State and God Save the Queen, all put together–but essentially the man was a fraud and his stories of a deprived childhood a tissue of ungrateful lies. In fact Bounderby's mother had doted on him and done her best to give him a good start in life while his later career had been greatly helped by a kind employer.

Bounderby's story illustrates an important point–the difference between myth and actuality in the social origins of the early factory masters. There were, indeed, many humble men among them but there were virtually none from the very bottom; most received vital financial assistance from friends and relations when they were setting out in the world. Similarly, although there were aristocrats and rich merchants who became factory owners, the notion that the mainspring of the Industrial Revolution was the reinvestment of profits from overseas trading and Enclosure is misleading. Until recently it was believed that the most important cause of the rapid development of the Clyde valley after 1780 was that Glasgow merchants, faced with the uncertainties of the American Revolution, decided to pour their money into the building of textile factories. In fact it was far more usual for the merchants to become bankers or landowners or to switch their trading interests to the West Indies.

## Religion Must Produce Industry

It is hard to generalise about the social origins of the new manufacturers and it is probably more sensible to think of the inventors, manufacturers and traders more as representatives of a distinctive personality type–which might be found at all levels of society–rather than as members of a social class. If manufacturers became 'middle class' as a result of their occupation it is by no means true that they were all middle class in origin. The origins of the most notable entrepreneurs were diverse. The Bridgewater Canal was, of course, financed by a duke; the great cotton magnate, Richard Arkwright, started life as a barber; while the iron master, Samuel Walker of Rotherham, began as a schoolmaster. There was change in all directions; some merchants (but not many) came to make the things they had previously only sold, scientists turned into industrialists, parsons into inventors, weavers and farmers into captains of industry.

The religious affiliations of the new entrepreneurial class has received a good deal of attention, both from contemporaries and from modern writers. There was a clear tendency for merchants–whose ancestors may have been advanced Dissenters in the seventeenth century–to drift from Chapel to Church. Although the complex of legislation which made up 'Dissenters' Disabilities' was often ignored, there remained a theoretical Anglican monopoly on town councils until 1828 and these bodies were essentially self-perpetuating oligarchies until 1835. The political influence of an alderman–even in towns which did not have a Member of Parliament–was considerable and it was possible to gain substantial economic advantage from the collection and assessment of local taxes. The merchant-dominated 'closed corporations' contained more diehard traditionalists than any other body, certainly more than among the aristocracy. No section of society could outdo them in their terror of Revolution, their contempt for 'Disaffected Ragamuffins', their horror of Catholic Emancipation or their hysterical veneration of the less worthy members of the royal family. Men bent on marrying their children into 'county' society had to reckon that landed gentlemen would prefer to marry a steady income rather than a larger but unstable fortune; a reliable income from the funds, requiring no attention, was more attractive than the risks and time-consuming demands of a manufacturing fortune. Above all, there was the over-riding social consideration; the English social code decreed that the nearer a man was to the actual process of production the less his claim to be a gentleman. It is not surprising that the average merchant, who probably used his profits to buy pictures, fine silver, wines, Consols, land, expensive clothes and prestigious education for his children–anything but reinvestment in his business–should have been reluctant to incur the expense of building factories and installing machinery. If anything, he wished to get further away from, not closer to, the loom and the workshop.

If there were occasional merchants who became manufacturers there was a strong possibility that such men would be nonconformists, men who had resisted the attractions of 'the National Whore'. Cobbett's antipathy to minority religious movements is well known. He refused to believe that the ranting, raving and howling that could be heard in Methodistical meeting houses could ever improve the morals of the people or make them more honest, industrious and public-spirited. The Methodists had never done anything which showed concern for public liberty and, by their constant emphasis on the Hereafter, detracted attention from glaring examples of exploitation and greed in this world. Similarly Cobbett was infuriated by attempts to abolish restrictions to prevent Jews from holding public office. If the proposals were carried England would cease to be a Christian country:

God knows, the Jews make free enough already, and certainly get more money together than any set of Christians. As if this were not enough, a clause was slipped into an Act of Parliament a few years back to enable them to possess a freehold property in England. It would not have passed so quietly I promise you, if I had been in Parliament... but what will the hon. and learned Gentlemen say if a Jew Judge is stuck up to try Carlisle or any other blasphemer? He is himself a blasphemer, and regularly, once a week blasphemes Jesus Christ in the Synagogue, and once a year crucifies him in effigy.[6]

Cobbett said much the same about Quakers and Unitarians. Accusations of blasphemy are an obvious cover for resentment at economic success and it is interesting that Cobbett was more sympathetic to the Roman Catholics, also a minority group, but not notable for their success in commerce or industry. But why should men who held un-orthodox religious opinions seem to do so well? Attempts have been made to find a connection between the theological content of a par-ticular religion and success in business; despite the ingenious theories, it seems unlikely that a man's opinions on the nature of the eucharist, on predestination and free will or on the relationship between the members of the Trinity, were really vital to making a fortune.

It is important to examine the nonconformist manufacturer in his social context. A man who remained loyal to the chapel would find it hard to gain acceptance in county society and a fairly limited political role would be open to him; thus the only avenue to an enhanced social importance was by amassing greater wealth. Similarly the prevalence of 'puritan' attitudes towards luxury and gracious living, at least among the founders of industrial dynasties, contributed greatly to rapid expansion. Wesley himself had seen the connection and was alarmed by it: 'Religion must necessarily produce both industry and frugality, and these cannot but produce riches. But as riches increase, so will pride and anger and love of the world. The Methodists in every place grow diligent and frugal; consequently they increase in goods, so, although the form of religion remains, the spirit is swiftly vanishing away.'

Men who held worldly vanities in contempt and who actually pre-ferred a simple way of life would have large sums of money available to invest in the further expansion of their business. Ploughed-back profits were the most important factor in the financing of economic growth during the Age of Cobbett. For many years Samuel and Aaron Walker, founders of a very profitable firm–valued at £122,000 in 1781–paid themselves a mere £105 per annum to cover living expenses. But perhaps the closest connection between plain living and commercial success was to be found in the Quaker community, a group described by Cobbett as 'the pestiferous sect of non-labouring, sleek and fat hypocrites'. The rules of Quaker living were set out in *The Book of Discipline;* pictures and looking glasses were expressly forbidden and there were bans on gambling, 'vain sports', visits to the theatre and 'books of an immoral tendency'. In the event of a death in the family no special mourning clothes were to be purchased and no memorial erected to the deceased. All clothes were to be plain and dark coloured and coats had to avoid vanities such as collars and lapels. Such a code avoided expenditure which less puritanically minded folk would take for granted. As Quakers grew richer some began to throw aside the old prohibitions; John Barclay wrote in 1817: 'I have been almost ready to blush for some, at whose houses I have been where pier glasses with a profusion of gilt carving and ornament about them, delicately papered rooms with rich borders, damask table cloths curiously worked and figures extremely fine, expensive cut glass, and gay carpets of many colours are neither spared nor scrupled at.'[7]

Many years were to pass before such backsliding would not provoke forthright criticism and even risk of expulsion. Those who conformed to the ways of the world were often stricken with conscience–in 1844 the immensely rich Quaker banker, Joseph John Gurney, accepted the admonitions of his co-religionists and ordered that all looking glasses should be removed from his mansion.

The Quaker movement was always a minority cult–about 20,000 in 1800–but Quakers were very prominent in business and industrial circles. There were the Peases who virtually controlled the economy of the north-east, Gurneys, Lloyds and Barclays in banking, Allen and Hanbury in pharmacy, Hornimans in tea, Reckitts in starch, Clarks in shoes, Crossfields in soap, Bryant and May in matches, Rowntrees, Cadburys and Frys in chocolate, and Whitbreads, Trumans and Hanburys in brewing. Such a galaxy of wealth and success cannot be completely explained by reference to *The Book of Discipline*. Despite critics like Cobbett, Quakers were generally esteemed by the rest of the population, at least by the end of the eighteenth century. Their reputation for honesty and probity in financial matters inclined others to do business with them and contributed to their success. Frederick Wendeborn, who did not approve of Dissenters on principle, could not deny their excellent qualities. Very few sects could be found which approached the Quakers in purity of morals, rectitude and virtue. During Wendeborn's stay in London he heard of no instance where a Quaker had been accused of a serious crime; there had been no Quakers in the dock at the Old Bailey for twenty years. Quarrels and disputes were infrequent and, if an outsider entered into an acrimonious dispute with a Quaker, he was likely to get the worst of the argument. The Quaker had the enormous advantage of being trained from early years to combat and subdue his passions and to maintain a cool temper whatever provocation he encountered.

In a more general way, the economic success of minority religions was caused by the fact that discrimination and a sense of being 'different' created a cohesiveness and cooperation. Quakers placed particular emphasis on mutual assistance based on trust and confidence; some were reluctant to buy government funds which might be used for warlike purposes and preferred to lend any surplus cash to members of their own faith. Such assistance enabled Quaker businessmen to raise sums far larger than their rivals could collect at short notice. In 1781 Thrales' Brewery in London was put up for sale at the enormous figure of £135,000; the brewery was bought by three Quakers, Robert Barclay, Sylvanus Bevan and John Perkins, who managed to borrow £70,000 from Quakers and £40,000 from other friends and connections. The readiness to lend money was reinforced by a trend to find marriage partners within the same social and religious group. The leading Quaker families developed into cousinhood which rivalled that of the old aristocracy in its complexity. In the Quaker community there was a ruling that any member who married a non-Quaker should be expelled; the dangers of too much interbreeding were recognised and there was a similar punishment for marriage between first cousins. Of course there were Quakers who broke these rules but to do so guaranteed a serious family crisis. Joseph John Gurney's son was expelled for 'marrying out'; the bewildered father wrote 'my heavens as well as earth have been strangely shaken'.

In view of the restrictions on marriage, it is possible that rich Quakers were forced to look for partners of lower social standing but who were members of their Society. In other words, religious exclusiveness may have been a mechanism for social mobility; the fact remains that during the Age of Cobbett the easiest way for a man to rise in the world was by marrying a woman who was his social superior. There were examples of industrious clerks who married the master's widow or daughter; in the absence of male heirs, such marriages were the best way of keeping a business going. Yet it would be wrong to exaggerate the degree of mobility involved. The clerks who married into the owner's family were not exactly Bob Cratchit types. Several of the clerks in Whitbreads brewery invested substantial sums in the business and had their portraits painted by Gainsborough and Romney. Although marriage restrictions may have produced a slightly greater degree of social mobility, it should be remembered that most minority groups did not cover a wide span of society. By the beginning of the nineteenth century, the Unitarians and Quakers were predominantly middle-class bodies, while the Methodists and Baptists had a strong 'labour aristocracy' basis. During the Age of Cobbett, when the labouring classes made up three-quarters of the total population, the same group made up only one-fifth of Quaker membership.

As the greatest advantage to a family fortune was marriage to an heiress, so the greatest disaster was a 'bad' marriage which brought no money and a decline in social status. The social institutions of the

The Enterprising and Frugal Capitalist

upper middle classes often seemed designed to reduce the chances of improvident marriage; the chapels were a way of protecting young members from dangerous contact with the population at large. Yet social exclusiveness was put before doctrinal soundness. In Oldham, Cobbett's constituency, the Methodist Riley family were happy to marry their children to Congregationalist Suthers and Anglican Fittons; all were wealthy. The ultimate was achieved when in some chapels iron railings were put up to divide the private pews from the ordinary seats– the honest rags of poverty from the rich attire of roguery. Religion may have helped a little, but the greatest advantage a man setting out in business could possess was to have friends and relations who were prepared–for whatever reason–to give him a helping hand.

## The Uneasy Class

Much of Cobbett's invective was directed against people who would now be described as 'middle class'; bankers, industrialists, civil servants, army officers, intellectuals, the lower clergy, lawyers, managers and even some clerical workers could be considered as members of this section of society. There has been much debate about when the middle classes 'rose'; Cobbett believed that the most decisive change came during the Napoleonic wars. The influence of the banker David Ricardo, a converted Jew, filled Cobbett with fury, but the gravest charge against Ricardo was not his race but the fact that he made a living in Change Alley. In the good old days, Lord Chatham had described such people as 'muckworms'. By 1819 the muckworm was no longer a creeping thing but with head raised aloft it struck terror into aristocrats of ancient lineage.[8] In general the middle classes were lashed by Cobbett; lawyers were 'toad eaters', civil servants 'tax eaters', country clergymen became 'magpies' and 'greedy, chattering, lying, backbiting, mischief-making and everlasting plagues'.

Cobbett had some pity for the lower middle classes because manual labour was more rewarding than a routine clerical job. Cobbett had experienced many hardships and vicissitudes, yet there was no part of his life which he looked upon with pain except the time he had spent as an attorney's clerk. In his colourful way he implored Fate to dispose of him rather by stretching him across the burning line or burying him beneath the snows of Zembe–to doom him to the wilds of Africa or the woods of America–to cast him, in short, wherever she might please between the poles; but 'Save,' he cried, 'Oh save me from the Attornies Office.'[9]

Of course there was a world of difference between an attorney's clerk and a rich industrialist; as there were divisions within the working classes, so the middle classes were an ill-defined group. The very word 'middle class' was not used before 1812 and only slowly replaced the older conceptions of 'ranks', 'orders' and 'interests'. Life was far from pleasant for a large number of people who today would be regarded as undoubted members of the middle classes. According to Edward Gibbon Wakefield there were three classes in England–the 'wealthy class', the 'uneasy class' and the 'miserable class'. Wakefield said of the middle, or uneasy class: 'Their existence is a continued struggle with difficulties. How to make the two ends meet, which way to turn, how to provide for one claim without neglecting another, how to escape ruin or at least what they consider degradation, how on earth to manage for their children; these are the thoughts which trouble and perplex them. The anxious, vexed or harassed class would be a better name for them.'[10]

Wakefield claimed that three-quarters, or rather nine-tenths of those engaged in trades and professions were decidedly 'uneasy'. Part of the trouble was due to over-population. There was a lot of talk about the 'superabundance of labourers', meaning ordinary workmen, but there was a much larger abundance of governesses, school teachers and clerks of every description. Despite all the unpleasant features of the job there were more girls from middle-class homes who wanted to be governesses than there were people who wished to employ them. The world seemed full of briefless barristers, qualified doctors who could not find patients, curates who could not find livings and ageing junior officers who would never be promoted. The prospects for such men were particularly daunting if they had a large family to provide for. The social values subscribed to by most of the middle classes demanded the trimmings of gentility. The pride and satisfaction with which a father might regard his first, and as yet only son, in the days of white frocks and curls, were changed into anxiety when some years later he found himself surrounded by half a dozen full-grown and fast-growing candidates for frock coats, polished top boots, walking canes, watches and cigars. But the prospects for the daughters were even more dismal.

Who will take her as wife that she will take for a husband? The general rule with daughters of men of small income whether fixed or not, is a choice of celibacy and marriage with one of the uneasy class. Now a great proportion of young men in the uneasy class dread marriage, unless there be a fortune in the case, as the surest means of increasing their embarrassment...There is not in the world a more deplorable sight than a fine brood of English girls turning into old maids one after another, first reaching the bloom of beauty, full of health, spirit and tenderness; next striving anxiously, aided by their mother to become honoured and happy wives, then fretting, growing thin, pale, listless and cross and at last–if they do not go mad or die of consumption–seeking consolation in the belief of an approaching millenium.[11]

The story might have been very different if something had turned up for papa at the right moment. Papa was probably as brave and resourceful an officer as men who became admirals or generals; he might be as learned as men who became judges or as eloquent and pious as men who became bishops–yet still promotion and success passed him by. The sad fact was that a good deal of professional advancement depended on the ability to buy one's way up and above all on having influential friends. A man with neither wealth nor friends was in a hopeless position.

The prospects of officers in the army and navy after the end of the war were particularly gloomy. War at least gave opportunities for men to distinguish themselves and there were a few instances of staff officers who had risen from humble beginnings. In peace time, the only criteria were seniority and the money to purchase a higher rank. Large sums were involved. In the Life Guards, a man had to spend a minimum of £7250 to become a Lieutenant-Colonel while in ordinary Regiments of the Line the sum was about £4500. But even when a post became vacant, there were so many applicants, all ready and eager to pay, that many would be disappointed. In theory, things were better in the navy where there was no purchase system, but critics claimed that this resulted in political calculations dominating the issue of whether to promote a man or not. It was not even just a question of promotion; in the 1820s reductions in the navy meant that many officers were 'stood down' and expected to live on half pay. It actually needed political influence to be seconded to a ship and thus return to full pay.

Yet there were sailors whose rise was positively meteoric; they tended to have famous names and be related to the political élite. In the Court Calendar of 1829 it appeared that Lord Edward Russell–son of the Duke of Bedford and brother of Lord John–had been made a Commander in 1828. At that time there were over seven hundred Commanders who were Russell's seniors; some had not been promoted since 1787.[12] If the Tories had remained in power Lord Edward's rise might have been less dramatic but the Whigs came into office in November 1830 and the Russells' influence was greatly increased. The Court Calendar of 1834 shows that Lord Edward Russell had been made a Post Captain in 1833–over the head of at least five hundred more senior Commanders who had remained in the service. It is not surprising that there were many officers in both army and navy who were embittered men; some were to take a prominent part in the Radical movements of the 1830s and a few actually threw in their lot with the Chartists.

The middle classes without wealth or influence were given a great deal of advice on how to ensure successful careers for their sons. J. C. Hudson's *The Parent's Handbook* makes depressing reading and must have provoked anguish in many middle-class households. Hudson pointed out that in many professions the expenses of training were considerable yet prospects of lucrative employment in the future was poor. Hudson calculated that the cost of keeping a boy at Sandhurst was £125 per annum. Even when the examinations had been passed and the commission purchased the rates of pay were abysmal. A Captain in a foot regiment received £3 a week and a Commander in the navy about £6. Pay was quarterly and in arrears. Some officers could indulge in profitable peculation at the tax-payers' expense but, against that, there were substantial mess bills which no one could avoid unless he was prepared to become the object of contempt and derision. Junior officers in 'smart' regiments needed substantial private incomes if they were to live in the style expected of them and yet remain out of the moneylenders' clutches. *Fraser's Magazine* declared:

You will see a languid boy, who a year ago was flogged at school, ring the bell for mess waiter and tell him 'For God's sake to bring something with plenty of cayenne in it.' The same evening, perhaps at mess, as the side dishes are one by one uncovered, he lifts his eyebrows, pulls down the corners of his mouth, and cries, 'Oh My God!' and this although he may have lived, up to the previous month, on plain joints and suet puddings. Perhaps he leans forward, with his elbows on the table, and with exquisite resignation, begs the president to 'show up the bill of fare'. It is astonishing how soon a mere child falls into these habits.[13]

The British army and the Royal Navy might be unequalled in discipline and in valour, but neither was suitable for the son of a poor man to enter as an officer. If a boy wanted to go to sea the merchant service offered better prospects than the navy. There were West India houses in Liverpool who would take on promising lads without a premium. The boy's outfit might cost about £30 but he would learn the skills of seamanship in the school of practical experience. It was necessary to dispel romantic visions before consigning one's son to such a career. There were boys whose passion for the sea was associated with the image of a clean and handsome young gentleman in a cap bounded with gold lace and a superfine blue cloth jacket, crowded with rows of gilt buttons, laid open to expose a white Kerseymere waistcoat and still whiter linen shirt collar, lightly held by the silken folds of a black neckerchief. Such a boy had to be told that if he wished to go to sea to learn his profession properly it would be better to imagine himself in a blue woollen shirt and a pair of canvas trousers, without shoes or stockings, his hands for ever at the tar bucket and his head covered, if at all, by a worsted nightcap in dry weather and by a thing called a 'sou-wester' painted white and resembling a coal heaver's hat during that part of the year when tropical rain poured down in pailfuls. His career might result in brilliant success or in disaster. 'Their subsequent career depends, as in all other stations in life, upon industry, prudence, intelligence and good fortune. They may sink into common sailors and by contracting evil habits, degenerate into vagabonds and paupers, or get pressed into the public service, and lose every chance of independence; on the other hand, they may become captains, shipowners, merchants, aldermen and lord mayors.'[14]

For those who preferred the arts of healing to the dangers of war and foreign trading the situation was not encouraging. At a conservative estimate it cost £500 to train to be a doctor and before that the medical student could not earn a single shilling. There were problems of buying a share of a practice and establishing a reputation; parents who thought of medicine as a career for their sons would do well to remember the old saying; 'By the time a physician earns his own bread and cheese he no longer has any teeth to eat them with.' The man who launched out on his own at an early stage of his career was as mad as the most unbalanced of his patients (not that he was likely to have any): 'Let him take a private house in any situation, however public, fix a lamp of red and green glass over the door, make known to the world by means of a brass plate that his name is Mr So and So and that he is a surgeon, accoucheur, &c. and fix up a bell handle on each side writing "Surgery Bell" under one and "Night Bell" under the other, and the probability is that twelve months will elapse before anybody will put his services in requisition.'[15]

Hudson could not find much to say for a career in the Civil Service. The vast majority of these appointments were controlled by the Secretary to the Treasury, the man who usually acted as Chief Whip of the government party in the House of Commons. The best way of establishing some claim to appointment was to have voted for a particular Member of Parliament through thick and thin; but it was also essential that the MP concerned should be a staunch supporter of the government and that he should be prepared to stir himself on behalf of the constituent concerned. If any of these vital requirements were not met, prospects of appointment were slender.

Even if a father was able to obtain a post for his son as a clerk in a government department the job was poorly paid. In most departments the salary was £100 per annum and rose painfully slowly. It was true that there were five chief clerks at the Treasury who received a handsome £1000 a year, but it was far more common to find men with thirty years' service behind them earning less than £300. Pay scales for clerks in the employ of the East India Company, the Bank of England, the private banks and insurance companies were similar and the chances of promotion scarcely better. It was possible for a young man to be articled to an architect or a prominent Civil Engineer but very heavy premiums of over 500 guineas were required.

There remained schoolmastering, the law and the church. The status of schoolmastering was so low that few middle-class parents desired their sons to enter such a despised occupation. It cost about £500 in fees and maintenance for a solicitor to become qualified and probably an additional £3000 to buy a partnership–thereafter, although much of the work was likely to be mundane, the rewards were substantial. The social prestige of a barrister was greater, and great advocates made fortunes which enabled them to buy country estates and rival the manufacturers and merchant princes. The expense of training for the bar was not excessive but the income was uncertain; the qualitied demanded by Hudson in order to bring success to a young barrister seem exacting. The young man would have to study diligently and have a natural capacity for digesting what he read. It was essential for him to be punctual and regular at his chambers, in court and on circuit. It would be wise to cultivate the most pleasing and popular manners and combine them with elegant taste, pure style and fluent delivery. He would have to avoid seeming aloof in his dealings with attorneys and solicitors yet at the same time it would never do for him to be suspected of deliberately setting out to catch their patronage. Yet with all these qualities a barrister would find himself with an income of only £500 a year, ten years after he had been called to the bar.

In many ways it is hard to escape the conclusion that for a middle-class youth without outstanding abilities the most sensible course was to enter the Church of England. The great thing about the church was that all the other occupations examined demanded a lot of hard work in order to make a success of the job. Once a clergyman had been duly inducted into a living by his bishop, he would have to behave really disgracefully before he was in any danger of being deprived of his position. Unless the incumbent was moved by missionary zeal, the work of a country parish was not unduly exacting, and at the same time the clergy were more acceptable in polite society than local doctors and solicitors. For a man in straitened circumstances, a son destined for the church had the great advantage of being cheap. The ancient universities were geared to the production of clergymen and, unlike the other professions, there were scholarships and exhibitions for those who intended to take holy orders.

It is true that there was a problem of obtaining a parish–the life of a mere curate was no better than that of a school teacher. It did not matter, however, if the family did not actually own a living themselves. It was possible to purchase the right of making the next presentation from the patrons through the intermediary of a firm of clerical agents. The right of presentation to a living yielding £300 a year could be purchased for under £1000. The living had to be chosen with care; the general advice was to act when the boy was about twelve and to select a parish whose present incumbent was in his early sixties. It was reasonable to suppose that the current rector would die about the time that the young man would be taking orders. Of course, there were elderly clergymen who died at inconsiderate times–either while the intended successor was too young, or, more likely in the case of Anglican clerics, living on into his eighties. The prudent parent took out an insurance policy to guard against this outcome. All in all, the church and the law stand out as the most promising careers for middle-class youths and if the young man concerned was neither intelligent nor hard-working, the church certainly offered the best return on investment. In general the outlook was gloomy, but the professional man did have one enormous advantage over the manual worker: 'Machinery cannot altogether supersede the function of hands; no machinery can unravel the intricacy of a law suit, or watch the variations of disease and suggest and apportion the appropriate remedy or scan the faculties of an individual man and place the truths of religion in the exact point of view in which they become visible and appreciable.'[16]

Despite this crumb of comfort, the general tone of Hudson's work is very depressing. It is certainly remarkable that he should have said so little about manufacturing and trading. It was only after discussing the generally dismal prospects for shorthand writers, newspaper reporters, musicians, painters and auctioneers, that Hudson turned his attention to this vital sphere. He was at pains to stress that nothing particularly heroic was required; the essential thing was to see the potential of mass demand for a new product, however humble, and then to have the courage of one's hunch to set up in business. In the London of the 1830s there were men who, much to Cobbett's disgust, were received into genteel society yet who had made their money from the manufacture of soda water, ginger beer or boot blacking.

Middle-class youths would be well advised not to be too 'delicate' in their choice of occupation. In the past, a man's social standing had depended on the public esteem (or otherwise) in which his profession was held. In future, it seemed, everything would depend on the size of his income, however acquired. Without money, there could be nothing. The clerk in a lawyer's office, harassed and overworked, had to know his place and keep his opinions to himself, just as much as the factory worker, perhaps more so. The clerk thought himself a gentleman; there could be no strikes or unions for him. He was on his own and would be a fool if he did not heed the words of Sydney Smith: 'It is always considered a piece of impertinence in England if a man of less than two or three thousand a year has any opinions at all on important subjects.'

Chapter Eleven

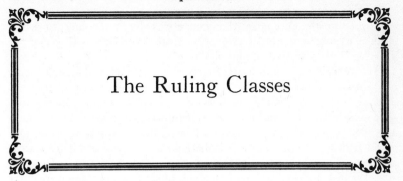

# The Ruling Classes

## Aristocratic Outrages

An examination of the economic and social conditions of the middle
and lower classes during the Age of Cobbett leads one to two main
conclusions. The total wealth of the nation was certainly increasing
and this enabled significant sections of both groups to enjoy a higher
standard of living–although there were groups of handicraft workers
as well as some professional people who suffered as a result of the
various changes which made up the Industrial Revolution. The debate
on living standards can never be finally resolved but those who argue
for an improvement probably have a slight edge over the 'pessimist
school'. If this is so, Cobbett was wrong to believe that the material
condition of most people had deteriorated during his lifetime.

Cobbett was right, however, in another equally important matter.
Both workers and many of their masters were losing a good deal of
their former freedom–they were compelled to do more monotonous
jobs, more regular hours, subscribe to a more rigid code of morality,
pay more deference to their social superiors and lead generally more
mechanical lives. As we have seen, some resisted these changes, while
others welcomed them, but there can be no doubt that economic and
social developments were taking much of the fun out of life. There was
a great deal of cruelty and brutality about the eighteenth century but
it had a rumbustious quality which it is hard not to find attractive.
More than any other writer, Cobbett appreciated the price that was
being paid for economic progress.

The interesting thing is that the same tendency towards respectability can be observed in groups which were not subject to the economic
stresses which have been examined in earlier chapters. Ladies and

The Price of Progress

gentlemen who received substantial incomes without working or even supervising the work of others also began to exhibit a more disciplined approach to life. Of course, the change was slow in coming; both the Prince Regent and Lord Byron seem to belong more to the Court of Charles II than to that of Queen Victoria.

Aristocratic marriages were often a matter of parental arrangement and, in such cases, tolerance of a partner's vagaries was probably the best recipe for success. Harmonious *ménages à trois* were not uncommon. The 5th Duke of Devonshire, his beautiful wife, Georgiana, and his blue-stocking mistress, Lady Elizabeth Foster, lived happily together and the Duchess included Lady Elizabeth in a family portrait by Gains-borough. The whole range of human vices was to be found in Regency society. Incest was common at all levels of society and there were cases both of male and female homosexuality. The Regent's brother, the Duke of Cumberland, was widely believed to have murdered his valet, Selis, after the man had discovered about Cumberland's unnatural tastes.

In some ways the moral climate was healthy; the excessive prudery of the mid-Victorian period was simply not possible in a world where there was not a single public lavatory in London. In case of necessity even rather grand ladies felt no particular embarrassment about using a deserted back street for this purpose. Masculine commentators frequently ascribed the degeneracy of their age to the freedom given to women and argued that adultery was encouraged by the easy-going laws on legitimacy. A child born to a married woman was assumed to be her husband's even if he repudiated it, and children were legitimate if born up to a year after the couple had ceased living together. Female vanity and extravagance in dress were believed to lead to misconduct– yet the law made a husband responsible for his wife's debts, even if contracted without his knowledge. But the advantage was not entirely with women; a man could commit adultery with relative impunity because his wife could not obtain a divorce on grounds of her husband's infidelity. A man who murdered his wife could be hanged whereas a woman who murdered her husband could still, in theory, be burned alive. In practice, however, this blatant piece of discrimination had long ceased to operate.

Another cause of trouble was the behaviour of young people, and Wendeborn thought that parental weakness was responsible for a great deal of evil: 'Fathers and mothers seem to be governed by their child-ren as they grow up, who laugh at the old ones along with the servants. It has even the appearance with some parents, as if they really believed that they must give way and not contradict the young ones who, indeed, are generally ready enough, not only to give hints to those who

A collier hewing coal. To the horror of reformers many miners worked naked. The presence of an unguarded candle flame increased the risk of explosion *Photo: Science Museum, London*

A cartoon against the suggestion for transporting destitute children. The cartoon highlights contemporary opinion that drinking among the lower classes was destroying family life *Radio Times Hulton Picture Library*

A cotton factory in the 1830s. The women are poorly clothed and a child crawling under moving machinery suggests a dangerous and poorly managed establishment *The Mansell Collection*

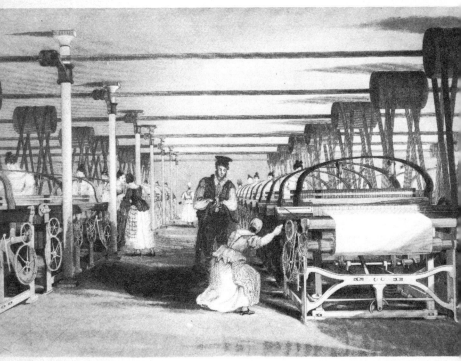

Power-loom weaving. The workers are better dressed and general conditions better than in the previous plate *Photo: Science Museum, London*

A bank clerk and customer in the 1780s. The lower middle classes were expected to be extremely deferential to their 'betters'  *Radio Times Hulton Picture Library*

Clerks in the General Post Office, 1809. This picture suggests an existence as boring and monotonous as that of any factory worker  *Radio Times Hulton Picture Library*

The Westminster Election, 1796. With open ballots, bribery and intimidation were common and would not disappear until the introduction of the Secret Ballot in 1872   *The Museum of London*

A pictorial representation of Cobbett's view of the unreformed political system. Taxes paid by poor people supported the indulgences of government pensioners whose services to the state were frequently of a dubious nature *Radio Times Hulton Picture Library*

are older, but even tell them to their faces, that times since their young days have greatly altered'.[1]

One of the most striking Regency vices was vanity, a trait which the Regent himself did much to foster. There were significant changes in men's fashions, most of them for the better. Wigs or natural hair heavily powdered had provided ideal homes for countless generations of lice. In 1795 the government introduced a tax on hair powder; men of fashion gave up using powder in protest and discovered that they were more comfortable than in the past. But the expense of a complete wardrobe was still prodigious; George Elers joined the 12th Regiment of Foot as a mere Lieutenant in 1796 but his wardrobe was expected to include at least six regimental jackets and a gross of shirts. His colonel had one hundred pairs of boots and two hundred jackets.[2]

Exquisite youths and dashing young men added interest and amusement to society but there was something repellent in older men who adopted the most extreme fashions to prove they were still young. The Regent himself had ruined his constitution by overdrinking, overeating and taking large doses of laudanum. His admirers might call him 'an Adonis of Loveliness'[3] but the effect was the result of tight corsets, face powder, rouge, false whiskers and hair dye. Upper-class Englishmen and women seemed to fear age more than death. The prospect of colds, rheumatism and gout seemed to offer no deterrent to the folly of wearing summer coats in winter.[4] One important merchant in poor health was forced to go to St Petersburg on business; when he returned he was much better and told Wendeborn: 'In Russia we guard ourselves against the raw season, but here they laugh at me, even when I put on a thin great coat, and I cannot help smiling at them when I am upon the Exchange and see how many of them are shivering with cold, because they fear that appearing in a warmer dress, they should look old, or impress the women with the notion as if they are not of a strong constitution.'[5]

Fear of old age was thought to be one of the reasons for the notorious propensity for suicide among the upper classes. A French guidebook to London claimed that the balustrades on bridges crossing the Thames were higher than on bridges in France, because the authorities were trying to reduce the enormous numbers who drowned themselves.[6] Among other causes the incidence of suicide was blamed on the damp climate, too much meat eating, too little control of the passions, excessive taxation or even a perverse desire for notoriety and a paragraph in the newspaper. Some critics made a significant point that Roman Catholicism was better suited to psychological needs than a cold and formal Protestantism. Societies which placed great emphasis on the confession and absolution seemed to be far less troubled by the problem of suicide.[7]

If a coroner's jury brought in a verdict of *Felo de se*, the property of the dead person was subject to confiscation and the body was buried at a crossroads with a stake driven through the heart. Enlightened opinion had long considered it absurd to try to punish a corpse and juries usually decided that a man who had taken his own life had been deranged. The dead man was thus eligible for Christian burial and his goods passed to his heirs in the usual way. There were a number of prominent suicides in the years after 1815 including the wealthy London brewer, Samuel Whitbread, the lawyer Romilly and–most sensational of them all–the Foreign Secretary, Viscount Castlereagh. Cobbett commented sourly on the contribution of aristocratic suicide to the cause of legal reform: 'We may thank God for disposing the hearts of our law-makers to be guilty of the same sins and foibles as ourselves...When a lord [Castlereagh], who was also a Minister of State, had cut his own throat, the degrading punishment of burial at cross-roads was abolished.'[8]

If wealthy people felt their lives were empty, it is not surprising that they should look for excitement to fill the void. In the war against France, when there should have been new opportunities, there seemed to be a distressing emphasis on ability as a prerequisite for promotion. To make matters worse, aristocratic parents were living longer than in earlier generations and an eldest son would be lucky to come into his estate by the time he was forty. Somehow the years of waiting had to be endured.

The need for excitement gave rise to the great English obsession with gambling; the preoccupation with 'chance' affected the rich and the poor alike. Wendeborn claimed that if two gentlemen found maggots in their walnuts after dinner, they could be relied upon to start betting on which maggot would crawl over the table quicker. The other diners would join in and soon hundreds if not thousands of pounds would be at stake on the speed of a maggot![9] Bets were often rather callous; wagers were taken more than once on whether a man who had fallen into the Thames would be drowned. Those who thought the man would drown protested strongly if a boat was sent to the rescue; they regarded this development as a monstrous interference with the fairness of the bet.

Of course, there were more conventional ways of betting. The world of horse racing was centred on Newmarket and had a feeling all its own, with a peculiar degree of social equality. There the difference was not between the gentlemen and the rest, but between those who knew about horses and those who did not. The boast of racing men was 'All men are equal on the turf and under it.' There was a sort of equality too in prizefighting where 'The Fancy' liked to match their skill and strength against a professional. Fighting was with bare fists and went on until one of the contestants could fight no more. It was a dangerous life but there were compensations. Moralists might dwell on the success of honest endeavour as exemplified in the life of James Brindley, but a boy who was strong might find the career of honest John Gully more instructive. Gully was an inmate of the Fleet Prison when his potential was first recognised by the champion of England, 'The Game Chicken', Henry Pearce.[10] In due course Gully became champion but, unlike some fighters, he used his purse well. He became a successful tipster and later owned a racehorse himself. In 1832 his colt, St Giles, won the Derby.[11] Gully achieved complete respectability. He became MP for Pontefract, the proprietor of a colliery and a close friend of Lord Fitz-william.

Other prizefighters gravitated towards the gaming clubs of St James's. The most famous were Crockfords and Almacks, but some political clubs like Brooks's (for Whigs) and White's (for Tories) really started life as gambling dens. Of course the clubs exemplified the most refined taste in architecture and provided the finest foods and wines. Captain Gronow described Crockfords in the 1820s:

No one can describe the splendour and excitement of the early days of Crockey...The members of the Club included all the celebrities of England, from the Duke of Wellington to the youngest ensign of the Guards; and at the gay and festive board, which was constantly re-plenished from midnight to early dawn, the most brilliant sallies of wit, the most interesting anecdotes interspersed with grave political dis-cussions and acute logical reasoning proceeded from the soldiers, scholars, statesmen, poets and men of pleasure, who, when the 'house was up' and balls and parties at an end, delighted to finish their even-ing with a little supper and a good deal of hazard at old Crockeys.[12]

The same listlessness which drove men into gambling clubs helped to spread the vogue of the seaside resort. 'The sea water cure' for glandular disease had been introduced by Dr Richard Russell, who built a house at Brighthelmstone about the middle of the eighteenth century. By 1800, a line of resorts, stretching from Sidmouth to Scarborough, vied for the favour of rich holidaymakers. Most of the resorts had been fishing villages, perhaps with a profitable sideline in smuggled brandy and lace. Now cottages became guest houses, and stuccoed terraces, assembly rooms, curio shops, theatres, circulating libraries and bandstands started to appear. The chief patron of the resort was the Prince Regent, and it was his enthusiastic support which made Brighton *the* place to go and, in the minds of some critics, the wickedest town in England. There was much truth in Cobbett's denunciations of the 'gingerbread' features of Brighton. A statue of the Regent was made of such inferior stone that the corrosive effects of sea air caused an arm to fall off. Thereafter guides simply told visitors that the statue had been erected to the memory of that great hero, Lord Nelson! The Prince's amours were widely reported in the London newspapers and helped to establish Brighton's dubious reputation.[13]

The Brighton Pavilion was constantly being altered and enlarged at public expense. The exotic food provided by Carême, the overheated rooms, the drapes and brocades, all hinted at a harem rather than the home of a Christian gentleman. The moral indignation exploded on 12 March 1816. Lord Stanley told Parliament that the squanderous and lavish profusion had more in common with the pomp and magnificence of a Persian satrap than with 'the sober dignity of a British prince, seated in the bosom of his subjects'.[14] Several speakers implied that the best historical parallel to Brighton under the Regency was Capri under the Emperor Tiberius. Of course there were scandals, masked ladies of quality giving birth in obscure cottages and ribald jokes based on misunderstandings about hotel rooms and bathing machines. A sober estimate, however, makes it hard to believe that Brighton's depravity could even rival that of Bath a couple of generations earlier.

For those suffering from boredom there were other remedies than sexual or culinary indulgence. Sentimental regard for animals was a possibility. Charles Lamb was disgusted by the attention ladies of fashion gave to the donkeys on Brighton beach. These 'sleek, foppish, combed and curled' creatures got pats and sweetmeats from women who would regard the underfed working donkeys of London with disgust.[15] There was fun to be had in a resort for those who could contrive to be permanent invalids–fuss and attention and opportunities for pleasurable tantrums. Elderly ladies seemed to attract personable young doctors–so long as the fees were good and there was a prospect of a legacy. Medicine was still a dangerous game and it is doubtful if hypochondriacs got such good value as those who worried about their souls. The resort might be very wicked, but that only made ostentatious religiosity more pleasurable. No serious resort was without a formidable array of chapels with charismatic preachers and eccentric theology. If life became too boring one could always have a good row with the minister and find another chapel more to one's taste.

The 'Evangelists', Henry Huntingdon and George Savage White, had large followings at Brighton. Huntingdon started life as a coal heaver whose cottage windows were frequently smashed by those who disliked his rantings. After he moved to London things improved, admirers built a chapel, gifts began to arrive from 'daughters in the faith' and Huntingdon eventually married the widow of a former Lord Mayor of London. The couple moved to Brighton and lived in considerable comfort. Huntingdon now affected a clerical-looking hat but he still preached in the old style and went around in a coach with 'SS' (Sinner Saved) painted on the panels.[16] As in the case of John Gully, the career of Henry Huntingdon shows that mechanical inventiveness was not the only or indeed the easiest way for a poor man to rise in the world.

Aristocratic decadence had a very short reign at Brighton or elsewhere; the enormities of the Regency Bucks would have passed unnoticed in the 1730s. Society was becoming more censorious both to the poor and to the rich. Charles Lamb was not impressed with the resorts; he found 'Worthing dull, Brighton duller and Eastbourne dullest'. Perhaps what Lamb meant was that the resorts were being taken over by the middle classes and middle-class values. Coach proprietors were offering special cheap rates from London to Brighton and by the late 1820s enterprising men were talking of a railway. By 1841 it had become a reality; only eleven years passed between the death of the Regent and the arrival of the family holiday and the day tripper.

## Godliness and Good Learning

In some ways Cobbett was a protagonist of the new order. His denunciations of the wickedness of the age, of the corruption of society and of the sin that abounded in spas and seaside resorts were echoed by many who repudiated his political views. There is an earnestness about Cobbett which is decidedly Victorian. On 30 September 1826 Cobbett rode into Cheltenham:

Which is what they call a 'watering place', that is to say, a place to which East India plunderers, West India floggers, English tax gorgers, together with gluttons, drunkards and debauchees of all descriptions, female as well as male, resort at the suggestion of silently laughing quacks, in the hope of getting rid of the bodily consequences of their manifold sins and iniquities. When I enter a place like this, I always feel disposed to squeeze up my nose with my fingers. It is nonsense, to be sure; but I conceive that every two-legged creature that I see coming near me is about to cover me with the poisonous proceeds of its impurities.[17]

Cobbett was more typical of his time than he would have cared to admit; in fact he was something of a prude. Shakespeare was dismissed as 'smutty'; *Tom Jones* was a pernicious book whose tendency was to make its readers despise virtue and to produce wretched objects who were simply a burden to the community.[18] Cobbett considered it immodest for women to employ male midwives; mothers who refused to breastfeed their children did so because they wanted 'to hasten back, unbridled and undisfigured, to those enjoyments, to have an eagerness for which a really delicate woman will shudder at the thought of being suspected'.[19] Cobbett was even disgusted at widows who remarried, and his opposition to Malthus owed a good deal to horror at the 'filthiness' of birth control.

Given those attitudes one might expect that Cobbett would welcome signs of greater respectability among the upper classes, but this was not so. Although there were some aristocratic Dissenters, the new moral fervour of parts of the ruling classes found clearest expression in 'The Saints', an Evangelical movement working within the Church of England. In politics, the Evangelicals were associated with Pitt the Younger and 'under the garb of sanctity' they had aided and abetted some of the changes which Cobbett deplored. The *Political Register* of 24 May 1811 portrayed the Evangelicals as being notable for 'the most infamous intrigues and the most rapacious plunder'.

The most outstanding Evangelical was William Wilberforce, the symbol of moral rectitude among the upper classes. Wilberforce's pamphlet 'An Appeal to the Religion, Justice and Humanity of the Inhabitants of the British Empire on behalf of the Negro Slaves in the West Indies' was described by Cobbett as 'a heap of shameless cant'. The seventy-seven pages contained 'a great deal of lying, a monstrous quality of hypocrisy and a great deal of that cool impudent falsehood for which the Quakers are famed'. Wilberforce argued that England must prove itself a Christian country by abolishing slavery and 'transmuting the wretched Africans into the condition of free British labourers'. Cobbett had grave doubts whether such a transmutation would be an improvement. There were thousands of 'white slaves' in England who would be happy to lick the dishes and bowls out of which the black slaves had eaten. The condition of the blacks in the sugar plantations might be deplorable and runaway slaves subjected to atrocious punishments by their masters—'this is perfectly damnable to be sure; this is tyranny; here is horrible slavery; the tyrants ought to be stricken down by thunderbolts and otherwise destroyed'—but were conditions in England so much better?

On 16 August 1819 a group of 'free British labourers', who had not run away from their masters or committed any other crime, were shot down in the 'Peterloo' massacre. Far from condemning such an outrage, Wilberforce supported a vote of thanks to the magistrates and soldiers involved. Whatever they might be in the West Indies, killing and wounding were obviously all right in Manchester. Slaves were certainly ill-treated but Wilberforce said nothing about the British soldiers, men who had helped to defeat Napoleon, who died after being flogged for some trivial misdemeanour. Wilberforce applauded when government spokesmen declared that Britain was 'the envy of surrounding nations, and the admiration of the world'.[20]

But Cobbett was wrong. There was hypocrisy and double standards but there can be no doubt that there was also a wider recognition among the upper classes of their duty to impose more exacting standards on themselves and to ameliorate the lot of the less fortunate. T. B. Macaulay wrote in 1823 that the most striking feature of the time was the proliferation of societies; 'there was scarcely one upper-class Englishman in ten who did not belong to some association for distributing books or for prosecuting them; for sending invalids to hospital, or beggars to the treadmill; for giving plate to the rich or blankets to the poor'. Many of the charities invite the derision of a more cynical age; among the organisations seeking aristocratic patronage were 'The Forlorn Female's Fund of Mercy', 'The Maritime Female Penitent Refuge for Poor Degraded Females' and 'The Ladies' Association for the Benefit of Gentlewomen of Good Family, Reduced in Fortune Below the State of Comfort to Which they have been Accustomed'. The patrons of some of the societies were probably chosen for their wealth and social position rather than for their goodness and blameless life. The Marquis of Hertford, one of the most notoriously immoral men of his generation, became President of the Lock Hospital for Persons Afflicted with Venereal Disease and of the Lock Asylum for the Reception of Penitent Females.

An explanation of this upper-class reformation of manners is essential to any understanding of the Age of Cobbett. Reports of the Terror in France had greatly alarmed Englishmen of wealth and power. Cobbett had encouraged these feelings of revulsion; in March 1795 his pamphlet *A Bone to Gnaw for the Democrats* gave minute descriptions of the atrocities which had taken place across the Channel–the butchering of prisoners in cold blood, the pleasure taken in seeing men, women and children die by inches, holes being dug in public squares to collect blood from the guillotine. Popular rule would result in tyranny, anarchy and death; the crowd would always be cruel. At the very name of 'democrat' humanity shuddered and modesty hid her head. Cobbett believed that the terrible events had been caused by the decline of religion. The cynicism, immorality and gross luxury of the Ancien Régime had been derived from the influence of the infidel philosophy of Voltaire and Rousseau. Might not Gibbon and Priestley have the same effect in England? In 1794, the text 'The fear of the Lord is the beginning of Wisdom' had a direct application; a return to religion and virtue at all levels of society, but particularly among the ruling classes, was the only way to save England from the fate of France.

The new aristocratic respectability was fundamentally conservative but it contained an element of utilitarianism. The traditional attitude was that the dissipations of a nobleman were his by right; the lower orders, and perhaps even God, had no business to find fault with a peer of the realm. But now some noblemen were taking up their Bibles again and read 'Unto whomsoever much is given, of him shall be much required.' The aristocracy could survive but only if its members proved useful members of society.

The institution of the Grand Tour had been the most important part of the education of a young gentleman. It was supposed to produce the complete civilised gentleman with a good knowledge of classical antiquities, speaking French and Italian, cutting an impressive figure on a horse and in the fencing school and generally exhibiting a high degree of social polish. The Grand Tour became difficult and then impossible as the French armies marched across Europe; much was lost but something was gained. Moralists had long believed that the Grand Tour corrupted promising young men. Flattery made them vain and idle; their minds were contaminated by notions of Popery and arbitrary government while their health (and breeding potential) was endangered by disease-ridden women.

The end of the Grand Tour meant that it was imperative to improve the quality of education available in this country. The great universities of Oxford and Cambridge had languished in the eighteenth century. When visiting Oxford in November 1821, Cobbett reflected upon the colleges 'devoted to what they call learning' whose real function was to shelter drones and send forth wasps with the rest of society. Some scholars might be evil but the prevailing characteristic was folly, emptiness of head and want of talent. The young men 'educated' at enormous expense were not fit to be clerks in a grocer's shop.[21] Other sources confirm this picture of neglect and ignorance; Edward Gibbon's tutor who 'well remembered he had a salary to receive and only forgot he had a duty to perform' was sadly typical.[22] Fellows of colleges were often socially inferior to their pupils and found it difficult to maintain order, let alone attention to work. The swaggering 'lounger', drinking, gambling and insulting strangers, was scarcely a good advertisement for institutions whose main purpose was supposed to be the 'breeding of godly and learned divines'.

But Dr Johnson observed when faced with a critic of Oxford: 'The members of a university may, for a season, be unmindful of their duty. I am arguing for the excellence of the institution.'[23] Johnson's point was underlined by the astonishing revival of the universities which took place in the 1790s. There were reforms in the examination system, a new spirit of scholarship and a new sense of purpose. By the time of Cobbett's bitter denunciation of the 1820s, the University of Oxford was already represented in Parliament by Sir Robert Peel–surely a 'Victorian' rather than a 'Regency' character. Cobbett had little time for the young man who delighted Parliament, charmed the drunkards and gluttons of the city and bewitched 'old debauched annuitants' with his promises to 'restore the currency of our ancestors';[24] but even Cobbett would have found it difficult to deny Peel's dedication to hard work. In his first year as an undergraduate, 1806–7, Peel was required to master a large proportion of Herodotus, Euripides, Livy, Horace, and Juvenal in their original languages; in mathematics his set books were Rowe's *Fluxions* and Robinson's *Conic Sections*.[25]

But probably the most dramatic change was an upsurge of active– rather than merely formal–religion. William Gladstone, the most high-minded of British prime ministers, grew up in the world of the Regency; he was to hold office as late as the 1890s but he matriculated at Christ Church in 1828–supposedly the golden age of dissipation and irreligion. Gladstone may have been unusual, but he seems to have had no diffi-culty in forming a circle of friends with similar views and commanded enough influence to be elected President of the Union. Of course, a pious young man encountered difficulties. Gladstone recorded that during the night of Wednesday 24 March 1830, a party of under-graduates invaded his rooms and attacked him. Yet the incident was seen as something to be thankful for: 'Because the incident must tend to the mortification of my pride, by God's grace: if at least any occur-rence which does not border on the miraculous can. Because I take it for granted that I shall be despised by some for it. I hardly know what to think of my own conduct myself. It is no disgrace to be beaten for Christ was buffeted and smitten–but though calm reasoning assures me of this, my impulses, my habit of mind, my vicious and corrupt nature, asserts the contrary–may it be defeated.'[26]

Both earlier and later generations would have found such sentiments embarrassing, or even nauseating, in a young man of twenty. The same trend of increasing respectability can be observed in the public schools.

Here, perhaps, things could only improve after the nadir in the mid-eighteenth century. Riots, followed by savage retaliation, were still a striking feature of school life. When George III met an Etonian his usual question was 'Have you had a rebellion lately, eh, eh?'[27] The campaigns seem to have more in common with those conducted by modern terrorist organisations than with the most disgraceful 'rag' of schoolboy fiction. George III was not exaggerating; the boys were in earnest and their behaviour certainly warranted the description of 'rebellion'. In 1797 the headmaster's study at Rugby was blown up by gunpowder, and eighteenth-century Harrovians were responsible for something like the modern car bomb when they destroyed the carriage of an unpopular governor. After the disturbances had been suppressed, perhaps with the assistance of the Yeomanry, headmasters would relish the prospect of beating boys for days on end. In some cases, this beating had unhealthy overtones and Dr Keate of Eton, having flogged eighty boys, merely regretted there were no more buttocks to birch. Conditions were crowded–two or three boys per bed–the food was terrible and there was a great problem of bullying. Even in the most prestigious schools there was a serious problem of understaffing. Few men became schoolmasters if another profession was possible; the job itself was a symbol of failure and there were too many teachers who found consolation in drink and cruelty.

The appointment of Dr Arnold, himself the product of the 'new' Oxford, as headmaster of Rugby in 1827 marked a new departure. Arnold did not spare the rod but his insistence on higher standards of teaching and his campaign against the most extreme forms of bullying did make life more tolerable for the public school boy. But Arnold's purpose was not so much to make great scholars but rather to produce a ruling class of good all-rounders, endowed with a powerful sense of Christian and moral duty. Arnold's disciple, Butler, later headmaster of Shrewsbury, declared that if he trained his pupils to be honourable and virtuous, he was doing more good to them and to society than any amount of learning could achieve. Again, the main spring of reform was religious. Arnold was convinced that by increasing the virtues of individuals he would automatically assist in the creation of a more virtuous society. In that ideal world, Anglicanism must continue to set the tone of the ruling élite, but it could do so only if the ruling classes recognised their faults and accepted the need for peaceful political change.[28] Thomas Arnold and his followers did much to adapt the upper classes to the new role expected of them and thus ensure their survival well into the twentieth century.

## Break Their Will Betimes

It is hard to believe that young men could have been thoroughly reformed if a similar process had not taken place among upper-class women. Eighteenth-century writers suggest a different set of attitudes to those associated with the Victorian matron, dutiful to her husband, prudish and entirely acquiescent in a world completely dominated by men. Continental writers usually had more fault to find with English-women than with Englishmen. Muralt's *Lettres sur les Anglois et les François* presents Englishwomen as spoilt creatures easily put out of humour and so addicted to laziness that they left all drudgery to their husbands who were foolish enough to submit to such treatment.[29] Wendeborn believed that the decline in the use of rouge and painting was a hopeful sign of increasing modesty but the large number of ladies attending sensational trials astonished and disgusted him:

It is also frequently observed that courts of judicature, when criminal cases are tried when female virtue and modesty must be put to the blush, have been crowded by those who as it was supposed would wish to be absent from motives of modesty and prudence; nay, even when the judges have cautioned and intreated them to retire, they have remained immoveable, and thought the covering their faces with a fan or a handkerchief, sufficient to declare their pudicity [i.e. modesty] and to hide tittering and laughing.[30]

Women who appeared so innocent would laugh heartily at doubtful jokes in theatres; they would look around in a brazen way and, even in church, their eyes were likely to wander from their devotions. Wende-born believed that the institution of the girls' boarding school was largely to blame. The main purpose of the education dispensed there seemed to be to produce 'a certain affected vivacity, liveliness, a smart-ness, and false wit sometimes bordering on pertness, a vanity in dress and fashions'.

Too much time was spent reading romantic novels which corrupted both mind and heart. However ignorant Victorian girls may have been, Wendeborn was convinced that in the London of the 1790s, most girls of twelve were well informed about matters which 'they would know early enough at the age of nineteen or twenty'.[31]

An impression of female depravity and rapacity can be derived from the careers of a number of ladies in the Regent's circle. There was Lady Hertford, more interested in power than in passion, who achieved her ambition of an affair with the Prince when she was well over forty. Lady Hertford was supplanted by Lady Conyngham who had been married for twenty-six years before she captured the Regent. There was something ridiculous about the association; the Prince pretended to be Romeo and Oberon while Lady Conyngham assumed the role of Juliet or Titania; considering the waist measurements of the parties involved, Falstaff and Mistress Quickly would have been more appropriate. Lady Conyngham grew very rich during her ascendancy over George IV. She stayed with him till the end, but during the last month of the King's life three whole wagon-loads of jewellery belonging to Lady Conyngham were removed from Windsor Castle–'first she packed and then she prayed, and then she packed again'.

The same force of character, the same independence and self-will can be observed in a wide variety of Regency women. If the career of Princess Charlotte, the Regent's only daughter, is anything to go by, Wendeborn's strictures on the disobedience of the young contain a good deal of truth. Early in 1814 arrangements were made for Charlotte to marry the Hereditary Prince of Orange. Charlotte did not like what she heard of the Prince and was furious when she discovered the terms of the marriage contract which stipulated that she should live in Holland until she became Queen, while some of her children would remain in the Netherlands permanently. Charlotte bluntly refused to accept the contract and got in touch with Henry Brougham to advise her on her legal rights. The Regent decided to play the heavy-handed father; Charlotte was to be put under house arrest at Cranbourne in Windsor Forest until she came to her senses. Charlotte had no intention of accepting treatment like that; before she was due to leave she slipped out of the house, hailed an ordinary hackney carriage and disappeared. She was eventually traced to Connaught House. A procession of the great and mighty was sent to reason with her–there was the Chancellor, the Bishop of Salisbury, Lord Ellenborough and many more. They made absolutely no impression and Charlotte was shaken only when Brougham told her that he had only to take her to the window, show her to the multitude, tell them her grievances and they would rise on her behalf. There would be a tremendous riot; Carlton House would be attacked and probably destroyed. The soldiers would be called out; by running away from her father's house Charlotte could cause the loss of hundreds of lives. Eventually Charlotte agreed to return, but only on condition that the marriage was dropped. There were difficulties to come, but, in the end, Charlotte was able to marry the man of her choice, Leopold of Saxe-Coburg. It was quite an achievement for a girl of eighteen.[32]

Yet for all these survivals of a brave, vigorous and rather earthy past, the image now cultivated by upper-class women was generally one of 'sensibility' as portrayed, somewhat ironically, in the novels of Jane Austen. Sensibility was not an easy attribute to define, although its symptoms included extreme fragility of health, headaches and 'spasms'. A new conception of beauty was developing; in the past the most attractive women had been plump, rosy-cheeked and fairly level-headed, but now the ideal woman was languishing, pale and given to morbid emotionalism both in love and religion. During the Regency, ladies died from causes that had not claimed a victim for centuries, if ever. There was poor Miss Anne Butler of Hackney (then a smart place to live) who died in January 1811 at the age of twenty. Miss Butler had recently received a proposal of marriage: 'But the too eager contemplation of the supposed scenes of future happiness which had recently opened upon her mind, the powerful effect produced by the congratulations of her friends, and the conflicting feelings created by the prospect of her union with one to whom she was attached and by her regret at leaving the parental roof gave rise to a nervous affection of her mind which as her constitution was delicate, speedily terminated in her death.'[33]

A great outlet for feminine sentimentality was to be found in the elaborate funeral pomp which accompanied death in the upper ranks of society. When persons of quality died, rooms were draped in black, family and servants wore mourning, long black ribbons trailed behind hats, black-edged writing paper was ordered and horses were adorned with black plumes. Friends who were unable to attend the funeral would send empty carriages to follow the procession. If the deceased had a coat of arms, a lozenge-shaped hatchment was exhibited on the front of the house–the heavy black frame powdered with silver drops to suggest tears. All curtains were drawn and the bereaved families, particularly the women, were expected to apply black-edged handkerchiefs to their eyes almost ceaselessly.

Earlier in the eighteenth century death seems to have been a somewhat masculine affair. Monuments often showing the deceased in a state of 'Classical' near nudity, were adorned with brash and confident verses. They boasted of worldly riches and success; some implied that God simply would not dare to refuse to admit such a man to Heaven. But fashions were changing; now there were veiled urns, heavy drapery and maidens with downcast eyes. The tone of epitaphs and funeral hymns, many written by women, became more fearful of Hell and more explicit on the horrors of the grave.

There were plenty of 'serious' women in the Age of Cobbett and perhaps the most serious was Hannah More, described by her friend Dr Johnson as 'the most powerful versificatrix' in the language, whose literary output was prodigious. No one could pretend that Hannah More was an original thinker but she knew exactly how to appeal to her audience. Her pamphlet *Thoughts on the Importance of the Manners of the Great to general Society* was virtually the manifesto of the Evangelical party. She was careful to emphasise that true religion was not austere and gloomy and certainly did not require the rich and powerful to renounce 'the generous and important duties of active life, for the visionary, cold and fruitless virtues of an hermitage, or a cloister'.[34]

In many ways Hannah More was a sane and agreeable woman, but she was ready to appeal to the prevailing morbidity, even at the expense of truth, in her efforts to bring about 'a reformation of the country'. One of her favourite devices was to produce what passed for a factual account of the death agonies of prominent atheists and 'infidels'. According to Hannah More, Tom Paine, the arch-unbeliever, called on God when he was dying–Paine is depicted as saying that he wished all his books had been burned and his last words given as 'If ever the Devil had an Agent on Earth, I am that Man.' Mrs More had no difficulty in consigning him to perdition:

On 8th of June 1809 died this miserable reprobate, aged 72 years, who, at the close of the eighteenth century, endeavoured to persuade the common people of England to think that all was wrong in that Government and in that religion which their forefathers had transmitted to them. For the sake of England and humanity it is to be wished that his impostures and his memory may rot together.[35]

Tom Paine's doctor resolutely denied that his patient had changed his religious views in the last moments of his life. Such fabrications seem distasteful and Hannah More's attitude to the poor would find scant support today. She did indeed found schools but her notions of the proper scope of education for the lower orders were very limited. She did not approve of domestic servants and 'charity children' learning to write. Such knowledge was useless, perhaps even dangerous, for people in a humble station. The rich certainly had a duty to instruct the common people but the object should be to provide 'a thorough knowledge of religion and some of the coarser arts of life by which the community may be best benefitted'.[36]

It is not surprising that Cobbett had little time for a woman who was trying to persuade the poor to accept their lot. He was good at making fun of empty-headed society women but he also found the blue-stocking rather ridiculous. He dismissed Hannah More as 'the Old Bishop in Petticoats'.[37] Although Hannah More had her faults, it is hard to avoid the conclusion that whatever a woman did, someone would find her ridiculous. Hannah may have been narrow-minded in her views on education for the poor, but she was much more modern when it came to the question of instructing upper-class girls. Her book *Strictures on the Modern System of Female Education* was a forthright attack on the view that the only education needed by young ladies was for them to learn how to dance, play the piano, sing, draw and sew. She was particularly contemptuous of the long hours wasted on entirely useless ornamental embroidery; chenille work, wafer work and crêpe work would have to go and be replaced by serious intellectual endeavour.

This, of course, was easier said than done. Wendeborn's strictures on girls' boarding schools were mild compared to those voiced by the Revd J. L. Chirol, who was particularly concerned at the dubious character of the teachers: 'Some have kept mistresses, cast off when the bloom of youth and beauty began to fade. Placed in a situation of reputed respectability they soon make their fortune through the patronage of their former *protectors*, who obtain a right of admittance to the young ladies committed to their care and thus not infrequently indemnify themselves with these for the loss of the charms of their quondam mistresses.'[38]

Chirol was being wildly alarmist and, in any case, the education of most girls was still in the care of a governess and based in the home. The governess, so often the object of derision and contempt, played a vital role in the education of the female part of the ruling classes. In many ways, hers was the least enviable position in the hierarchy of a great house. The governess was usually the daughter of an impoverished clergyman. In a society where far more women than men survived to reach a marriageable age, the absence of rich parents and a dowry was a serious disadvantage. Unless she was a woman of exceptional beauty and charm, a governess was most unlikely to receive a proposal of marriage from a 'gentleman'. From her earliest years she had been told she was a lady and taught to despise ordinary uncultivated men who, in turn, were unlikely to take much interest in a blue-stocking. There were governesses who were the willing victims of their masters' lusts but, on the whole, they were women of unshakeable virtue. In day-to-day life their most acute problem was that they were neither fish nor fowl. The governess was probably disliked by the servants for giving herself airs, yet she was liable to be despised–or insensitively patronised–by the lady of the house on account of her poverty and poor marriage prospects. In such depressing circumstances, it is at least understandable that so many governesses took refuge in the reading and writing of romantic novels.

In really grand households it was considered the height of bad manners to treat the governess as a servant. Selina Trimmer was governess to the group of children at Devonshire House and Chatsworth and did her best to shield her charges from the immorality of their elders. Although Selina did not approve of the life style of the Devonshires she was treated with great kindness and very much as an equal. She retained her apartments at Chatsworth even after her charges grew up and was to be a valued confidante and adviser of former pupils who were now grown women. Obviously there were difficulties, and Selina compared Lady Elizabeth Foster–the Duke's mistress and second wife–to the north-east wind which 'in the brightest sunshine still has some chill in it'. But Selina cannot have been all that unhappy; when she was offered the most illustrious job of her profession–sub-preceptress to Princess Charlotte–she had no hesitation in refusing.

Perhaps the position of the governess was most difficult when her employers came from the increasing numbers of the *nouveaux riches*. Such people were inclined to think of a governess as a status symbol like a carriage, rather than as a person who had a vital role to play in the education of their children. Some believed–quite erroneously–that the best way to gain the acceptance of the county gentry was to treat governesses and domestic staff badly. In some cases, the reaction was defensive. It is easy to sympathise with the poor governess but we should also spare a thought for the lady of a successful manufacturer who found it difficult to adapt to her new opulence and grandeur. In particular she might be acutely aware that her children's governess was better born, better educated and generally more lady-like than she.

The alacrity with which the upstart middle classes took to employing governesses was the sort of development which men like Cobbett considered the embodiment of pretence and humbug gentility. His views on the education of the upper classes were summarised in his *Advice to Young Men and (incidentally) to Young Women in the Middle and Higher Ranks of Life*. One of the main purposes of a governess was to instruct young ladies in the French language. Although Cobbett was not opposed to the teaching of French, the qualities he thought most attractive in women were–in that order–chastity, sobriety, industry, frugality, cleanliness, knowledge of domestic affairs, good temper and beauty. The purpose of female education should be to produce young women who approximated to these ideals. There were grave dangers in education by governesses.

With regard to young women, too, to sing, to play on instruments of music, to draw, to speak French, and the like are very agreeable qualifications; but why should they *all* be musicians and painters and linguists? Why *all* of them? Who, then, is left *to take care of the houses* of farmers and traders? But there is something in these 'accomplishments' worse than this; namely, that they think themselves *too high* for farmers and traders; and this, in fact, they are; much *too high*; and therefore the servant girls step in and supply their place.[39]

But Cobbett's views on education were often more liberal than those entertained by governesses. When in Philadelphia in the 1790s, he had been influenced by Rousseau's *Émile*. He still believed that children developed spontaneously and were best taught with the minimum of restraint and scolding. His own children were each given a little garden to cultivate; the essential task was to get them interested in *things*; book learning would follow naturally. Of course, Cobbett's own family could scarcely be described as upper class, but in the days at Botley, before he was sent to prison, he lived the life of a prosperous farmer with the same sort of income as many who were busy turning their daughters into 'ladies'. The scene at Botley about 1808 seems very attractive:

A large strong table in the middle of the room, their mother sitting at her work, used to be surrounded with them, the baby, if big enough, set up in a high chair. Here were ink-stands, pens, pencils, India rubber, and paper, all in abundance, and everyone scrabbled about as he or she pleased. There were prints of animals of all sorts; books treating of them: others treating of gardening, of flowers, of husbandry, of hunting, coursing, shooting, fishing, planting and, in short, of everything with regard to which we had something to do. One would be trying to initiate a bit of my writing, another drawing the pictures of some of our dogs or horses, a third poking over *Bewick's Quadrupeds*, and picking out what he said about them.[40]

Cobbett's enthusiasm for 'sweet air' and rural life would have found only qualified enthusiasm in the world of governesses and young ladies; there was always the danger that impressionable girls might draw unfortunate conclusions from the activities of farm animals. The advance of 'refined delicacy' had been such that farmers' daughters were expected to blush and look shocked at the mention of a bull; yet well within Cobbett's memory, good women had spoken of animal breeding as freely as about milking or spinning. The ultimate in absurdity was achieved when a jury actually awarded damages to a man 'calling himself a gentleman', because a neighbour had a bull in an adjoining yard. The plaintiff alleged that this was so offensive to his wife and daughters that unless the animal were removed he would be compelled to brick up his windows or sell his house. Cobbett knew how to make the most of a case like this.

If I had been the father of these, at once, *delicate* and *curious* daughters, I would not have been the herald of their purity of mind; and if I had been the suitor of one of them, I would have taken care to give up the suit with all convenient speed; for how could I reasonably have hoped ever to be able to prevail on delicacy, *so exquisite*, to commit itself to a pair of bridal sheets? In spite, however, of all this 'refinement in the human mind' which is everlastingly dinned in our ears; in spite of the 'small-clothes' and of all the other affected stuff, we have this conclusion, this undubitable *proof*, of the falling off in *real* delicacy; namely that where there was one illegitimate child only fifty years ago, there are now *twenty*.[41]

Whether Cobbett was right or not, there can be no doubt that much greater care was taken in the education of the young. There were bound to be rebels against the tighter regime; Selina Trimmer was an excellent governess in every way but one of her pupils was the notorious Lady Caroline Lamb. In general, it seems likely that the greater delicacy of education produced a generation which was more inhibited in its conduct than was usual in the eighteenth century. One of the most striking features of the age was the production of school books which shielded children from the slightest hint of indelicacy. Selina Trimmer's mother, Mrs Sarah Trimmer, considered the Bible far too explicit in some matters; accordingly, she produced *A Sacred History selected from the Scriptures with Annotations and Reflection adapted to the comprehension of Young Persons.*

Mrs Trimmer's magazine *The Guardian of Education* reviewed books for children and tried to ensure that only the suitable ones found their way into well-conducted households. It is easy to pour scorn on Mrs Trimmer and her kind yet even some twentieth-century progressives might entertain doubts about a book like *Boyer's Royal Dictionary*. The work dated from the middle of the eighteenth century, but a new and 'improved' edition was published in 1803. The dictionary was 'specially designed to afford help to young students of French'; those young students were given what in many ways was an excellent course but it is unlikely that Mrs Trimmer would have approved of some of her examples. With great solemnity the dictionary explained that 'his arse makes buttons' should be translated as 'il chie de peur'; there were actually two ways of saying 'he is the crack-fart of the nation'–'C'est un homme qui franche hautement sur les affaires d'état' or 'un homme qui se mêle de régler l'état'. Perhaps Mrs Trimmer had a point after all.

The Ruling Classes

However much credit was given to *The Guardian of Education*, Mrs Trimmer overdid things. One of her favourite themes was the unsuitability of fairy stories for young girls. Cinderella aroused her particular fury; the tale seemed designed to encourage envy, jealousy and dislike for stepmothers and half-sisters, together with a glorification of vanity and fine dresses. In short, even young girls and children were expected to reflect the increasing seriousness of the times. In Evangelical households the notion of original sin and the inherent wickedness of young people was fast gaining ground. Hannah More declared that it was 'a fundamental error to consider children as innocent beings'.[42] Yet perhaps no more than half of the children born to rich parents would survive until adulthood; what good were all the restraints, privations and character-forming punishments for those who died young? Life may have always been better for the rich but children and young girls do not seem to have had a particularly good deal. No doubt parents thought they were doing the right thing. As they raised their canes some of them may have recalled the chilling advice of John Wesley: 'Break their wills betimes. Begin this work before they can run alone, before they can speak plain, perhaps before they can speak at all. Let a child from a year old be taught to fear the rod and to cry softly; from that age make him do as he is bid, if you whip him ten times running to effect it. Break his will now and his soul shall live, and he will probably bless you to all eternity.'[43]

## The Name of William Cobbett

William Cobbett had no illusions about the godliness and piety which was so popular. It was simply being used to justify an abominable social system. Cobbett produced a parody of a chapel hymn:

> *Come little children, list to me,*
> *While I describe your duty,*
> *And kindly lead your eyes to see,*
> *Of lowliness the beauty.*
>
> *'Tis true your bony backs are bare*
> *Your lips too dry for spittle*
> *Your eyes as dead as whitings are*
> *Your bellies growl for victal.*
>
> *At parching lips when you repine*
> *And when your belly hungers*
> *You covet what by right Divine*
> *Belongs to Borough Mongers*

179

*Let Dungeons, gags and hangman's noose*
*Make you content and humble*
*Your heavenly crown you'll surely lose*
*If here on earth you grumble.*[44]

Cobbett was a bitter man in his later years, as this 'hymn' suggests. Hopes of the collapse of 'The Thing', the destruction of the parasite fundholders, the levelling of wens, the overthrow of Enclosures, the reduction of taxation, the abolition of borough-mongering and corruption and a general return to the Good Old Days buoyed Cobbett up in adversity. From 1816 until the end of his life, he made war on what he called 'The Usurpation'. The real power in the country was not the monarchy, not the aristocracy and not the people, but a band of great nobles who by sham elections, and by means of all sorts of bribery and corruption, had obtained sway in the country. Underneath this group, purely for the purposes of show and election, they had a thing called a king, a set of sharp and unprincipled fellows whom they called ministers, a mummery which they called a church, experienced and well-tried and steel-hearted men whom they called judges, a company of false money makers whom they called a bank, numerous bands of brave and needy persons whom they called soldiers and sailors, and a talking, corrupt and impudent set whom they called a House of Commons.[45]

In the years after 1815 there were several times when it seemed that Cobbett's hopes would be realised. Cobbett was forced to flee to the United States, largely to escape his creditors, in 1818 and when he returned he found the country obsessed with George IV's attempts to divorce Caroline of Brunswick. There was enormous popular sympathy for the Queen, and together with economic difficulty, this attitude greatly strengthened those who demanded drastic changes in the system. Cobbett was genuinely sympathetic to Caroline and believed her to be entirely innocent of the charges of adultery made against her, but he was always adamant that the Queen's affair was only a means to the greater end of fundamental social and political change.

But opinion turned against Caroline and the operation of the Six Acts pruned the *Political Register* of its more explosive passages. It was this situation which forced Cobbett to try to reach his audience by word of mouth by addressing public meetings up and down the country. The travelling required by this direct approach to the people was a considerable achievement for a man in his sixties and it was an even greater achievement to turn the impressions of country town meetings and deserted bridleways into the literary masterpiece *Rural Rides*. Everything Cobbett saw convinced him that the present state of things could not last. Near Great Bedwin in Wiltshire he saw some very pretty girls 'ragged as colts and as pale as ashes'. Only the heart of a seat seller or a loan jobber would not ache at the sight of their blue arms and lips as they worked in the frost of the early morning. A visit to Dartford, the garrison town in Kent, confirmed Cobbett's view that the artificial system created by the wars against France was already falling apart:

This is a little excrescence that has grown out of the immense sums which have been drawn from other parts of the Kingdom to be expended on Barracks Magazines, Martello-Towers, Catamarans, and all excuses for lavish expenditure, which the war for the Bourbons gave rise to. All things will return; these rubbishy flimsy houses on this common will just be deserted then crumble down, then be swept away, and the cattle, sheep, pigs and geese will once more graze upon the common, which will again furnish heath, furze and turf for the labourers on the neighbouring lands.[46]

Cobbett's hopes were highest in 1825 and 1826 when he was convinced that universal bankruptcy and distress would compel the ministers to repudiate the National Debt–and thus pull down the social, economic and political system he had so long denounced. A great feast was held at The London Tavern on 6 April 1826 to celebrate the coming victory. Cobbett gave the toast–'The industrious and labouring people and may their food and raiment cease to be taken from them by the juggling of the paper money system.' Full of optimism, Cobbett stood for Parliament at the general election of 1826, but despite the fairly wide franchise at Preston, the campaign was a disaster and was marred by bitter quarrels among the Radicals. Cobbett came bottom of the poll and some observers were ready to write him off as a has-been. Heine wrote: 'He is a chained house-dog who falls with equal fury on every one whom he does not know, often bites the best friend of the house. barks incessantly and just because of this incessantness of his barking cannot get listened to, even when he barks at an actual thief...This makes the dog furiously savage, and he shows all his hungry teeth. Poor old Cobbett! England's watch dog!'[47]

Cobbett and the earlier generation of Radicals had seen unfair taxation as the main cause of distress among ordinary people and had agreed that this evil sprang from the system of pocket borough representation in Parliament. Younger men were arguing that the poor were the victims of the economic process itself. Cobbett, however, clung to his conviction that it was government taxes on food, drink, clothes and houses which kept working men and producers poor yet propped up an idle class of pensioners, spies, borough-mongers and standing armies.

Thus the essential division in society was between the productive classes and the unproductive. Despite his distaste for cotton factories, lords of the loom and similar manifestations of the nineteenth century, Cobbett was sufficiently old-fashioned to regard manufacturers as part of the productive classes. According to Cobbett, most wrongs could be righted if taxes were reduced by means of a reformed Parliament and an enlarged electorate. At the height of agitation in 1819 and 1820 these doctrines were put forward not only in 'The Twopenny Trash' but also in T. J. Wooler's *Black Dwarf* and T. Davidson's *Medusa*. All three argued that priests were the chief buttresses of the system, living off its rates, tithes and taxes and–worst of all–persuading people to acquiesce in injustice. Like pickpockets the priests took what did not belong to them, like highwaymen they took it by force and like libertines they spent it in criminal voluptuousness. If they met with any opposition 'they bid the constable seize, and the soldiers shoot and the hangman hang'.

Yet Cobbett always limited his attacks to the political aspects of the Church of England and indeed remained an Anglican throughout his life. To him religion was a matter of day-to-day kindness and mercy, not of ecstatic conversion, grace and revelation. A parson once said to Cobbett that his religion was 'altogether political'. Cobbett replied that he was no Doctor of Divinity and that he was in favour of a religion, any religion, that tended to make men innocent and benevolent and happy. Cobbett's underlying traditionalism in social and personal values–home and hearth, rural pastimes and 'proper' social distinction–inhibited his attacks on the system. To the end Cobbett retained his early anti-Republicanism; he was for a government of King, Lords and Commons, for the freedom, happiness and greatness of England, and, above all, for the good feeding and clothing of those who raised all the food and made all the clothing.

It was rousing stuff but too simplistic; by the late 1820s some Radicals came to see that the Cobbett programme of tax reform would leave the existing system intact in all essentials. Younger men began to proclaim that so long as there were enormous inequalities of wealth, government would remain in the hands of the rich. They claimed that it was really profits, not taxes that kept the poor impoverished. Cobbett believed that the working man was oppressed, Hetherington, Carpenter and O'Brien thought it was more important that he was exploited. In this scheme of things manufacturers could no longer belong to the productive classes. In such a world Cobbett's idea of factories as essentially peripheral and exotic manifestations subordinate to 'the accursed paper money system', seemed absurdly old-fashioned. For

Bronterre O'Brien taxes were 'a molehill' compared to the 'Mont Blanc' of capitalist robbery. The real cause of distress was the appropriation by capitalists and middlemen of the fruits of the working man's labour.

It followed, therefore, that any scheme of reform which did not touch this central issue was probably a trick by the middle classes to enlist the workers in their campaign to wrest the remnants of power retained by the feudal aristocracy. While Cobbett had specifically defended the small profits made by bakers and millers–'This useful, this necessary class of men'–O'Brien declared that the line-up of forces was 'the monarchy, aristocracy, millocracy and shopocracy against the insulted and all-sustaining democracy'. Shopkeepers were indeed the greatest foes of the working man because on the one hand they were the sycophants of the aristocracy and on the other they tyrannised and exploited the poor: 'All that is mean, and grovelling, and selfish, and sordid and rapacious and hard and cold and cruel and usurious belongs to this huxtering race.'

The younger men wrote from a point of view which saw a clear-cut division between those who benefited from the existing system and those who did not. Cobbett's sympathies were with the small producer who combined some capitalist and some proletarian aspirations. There were still thousands of small producers in farms and workshops, even in mining, in the England of 1835. But the trend towards a reduction in numbers was clear; it would be premature to say that a modern proletariat existed in 1835 but it was clearly in the making. Cobbett tried to ignore this development; did he not say that he never liked to see machines in case he should be tempted to understand them?

But there was no comfort for those who thought that Cobbett's influence was at an end; his critics were told that the 'poor old man' could still travel five hundred miles on horseback in a speech-making tour, make two or three long speeches every day for a month; he could put down the saucy, the rich, the tyrannical and make them hang their heads for shame in his presence. He might be defeated at an election but he could return home 'through forty miles of huzzahs from the lips of a hundred and fifty thousand people'. Nothing, it seemed, could dent Cobbett's self-esteem; he wrote in 1833: 'I have always led the way at a great distance forward; I have foreseen, foretold, every event, every effect my predictions have in due succession become history: I have been the teacher of the nation.'

Of course, things did not turn out as Cobbett hoped but he was always a man to excite interest. Those who had expected a fiery demagogue were surprised by Cobbett on his lecture tour of the Midlands and the North in November 1832. The thin white hairs and high forehead, the humour lurking in his eyes and dancing about his lips certainly suggested more than an old farmer in his best suit but the overall impression was very respectable. Cobbett was clearly a superb public speaker—his voice clear and flexible and very skilfully modulated so that his audience did not miss a word. He was always master of any hecklers and never at a loss for a witty and sometimes sharp reply. Many considered Cobbett a comic actor of genius whose power of imitation went far beyond mere voice patterns—he seemed to be able to get into a man's mind and character as well. Even if they did not agree with him, people came for miles to hear Cobbett's turn on Lord Althorp. His very solemn irony, blistering sarcasm, sly hints and apparently random points made against the government always told with great effect. Cobbett may have overrated his own importance but he certainly was a man who could never be ignored.

Of course there was an absurd side to Cobbett; it is hard not to smile at his claim that, compared with defeating him, defeating Napoleon was a mere trifle. His attitude to many of the necessary changes which were taking place was often utterly blinkered. There have been commentators who have claimed that Cobbett's emphasis on traditional social and personal values—home, hearth, rural pastimes and an essentially hierarchic society—would have made him a Fascist if he had been alive in the twentieth century. Such a judgement displays very little understanding of the sort of man William Cobbett was. It is hard to detect any hint of 'Fascism' in Cobbett's election manifestos calling for the abolition of sinecures and tithes, the liquidation of the National Debt through the sale of church lands, a reduction of the army, adjustment of the currency and above all reform of Parliament.[48] It was because of views like this that Cobbett was elected to Parliament by the people of Oldham. When Cobbett died, even the condescending *Times* was forced to admit that in many ways 'this self-taught peasant' was among the most remarkable men of the age. It was partly the things that Cobbett said and partly the way he said them. When asked to explain the incessant bustle and activity of England, Cobbett was careful to include beasts as well as men.

The lawyers, doctors, parsons, merchants are alike; and as to the shopkeepers and tradesmen, they know not what leisure or pleasure means. The gentlemen are as busy as the rest. They are half their lives on horseback. Hunting and shooting are their labour and hard labour too. In everything where horses are the chief instruments (and horses are second only to men) the English so far surpass all the rest of the world that there is no room for comparison. The man who has a mind to know something of England, in this respect, should walk from the Tower of London to Charing Cross a little after day light in the morning while the streets are clean of people. He would then see the teams of immense horses drawing up from the banks of the Thames, coals, timber, stone and other heavy materials. One morning last summer I counted in various places more than an hundred of these teams, worth each of them little less than a thousand pounds.[49]

The great thing about Cobbett was that, even when he was wrong, he wrote with a clarity and perception, an almost childlike interest in everything, which makes him into a powerful searchlight compared to the flickering candles of others who tried to illuminate the bewildering things which were happening to England in the first three decades of the nineteenth century. Cobbett believed that England had been the happiest country in the world, the country of roast beef, distinguished above all things for the good food, good raiment and good morals of its people. Now through greed and ignorance, it had become as much distinguished for the opposites of all these good things. When Cobbett died on 18 June 1835, it did seem that all of the things he had opposed were triumphant, the 'muckworm' manufacturing and commercial bourgeoisie had forced the ordinary people to accept a position which may have given them greater affluence but left them with very much less freedom. It looked as if the muckworm would go on to humble the throne as well–but then Cobbett never had any illusions about the role of the monarchy in England after 1688. It certainly might seem strange that the Kings of England should be a race of foreigners and that royal marriages should be so arranged that no sovereign had a single drop of English blood in his veins. If one thought, however, of these apparent sovereigns as nothing more than mere puppets in the hands of a parasite aristocracy and *nouveau riche* merchants, then everything made much more sense. It was in the interest of the ruling classes to have a family on the throne for whom the people had no regard.[50] Nothing would have surprised Cobbett more than the popular veneration which Queen Victoria eventually inspired.

The triumph of elements in society which he despised and the inaccuracy of many of his predictions does not make the period between 1780 and 1835 any less 'The Age of Cobbett'. In one prediction, at any rate, he was absolutely right:

Some generations, at least, will pass away, before the name William Cobbett will cease to be familiar in the mouths of the people of England, and, for the rest of the world, I care not a straw.[51]

# Notes

### Chapter 1: William Cobbett: The Bantering Countryman

1. William Cobbett, *Autobiography*; W. Reitzel (ed.), London 1933, p. 12.
2. Ibid., p. 71.
3. *Victoria County History*: Surrey, i, London 1956, pp. 428–9.
4. W. Marshall, *The Rural Economy of the Southern Counties*, ii, London 1798, p. 74.
5. Cobbett, *Autobiography*, pp. 99–100.
6. Ibid., p. 15.
7. Ibid., p. 10.
8. Ibid., p. 15.
9. Ibid., p. 16.
10. Ibid., p. 17.
11. Ibid., p. 15.
12. William Cobbett, *Rural Rides*; A. Briggs (ed.), i, London 1956, p. 22.
13. Ibid., i, p. 7.
14. Ibid., i, p. 74.
15. Ibid., ii, p. 84.
16. Samuel Bamford, *Passages in the Life of a Radical*, London 1844, p. 18.
17. *Rural Rides*, i, p. 159.
18. *Political Register*, 3 November 1816.

### Chapter 2: Agriculture and Population

1. M. A. Havinden, 'Agricultural Progress in Open Field Oxfordshire', *Agricultural History Review*, vii, 1961, pp. 73–83.
2. A. Young, *General View of the Agriculture of Oxfordshire*, London 1806, p. 93.
3. Ibid., pp. 100–103.
4. A. Young, *Farmer's Tour*, 3rd edn, London 1793, pp. 150–51.
5. *Rural Rides*, i, p. 54.
6. M. Williams, *The Draining of the Somerset Levels*, Cambridge 1970, pp. 128–40.

# Notes

7. W. Marshall, *The Rural Economy of Norfolk*, London 1795, ii, p. 209.
8. Ibid., ii, p. 239.
9. A. H. John, 'Farming in Wartime' in E. L. Jones and G. E. Mingay (eds), *Land, Labour and Population*, London 1967, p. 33.
10. T. Malthus, *First Essay on Population*, London 1798, reprinted London 1926, p. 73.
11. Ibid., pp. 21–4.
12. *Rural Rides*, i, p. 136.
13. R. Price, *An Essay on the Population of England*, London 1780.
14. F. Eden, *An Estimate of the Number of Inhabitants in Great Britain*, London 1800, p. 92.
15. P. Deane and W. A. Cole, *British Economic Growth 1688–1959*, Cambridge 1962, p. 8.
16. Malthus, op. cit., p. 64.
17. Ibid., p. 69.
18. E. A. Wrigley 'Family Limitation in Pre-Industrial England' in M. Drake (ed.), *Population and Industrialisation*, London 1969, p. 164.
19. James Woodforde, *Diary of a Country Parson*, J. Beresford (ed.), Bath 1924–31, ii, p. 297.
20. Quoted in E. A. Wrigley, *Population and History*, London 1969, p. 125.
21. J. L. and B. Hammond, *The Village Labourer 1760–1832*, London 1911, pp. 164–5.
22. Malthus, op. cit., p. 415.

### Chapter 3: The Agricultural Community

1. Cobbett, *Autobiography*, p. 114.
2. G. D. H. Cole, *The Life of William Cobbett*, London 1924, p. 104.
3. A. Hawkins, *Whitsun in Nineteenth-Century Oxfordshire*, Oxford 1973, p. 4.
4. B. Reaney, *The Class Struggle in Nineteenth-Century Oxfordshire*, Oxford 1970, p. 7.
5. D. McClatchey, *Oxfordshire Clergy 1777–1869*, Oxford 1960, p. 93.
6. *Oxford University and City Herald*, 25 September 1830.
7. W. E. Tate, *The English Village Community and the Enclosure Movements*, London 1967, p. 85.
8. McClatchey, op. cit., p. 98.
9. Ibid., p. 109.
10. *Annual Register*, 1799, Chronicle, p. 55.
11. Reaney, op. cit., p. 38.
12. E. J. Hobsbawm and G. Rudé, *Captain Swing*, London 1969, p. 218.
13. Ibid., p. 246.
14. *Political Register*, 13 November 1830.
15. G. D. H. Cole, op. cit., p. 365.
16. Quoted in Lewis Melville, *Life and Letters of William Cobbett*, London 1913, ii, p. 234.
17. *Commercial and Agricultural Magazine*, September 1800.

The Price of Progress

*Chapter 4: The Wens*

1. Robert Southey, *Letters from England*, Letter 36.
2. Ibid., Letter 61.
3. 8 January 1822; *Rural Rides*, i, p. 64.
4. G. F. Wendeborn, *A View of England*, London 1791, i, p. 262.
5. Ibid., i, p. 336.
6. Quoted in B. I. Coleman (ed.), *The Idea of the City in Nineteenth-Century Britain*, London 1973, p. 39.
7. Quoted in J. J. Tobias, *Crime and Industrial Society in the Nineteenth Century*, London 1967, p. 94.
8. As note 7.
9. M. D. George, *London Life in the Eighteenth Century*, London 1925, p. 4.
10. J. P. Malcolm, *Anecdotes of the Manners and Customs of London*, London 1808, p. 119.
11. Francis Place, *Autobiography*, Mary Thrale (ed.), Cambridge 1972, p. 51.
12. Ibid., p. 78.
13. Ibid., p. 63.
14. Malcolm, op. cit., p. 205.
15. Ibid., p. 481.
16. Ibid., pp. 485–6.
17. Place, op. cit., p. 87.

*Chapter 5: The Poor and Indigent*

1. Quoted in M. Brander, *The Georgian Gentleman*, London 1973, p. 82.
2. E. Sigsworth 'A Provincial Hospital in the Eighteenth and Early Nineteenth Centuries', *College of General Practitioners' Yorkshire Faculty Journal*, June 1966.
3. Quoted in Brander, op. cit., p. 2.
4. James Woodforde, *Diary of a Country Parson*, iv, p. 262.
5. 'The Trial of Burke and Hare' in *Notable Scottish Trials*, Edinburgh 1921, p. 186.
6. Francis Place, *Autobiography*, p. 51.
7. Ibid., p. 52.
8. Ibid., p. 78.
9. Ibid., p. 79.
10. Ibid., p. 87.
11. Ibid., p. 110.
12. Ibid., p. 54.
13. *Rural Rides*, ii, p. 13.
14. Cobbett, *Autobiography*, p. 62.
15. Sir Frederick Eden, *State of the Poor*, London 1798, iii, p. 45.
16. Ibid., iii, p. 31.
17. Quoted in J. L. and B. Hammond, *The Village Labourer*, p. 83.
18. Cobbett, *Autobiography*, p. 115.
19. Quoted in Hammond, op. cit., p. 49.
20. W. Cobbett, *Collected Works*, J. M. Cobbett (ed.), London 1835, iv, p. 128.

# Notes

21. Sir Frederick Eden, op. cit., iii, p. 23.
22. Tobias Smollett, *Sir Launcelot Greaves*, London 1762, ch. III.
23. Cobbett, *Autobiography*, p. 130.
24. John Scott, *Observations on the Present State of the Parochial and Vagrant Poor*, London 1773, p. 36.
25. Dr J. Trotter, *Observations on the Poor Laws*, London 1775, p. 52.
26. *Reports from Committees of the House of Commons*, ix, pp. 258–9.
27. *Middlesex County Records*, J. C. Jeafferson (ed.), London 1887, ix, p. 364.
28. *Hertfordshire County Records*, W. J. Hardy (ed.), London 1907, i, p. 183.
29. *Northamptonshire Notes and Queries*, Northampton 1929, iii, p. 26.
30. Quoted in Paul Mantoux, *The Industrial Revolution*, revised by T. S. Ashton, London 1964, p. 433.
31. Quoted in D. Marshall, *The English Poor in the Eighteenth Century*, London 1928, p. 193.
32. Quoted in J. Sambrook, *William Cobbett*, London 1973, p. 26.

### Chapter 6: Prodigious Rapidity

1. F. A. Wendeborn, *A View of England*, i, p. 412.
2. Carl Philip Moritz, *Travels through Several Parts of England in 1782*, London 1795, p. 248.
3. J. Copeland, *Roads and their Traffic 1750–1850*, Newton Abbot 1968, p. 94.
4. *The Torrington Diaries*, C. B. Andrews (ed.), London 1936, iii, p. 7.
5. Copeland, op. cit., p. 117.
6. Quoted in Copeland, op. cit., p. 129.
7. The Petre Papers in the Essex Record Office, Chelmsford.
8. M. Brander, *The Georgian Gentleman*, p. 168.
9. Horace Walpole to the Countess of Ossory, 7 October 1781; *Letters of Horace Walpole*, Mrs Paget Toynbee (ed.), London 1904, xii, p. 62.
10. Copeland, op. cit., p. 44.
11. Genesis 24:60.
12. James Phillips, *General History of Inland Navigation*, London 1792, pp. vi–viii.
13. Charles Hadfield, *The Canal Age*, London 1968, p. 47.
14. Erasmus Darwin, *The Botanic Garden, Containing the Economy of Vegetation, a Poem with a Philosophical Note*, London 1791, p. 141.
15. Phillips, op. cit., pp. 89–91.
16. Hadfield, op. cit., p. 19.
17. Ibid., p. 29.
18. H. J. Dyos and D. H. Aldcroft, *British Transport, an Economic Survey*, Leicester 1969, p. 108.
19. *The Creevey Papers*, Sir Herbert Maxwell (ed.), London 1903, ii, p. 204.

### Chapter 7: Experiments and Processes

1. H. Arnot, *History of Edinburgh*, Edinburgh 1779, p. 403.

2. J. P. Muirhead, *The Origin and Progress of the Mechanical Inventions of James Watt*, London 1854, i, p. xxi.
3. *Municipal Commission Report*, 1835.
4. 'Observations on Priestley's Emigration' in Cobbett, *Works*, i, p. 17.
5. A. Ure, *The Philosophy of Manufacturers*, 2nd edn, London 1861, pp. 10–11.
6. Ibid., pp. 27–8.
7. *Political Register*, 19 November 1807.
8. Ibid.
9. Ibid.
10. Wendeborn, *A View of England*, i, p. 191.
11. Ibid., i, p. 225.
12. R. James, *Josiah Wedgwood*, Aylesbury 1972, p. 9.
13. Ibid., p. 26.
14. See D. E. C. Eversley, 'The Home Market and Economic Growth' in E. L. Jones and G. E. Mingay (eds), *Land, Labour and Population*, pp. 206–59.
15. Ure, op. cit., p. 372.
16. Wendeborn, op. cit., i, p. 85.
17. Cobbett, *Autobiography*, p. 23.
18. Ibid., p. 25.
19. *Political Register*, 6 July 1809.
20. Wendeborn, op. cit., i, p. 90.
21. *Victoria County History*: Kent, ii, London 1962, pp. 385–90.
22. Samuel Smiles, *Industrial Biography*, London 1863, pp. 114–20.
23. Quoted in B. Trinder, *The Industrial Revolution in Shropshire*, London 1973, p. 192.
24. Smiles, op. cit., p. 116.
25. W. H. Court, *The Rise of the Midland Industries*, Oxford 1938, pp. 189–90.
26. Cobbett, *History of the Protestant Reformation*, London 1827, para. 15.
27. I. Grubb, *Quakerism and Industry before 1800*, London 1930, p. 132.
28. *Rural Rides*, i, pp. 42–3.
29. Trinder, op. cit., p. 233.
30. J. R. Randall, *The Severn Valley*, London 1862, pp. 160–61.
31. M. Elsas (ed.), *Iron in the Making*, London 1960, p. 7.
32. Quoted in J. Gloag and D. Bridgwater, *A History of Cast Iron in Architecture*, London 1948, p. 116.

### Chapter 8: Automatic Labour

1. *Parliamentary Papers* (Select Committee on Handloom Weavers), 1840, xxiv, p. 649.
2. *Political Register*, 17 November 1824.
3. F. Engels, *Condition of Working Class in England*, trans. and ed. by W. O. Henderson and W. M. Chaloner, Oxford 1958, p. 187.
4. Engels, op. cit., p. 192.
5. Thomas Carlyle, *Chartism*, 2nd edn, London 1842, p. 28.
6. Quoted in Engels, op. cit., p. 82.

7. Ure, *The Philosophy of Manufacturers*, p. 278.
8. Ibid., p. 301.
9. Ibid., p. 401.
10. Ibid., p. 343.
11. Ibid., p. 279.
12. Ibid., p. 397.
13. Ibid., p. 306.
14. *Political Register*, 17 November 1824.
15. *Parliamentary Papers* (Select Committee on Handloom Weavers), 1840, xxiv, p. 645.
16. See E. P. Thompson, 'Time, Work-Discipline and Industrial Capitalism', in *Past and Present*, 38, 1967, pp. 56, 97.
17. Ure, op. cit., p. 15.
18. Ibid., pp. 22–3.
19. Philip Gaskell, *Artisans and Machinery*, London 1836, p. 105.
20. Ibid., p. 107.
21. Ibid., p. 111.
22. *Hansard*, 15 March 1844, 3rd Series, lxxiii, pp. 1093–4.
23. Ibid., p. 1096.
24. Ibid., p. 1097.
25. Quoted by Ashley in *Hansard*, lxxiii, p. 1097.
26. Quoted in A. Clayre, *Work and Play*, London 1974, p. 124.

## Chapter 9: Oppression and Slavery

1. *Political Register*, 17 November 1824.
2. F. Engels, *The Condition of the Working Class in England*, p. 10.
3. J. L. and B. Hammond, *The Skilled Labourer 1760–1832*, London 1919, p. 58.
4. Wendeborn, *A View of England*, i, pp. 234–5.
5. *Political Register*, 1 December 1830.
6. *Political Register*, 8 November 1816.
7. F. O. Darvall, *Popular Disturbances and Public Order in Regency England*, Oxford 1934, p. 260.
8. Quoted ibid., p. 53.
9. Quoted ibid., p. 55.
10. Quoted ibid., p. 72.
11. Ibid., p. 169.
12. Quoted in Hammond, *The Skilled Labourer*, p. 127.
13. *Parliamentary Papers* (Select Committee on Handloom Weavers), 1840, xxiv, p. 75.
14. *Parliamentary Papers* (Royal Commission on the Employment of Women and Children in Mines and Factories), 2nd Report, 1843, xiii, p. 122.
15. *Political Register*, 14 August 1807.
16. *Parliamentary Papers* (Royal Commission on the Employment of Women and Children in Mines and Factories), 1st Report, 1842, xv, p. 91.

17. Ibid.
18. Ibid., p. 94.
19. Ibid., p. 71.
20. Ibid., p. 135.
21. Ibid., p. 146.
22. Ibid., p. 189.
23. Ibid., p. 157.
24. Royal Commission on the Employment of Women and Children...
    2nd Report, 1843, xiii, p. 157.
25. Ibid., p. 198.
26. Quoted in J. F. C. Harrison, *The Early Victorians*, London 1971, p. 111.

*Chapter 10: The Enterprising and Frugal Capitalist*

1. Quoted in J. Sambrook, *William Cobbett*, p. 179.
2. Ure, *The Philosophy of Manufacturers*, p. 407.
3. Ibid., p. 411.
4. Ibid., p. 416.
5. Gaskell, *Artisans and Machinery*, p. 97.
6. *Hansard*, 8 March 1833, xvi, p. 12.
7. E. Isichei, *Victorian Quakers*, Oxford 1970, p. 25.
8. *Political Register*, 4 September 1819.
9. Quoted in J. C. Hudson, *The Parent's Handbook*, London 1842, p. 200.
10. E. G. Wakefield, *England and America*, London 1833, p. 93.
11. Ibid., p. 103.
12. Hudson, op. cit., p. 60.
13. *Fraser's Magazine*, xxxvi, p. 598.
14. Hudson, op. cit., p. 66.
15. Ibid., p. 89.
16. Ibid., p. 220.

*Chapter 11: The Ruling Classes*

1. Wendeborn, *A View of England*, i, p. 419.
2. M. Brander, *The Georgian Gentleman*, p. 42.
3. *Morning Post*, 18 March 1812.
4. Wendeborn, op. cit., i, p. 421.
5. Ibid., p. 422.
6. H. Grosley, *Londres*, Paris, n.d., i, p. 398.
7. Wendeborn, op. cit., i, p. 399.
8. *Rural Rides*, 19 April 1830, ii, p. 256.
9. Wendeborn, op. cit., i, p. 413.
10. H. Blyth, *Hell and Hazard*, London 1969, pp. 241-6.
11. Ibid., p. 135.
12. Quoted ibid., p. 117.
13. Clifford Musgrave, *Life in Brighton*, London 1970, p. 88.
14. *Hansard*, xxxiii, p. 201.
15. D. M. Stuart, *Regency Roundabout*, London 1943, p. 63.

16. Ibid., pp. 50–51.
17. *Rural Rides*, ii, p. 126.
18. Cobbett, *Advice to Young Men and (incidentally) to Young Women in the Middle and Higher Ranks of Life*, London 1829, paras. 311–12.
19. Ibid., para. 233.
20. 'To William Wilberforce on the State of the Cotton Factory Labourers', *Political Register*, 27 August 1823.
21. *Rural Rides*, i, p. 35.
22. E. Gibbon, *Memoirs of My Life*, G. A. Bonnard (ed.), London 1966. p. 49.
23. J. Boswell, *Boswell in Search of a Wife*, F. Brady and F. A. Pottle (eds), London 1957, p. 163.
24. N. Gash, *Mr Secretary Peel*, London 1961, p. 240.
25. Ibid., p. 55.
26. M. R. D. Foot (ed.), *The Gladstone Diaries: Volume 1 1825–32*, Oxford 1968, pp. 290–91.
27. Brander, op. cit., p. 16.
28. N. Hans, *New Trends in Education*, London 1951, p. 209.
29. G. Muralt, *Lettres sur les Anglois et les François*, Cologne 1727, p. 13.
30. Wendeborn, op. cit., i, p. 437.
31. Ibid., i, p. 438.
32. C. Hibbert, *George IV*, London 1973, pp. 68–72.
33. Stuart, op. cit., p. 21.
34. H. More, *Works*, London 1830, ii, p. xvi.
35. Printed in *New Times*, November 1809.
36. H. More, 'A Cure for Melancholy', *Stories*, London 1818, i, p. 356.
37. *Political Register*, 20 April 1822.
38. Quoted in Stuart, op. cit., p.22.
39. Cobbett, *Advice to Young Men...*, para. 327.
40. Ibid., para. 291.
41. Ibid., para. 239.
42. H. More, *Strictures on the Modern System of Female Education*, London 1799, p. 44.
43. R. Southey, *Life of Wesley*, London 1890, p. 561.
44. E. Smith, *William Cobbett*, London 1878, p. 230.
45. *Political Register*, 6 June 1816.
46. *Rural Rides*, i, p. 37.
47. Quoted in Sambrook, *William Cobbett*, p. 140.
48. *Address to Electors of Manchester*, September 1831.
49. *Political Register*, 18 May 1824.
50. *Political Register*, 8 June 1816.
51. *Political Register*, 21 July 1833.

# Selected Reading List

H. Blyth, *Hell and Hazard*, London 1969.

M. Brander, *The Georgian Gentleman*, London 1973.

W. Cobbett, *Autobiography*; W. Reitzel (ed.), London 1933.

W. Cobbett, *Rural Rides*, A. Briggs (ed.), London 1956.

G. D. H. Cole, *The Life of William Cobbett*, London 1924.

B. I. Coleman (ed.), *The Idea of the City in Nineteenth-Century Britain*, London 1973.

J. Copeland, *Roads and their Traffic 1750–1850*, Newton Abbot 1968.

W. H. Court, *The Rise of the Midland Industries*, Oxford 1938.

P. Deane and A. A. Cole, *British Economic Growth 1688–1959*, Cambridge 1962.

M. Drake (ed.), *Population and Industrialisation*, London 1969.

F. Engels, *Condition of the Working Classes in England*, trans. and ed. by W. O. Henderson and W. M. Chaloner, Oxford 1958.

M. D. George, *London Life in the Eighteenth Century*, London 1925.

C. Hadfield, *The Canal Age*, London 1968.

J. L. and B. Hammond, *The Village Labourer 1760–1832*, London 1911.

N. Hans, *New Trends in Education*, London 1951.

E. J. Hobsbawm and G. Rudé, *Captain Swing*, London 1969.

R. James, *Josiah Wedgwood*, Aylesbury 1972.

E. L. Jones and G. E. Mingay (eds), *Land, Labour and Population*, London 1967.

D. Marshall, *The English Poor in the Eighteenth Century*, London 1928.

P. Mathias, *The First Industrial Nation*, London 1966.

D. McClatchey, *Oxfordshire Clergy 1777–1869*, Oxford 1960.

F. Place, *Autobiography*, Mary Thrale (ed.), Cambridge 1972.

J. Sambrook, *William Cobbett*, London 1973.

D. M. Stuart, *Regency Roundabout*, London 1943.

W. E. Tate, *The English Village Community and the Enclosure Movement*, London 1967.

E. P. Thompson, *The Making of the English Working Class*, London 1956.

# Selected Reading List

J. J. Tobias, *Crime and Industrial Society in the Nineteenth Century*, London
    1967.
J. Woodforde, *Diary of a Country Parson*, J. Beresford (ed.), Bath 1924.
E. A. Wrigley, *Population and History*, London 1969.

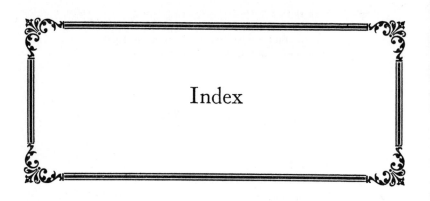

# Index

# Index

# Index

# Index

Index

Vidler, John 77
Village life 6, 30, 31

Wakefield, Edward Gibson 152
Walpole, Horace 79
Walsingham, Lord 34
Warwickshire 134
  Coventry 90, 130
Ware, Issaac 100
Watt, James 90
Wedgwood, Josiah 85, 91, 93, 97, 98
Wellington, Duke of 100, 139
Wendeborn, Frederick 42, 43, 74, 96,
  99, 101, 127, 160, 161, 171
Wesley, John 55, 179
West India Dock Company 60
Whitbread, Samuel 67, 162
Wilberforce, William 67, 166, 167
Wilkinson, John 105
William IV 131

Wiltshire
  High Clere 19
  Chippenham 75
  Great Bedwin 181
Winchester, Bishops of 3–5
Windsor Castle 139
Wing, William 32
Wingate, Edward 71
Woodforde, James 15, 21, 54, 56
Wordsworth, William 7, 39, 84
Worlidge, John 11
Wyllie, John 107

Yorkshire
  Beverley 69
  York 75, 76, 118
  Leeds 76
  Huddersfield 135
Young, Arthur 3, 12, 13–15, 62,
  65